P9-AEY-989

Northeast Lakeview College
33784 0001 2783 7

AUDIT PLANNING

AUDIT PLANNING

A Risk-Based Approach

K.H. SPENCER PICKETT

John Wiley & Sons, Inc.

This book is printed on acid-free paper. ♾

Published by John Wiley & Sons, Inc., Hoboken, New Jersey.
Published simultaneously in Canada.

For general information on our other products and services, or technical support, please contact our Customer Care Department within the United States at 800-762-2974, outside the United States at 317-572-3993 or fax 317-572-4002.

Wiley also publishes its books in a variety of electronic formats. Some content that appears in print may not be available in electronic books.

For more information about Wiley products, visit our Web site at *http://www.wiley.com.*

Library of Congress Cataloging-in-Publication Data:

Pickett, K.H. Spencer.
Audit planning: a risk-based approach / K.H. Spencer Pickett.
p. cm.
Includes index.
ISBN-13: 978-0-471-69052-8 (cloth)
ISBN-10: 0-471-69052-X (cloth)
1. Auditing, Internal. 2. Risk management—Auditing. I. Title.
HF5668.25.P5286 2006
657'.458—dc22

2005023681

Printed in the United States of America

10 9 8 7 6 5 4 3 2 1

ABOUT THE INSTITUTE OF INTERNAL AUDITORS

The Institute of Internal Auditors (IIA) is the primary international professional association, organized on a worldwide basis, dedicated to the promotion and development of the practice of internal auditing. The IIA is the recognized authority, chief educator, and acknowledged leader in standards, education, certification, and research for the profession worldwide. The Institute provides professional and executive development training, educational products, research studies, and guidance to more than 80,000 members in more than 100 countries. For additional information, visit the Web site at *www.theiia.org*.

This book is dedicated
to the memory of my father, Harry Pickett.

CONTENTS

PREFACE

Auditing New Horizons is a new series of short books aimed primarily at internal auditors, but this series will also be useful to external auditors, compliance teams, financial controllers, consultants, and others involved in reviewing governance, risk, and control systems. Likewise, the books should be relevant to executives, managers, and staff as they are increasingly being asked to review their systems of internal control and ensure that there is a robust risk management process in place in all types of organizations. Each book provides a short account of important issues and concepts relevant to the audit and review community. The series will grow over the years, and John Wiley and Sons, Inc., is working alongside the Institute of Internal Auditors, Inc., to ensure that each new title reflects both current and emerging developments. The framework for Auditing New Horizons is illustrated in Figure P.1.

Figure P.1 The Auditing New Horizon Book Series

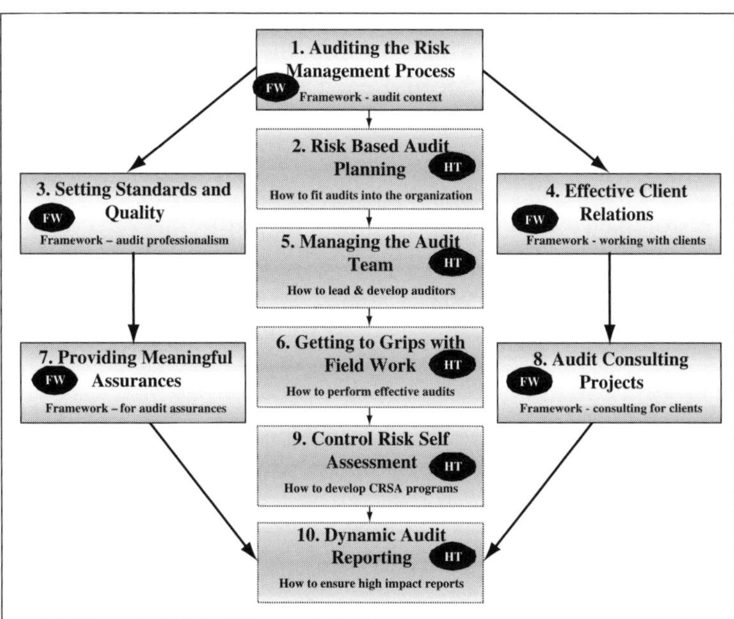

Each book in the series contains eight key models that are developed throughout the relevant chapters and that can be employed to ensure that best practice pointers can be assessed for their impact on current practice. Some of the titles establish important frameworks for the audit function, while others are more concerned with how to deliver the audit product within the defined framework. The books also contain checklists and short case studies that can be used to implement aspects of the relevant underlying models. The books are extensively based on the Institute of Internal Auditor's Professional Practices Framework in terms of their published standards, advisories, and assorted guidance. Because the books are fairly succinct, reference to other sources will be limited. There are no detailed case studies taken from well-known companies in this book series because of the fast changing pace of business, where current material quickly falls out of date. The books do, however, refer to many short examples of what happens in different organizations, as a way of illustrating important points. The dynamic nature of the governance, risk, and control context means that some new book titles for the Auditing New Horizons series may change over the coming years. We hope that readers find the series both interesting and stimulating and that they provide a reference source that adds value to internal auditing, external auditing, and other review functions.

The second book in the Auditing New Horizons Book Series, *Risk-Based Audit Planning*, fits well with the first book on *Auditing the Risk Management Process*. The risk management process feeds into the audit planning cycle, which informs the risk management process. Each complements the other and each needs to be considered in the context of the other. A feature of the Auditing New Horizons book series is that the short books build on the previous titles in such a way that an overall picture of important audit issues is developed. As each book is completed, further layers will be added to this picture so that it eventually forms an entire resource.

LIST OF ABBREVIATIONS

BASEL: Committee on Banking Supervision

CAATs: Computer Assisted Audit Techniques

CAE: Chief Audit Executive

CEO: Chief Executive Officer

CFO: Chief Finance Officer

COSO: Committee of Sponsoring Organizations

CRO: Chief Risk Officer

CRSA: Control Risk Self-Assessment

CSA: Control Self-Assessment

ERM: Enterprise Risk Management

H&S: Health and Safety

IIA: Institute of Internal Auditors

IS: Information Systems

IT: Information Technology

KPI: Key Performance Indicators

OECD: Organization of Economic Cooperation and Development

PPF: Professional Practices Framework

PR: Public Relations

RA: Risk Assessment

RI: Risk Identification

RM: Risk Management

RO: Risk Owner

SEC: Securities and Exchange Council

SIC: Statement on Internal Control

1

WHY RISK-BASED AUDIT PLANNING?

> The chief audit executive should establish risk-based plans to determine the priorities of the internal audit activity, consistent with the organization's goals.
>
> —IIA Standard 2010

INTRODUCTION

Internal auditing has grown tremendously over the years to reflect its new high-profile position in most large organizations. It has shifted from back-office checking teams to become an important corporate resource. The focus on professionalism and objectivity has driven the new-look auditor toward high-impact work that can really make a difference. *Risk-Based Audit Planning* is the second book in the Auditing New Horizons book series. The first book set out a framework for audit's role in ERM, while this second book describes how to put these aspirations into action.

The practical focus of this book has necessitated a greater use of case studies and checklists. Note that the same format of building purpose-made models for each chapter as exists in *Auditing Risk Management* is applied and this format will apply to all the books in the Auditing New Horizons series. *Risk-Based Audit Planning* draws on a number of important sources of information and guidance. First and foremost is the Institute of Internal Auditor's (IIA) professional practices framework that includes research, position papers, and noted textbooks as well as the standards, code of ethics, practice advisories, IIA publications, and pronouncements. This second book becomes more detailed as we consider how the auditor prepares the actual strategy for delivering audit's role. We will be discussing the way plans are prepared by the auditor to ensure that audit's role is properly discharged in a professional manner.

The growing demands for better accountability from all types of organizations in both the public and private sectors has led to great pressures on the internal and external auditors to perform. The starting place, assuming there is a professional audit shop in place, is to prepare a well-appointed strategy that supports first-class audit plans. There is little scope for delivering the goods, unless and until there has been enough time and effort spent on working out where to focus this effort. There are many documented cases where auditors have failed in this respect, not the least being the WorldCom case where at the bankruptcy hearing it was suggested that:

> Of concern is the lack of any effective participation by the Audit Committee in reviewing the adequacy of the annual internal audit plan, with the Audit Committee appearing to have approved the final plan as a formality. Based upon requests of Management, other audits, not part of the Audit Committee-approved plan, were added while some audits originally scheduled were not completed. At most, the Audit Committee was advised of such changes after the fact. Under such circumstances, senior management could influence the focus of the Internal Audit Department away from sensitive areas without the oversight that the Audit Committee would normally be expected to provide.[1]

This criticism of the internal audit approach to planning audit work may well cast a shadow over the future of the internal audit process. There is now less room for failure in terms of developing and implementing an effective process for assigning the right audit resources to the right work. Risk-based audit planning has come to the rescue as a way of targeting high-risk areas and helping the auditors achieve maximum value for their efforts. Before launching our first model, we need to outline the formal definition of *internal auditing* from the IIA:

> Internal auditing is an independent, objective assurance and consulting activity designed to add value and improve an organization's operations. It helps an organization accomplish its objectives by bringing a systematic, disciplined approach to evaluate and improve the effectiveness of risk management, control, and governance processes.[2]

As is clear from this definition, the auditor has a crucial role to play in helping the organization meet the growing demands for better governance, which incorporates the need for effective risk management and reliable controls. Risk drives the entire economy and also public services. Companies face the risk of collapse, public services risk failing to meet their customers' needs, while not-for-profit organizations risk not achieving their various mandates. Meanwhile, audit faces the risk of expressing an inappropriate opinion owing to:

- Performing the wrong audit
- Employing the wrong audit approach
- Using the wrong staff
- Breaching professional standards
- Performing work at the wrong time
- Issuing the wrong reports and delivering the wrong underlying assurances

These risks become huge when set against the background of the new corporate context driven by Sarbanes-Oxley (SOX) and the demands placed on boards and audit committees for full and accurate disclosures on governance arrangements and financial controls. Audit teams are being asked to rally round the "big issue" of how to keep the executive team safe by helping it manage the risk of falling foul of SOX or whatever regulatory rules impact the sector in question. This chapter looks at the overall concept of audit planning and reinforces the important value that derives from well-researched plans and a robust audit-planning process. Risk-based audit planning may be seen as an approach to audit work that focuses on strategic, regulatory, financial, and business risks that confront an organization, and which uses these risks to steer the audit process in a way that maximizes the impact of audit's assurance and consulting work. Planning takes time and effort and the model that is developed in this chapter seeks to address the question: "Why bother to spend a great deal of time planning?"

RISK-BASED AUDIT-PLANNING MODEL: PHASE ONE

Our first model appears in Figure 1.1.

Each aspect of the model is described in the following paragraphs.

Figure 1.1 Risk-Based Audit-Planning Model: Phase One

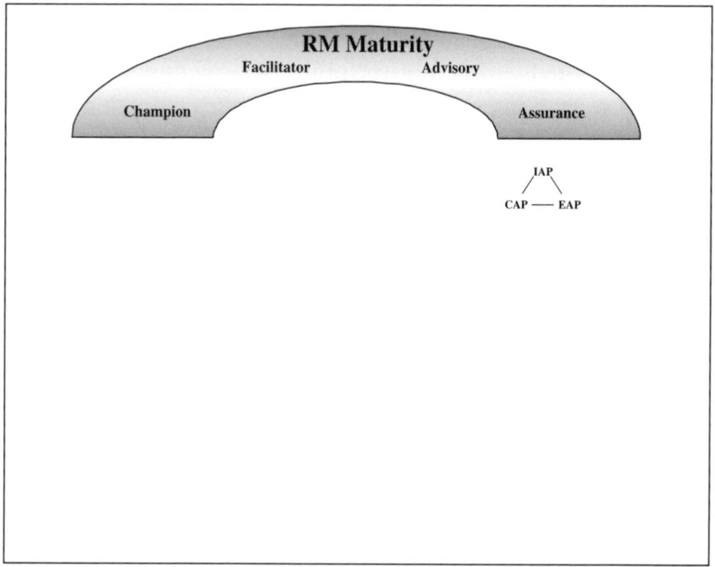

Champion

The model builds on the first book in the Auditing New Horizons series, *Auditing the Risk Management Process*. It does this by using the risk management maturity model that starts on the left (i.e., risk immaturity) and moves through to full risk maturity on the right. Meanwhile, audit's role in the risk management process moves through various stages that are described in our first model in Figure 1.1, starting with a consulting role as risk champions. Organizations that have not made much progress in establishing an effective risk management process are asking their audit teams to help kick-start the task. In this scenario, annual audit plans have been torn up and replaced by a wholesale effort to resource the risk champion role. The IIA has studied this dilemma and considered the impact of SOX on audit's role:

> Internal auditors may provide training and/or information on internal control identification and assessment, risk assessment, and test plan development without impairment to objectivity. As the organization's control experts, this would be a natural role.[3]

The SOX bandwagon is unstoppable and there are good reasons why audit plans are becoming immersed in work related to complying with the various spin-offs including the need to document risk management arrangements and internal controls. Research into the impact of SOX reports the following main benefits:

> Three quarters of the financial executives in the Oversight Systems survey said that their company had realized a benefit from Sarbanes-Oxley compliance. The main ones were that it:
>
> Ensures the accountability of individuals involved in financial reports and operations.
>
> Decreases the risk of financial fraud.
>
> Reduces errors in their financial operations.
>
> Improves the accuracy of financial reports.
>
> Empowers the board audit committee by providing it with deeper information.
>
> Strengthens investors' view of the company.[4]

Facilitator

The next stage of our model in Figure 1.1 moves the risk management process forward and involves the auditor adopting a facilitating role. Facilitation is about helping people in the organization adopt and employ Enterprise Risk Management (ERM) to inspire better business results and to embed good accountability throughout the business. Again, many standard audit plans are being revised to focus on this newly appointed task as audit teams start to focus on facilitating ERM as part of their overall mission in life. The IIA paper on audit's role in SOX makes it clear that audit can have a major impact on the way managements develop procedures for making their Section 404 assertions regarding their internal controls over financial reporting, and the way the external auditor, in turn, makes attestations of these management assertions. Section 302 focuses on quarterly reporting of financial reporting controls, and disclosure controls and procedures. While these reporting obligations are clearly the management's responsibilities, internal audit, as the expert in control systems, is seen as having a legitimate role in assisting the projects that must underpin these new disclosures so long as it does not impair audit independence. The traditional 10% planning allowance for contingencies and management requests for additional help falls far short of the usual level of support that audit is being asked to provide for helping set up the procedures for managing disclosure and regulatory risk as well as the normal risks of managing the business. When setting up the consulting role, the auditor needs to be aware of IIA Practice Advisory 1000.C1-2, which suggests that the auditor needs to consider several factors when deciding whether to take on large consulting projects:

- The needs of management officials, including the nature, timing, and communication of engagement results.
- The possible motivations and reasons of those requesting the service.
- The extent of work needed to achieve the engagement objectives.
- The skills and resources needed to conduct the engagement.
- The effect on the scope of the audit plan previously approved by the audit committee.
- The potential impact on future audit assignments and engagements.
- The potential organizational benefits to be derived from the engagement.[5]

It is one thing to help the management get on top of the risk management agenda, but this must be done carefully, as made clear in Practice Advisory 1000.C1-2:

> Care should be taken, particularly involving consulting engagements that are ongoing or continuous in nature, so that internal auditors do not inappropriately or unintentionally assume management responsibilities that were not intended in the original objectives and scope of the engagement.[6]

It is a good idea to check with the audit committee, before throwing the annual audit plan out the window, about diverting chunks of planned work to the risk management project. Most organizations ensure that the audit committee is built into the audit-planning process as indicated by one commentator:

> The Audit Committee has delegated authority to the Senior Vice President—Internal Audit to make/approve changes that meet certain criteria, and report those changes to the Committee. Any changes outside those criteria must be approved by the Audit Committee before adjusting the work plan.[7]

CASE STUDY

Refocusing the Audit Plan

A large public sector internal audit department made many references to the lack of good internal control awareness among business unit managers in all parts of the organization. One of these remarks was featured in the annual report to the governing board, and caused some concern among the senior management team. The proposed annual audit plan submitted to the audit committee focused on follow-up audits in areas in which previous audits had found poor compliance, high levels of error, inconsistent local decisions, and generally unreliable controls. As part of the consultation applied to the draft audit plan, the Chief Audit Executive (CAE) met with the CEO and discussed the problems at the business unit level. It was felt that these concerns related to a generic failure to appreciate the value of good controls and ensure that procedures are applied in a consistent and transparent manner. The CAE asked that the audit plan be reframed to include a large project for promoting better control awareness among managers and supervisory staff levels. It was felt that the follow-up audits would simply confirm that there were ongoing problems resulting from a poor control culture and that the year-long project would aim to tackle the root cause of this problem. The second round of consultation on the proposed audit plan generated much more enthusiasm and it was decided by the audit committee as the best use of the audit resource, for the year in question.

Advisory

The ERM maturity spectrum in Figure 1.1 moves further right as the organization develops more confidence in the way it establishes ERM. In this scenario, audit teams are able to move back from the intense championing and facilitating positions and simply assume an advisory role as the audit consulting arm takes a back seat. The gaps that the consulting work had been causing in annual audit plans can be made good and audit teams may embark on more formal planning schemes as envisaged by good commercial practice:

> Typically, an annual audit planning process should start with the review of a company's audit universe, which is a risk-rated, comprehensive list of all auditable areas within a company. Risks should be assessed based on the perceived strengths and weaknesses of the internal controls, the security over systems, and the reliability of the personnel responsible for such controls and systems.[8]

Assurance

Our model in Figure 1.1 suggests that assurance services are reinforced when the organization has arrived at some degree of risk maturity. Audit can now turn to providing a formal opinion on the state of risk management and reported disclosures. Assurance services are defined by the IIA as:

> An objective examination of evidence for the purpose of providing an independent assessment on risk management, control, or governance processes for the organization. Examples may include financial, performance, compliance, system security, and due diligence engagements.[9]

The key word in this definition is *independent*. It is independence that makes the audit input invaluable to the board and its audit committee by providing an objective perspective on the way risk is being managed within the organization. Before audit plans can be properly formulated within a changing governance context, it needs to be made clear that audit has to step back from aspects of the business projects that it was previously immersed in. It is not simply a case of moving from a consulting role to an assurance role as the organization comes to grips with its risk management process. Audit standards make clear the need to ensure that this distancing task is properly managed. Practice Advisory 1130.A1-1 deals with assessing operations for which internal auditors were previously responsible and can be used to deal with the transition from being the corporate risk champion to providing formal assurances on the state of risk management. The practice advisory suggests that:

> Objectivity is presumed to be impaired when internal auditors audit any activity for which they had authority or responsibility within the past year. These facts should be clearly stated when communicating the results of an audit engagement relating to an area where an auditor had operating responsibilities.
>
> Persons transferred to or temporarily engaged by the internal audit activity should not be assigned to audit those activities they previously performed until a reasonable period of time (at least one year) has elapsed. Such assignments are presumed to impair objectivity, and additional consideration should be exercised when supervising the engagement work and communicating engagement results.
>
> The internal auditor's objectivity is not adversely affected when the auditor recommends standards of control for systems or reviews procedures before they are implemented. Objectivity is considered to be impaired if the auditor designs, installs, drafts procedures for, or operates such systems.

> The occasional performance of non-audit work by the internal auditor, with full disclosure in the reporting process, would not necessarily impair independence. However, it would require careful consideration by management and the internal auditor to avoid adversely affecting the internal auditor's objectivity.[10]

If the audit department is going to lead on a SOX/ERM project, then it may be a good idea to use a consulting-based audit team that is differentiated from the assurance work performed by the other teams. In this way, the consulting role can be carried out by people who will not immediately perform assurance work on the SOX/ERM arrangements in line with the remit of the practice advisory. There is a great deal of help and assistance that auditors can provide without being deemed as interfering with the formal assurance role. One further consideration is the need to ensure that any project work does not impair the reporting arrangements so that audit report to line personnel and do not fall foul of Practice Advisory 1110-2:

> The CAE should also ensure that appropriate independence is maintained if the individual responsible for the administrative reporting line is also responsible for other activities in the organization, which are subject to internal audit. For example, some CAEs report administratively to the chief financial officer, who is also responsible for the organization's accounting functions. The internal audit function should be free to audit and report on any activity that also reports to its administrative head if it deems that coverage appropriate for its audit plan. Any limitation in scope or reporting of results of these activities should be brought to the attention of the audit committee.
>
> CAEs should also consider their relationships with other control and monitoring functions (risk management, compliance, security, legal, ethics, environmental, external audit) and facilitate the reporting of material risk and control issues to the audit committee.[11]

Audit departments that assume the risk management role along the lines of, say, forming a department called *Internal Audit and Risk Management* must bear in mind the difficulty in subsequently auditing the work of the risk management function. Some audit teams kick-start the risk management function and possibly transfer a couple of audit staff into the new team. But they then encourage a degree of distance from the team as, over time, it settles down and forms a reporting line to defined parts of the business, such as corporate planning or finance. Whatever the approach, it is important to help build the progress that the organization is making on SOX/ERM and ensure that the changing inputs from internal audit are built into the audit-planning process. ERM has been placed alongside SOX not just as a convenience but as a way of recognizing the important link between these two concepts. SOX creates tighter governance arrangements that drive better accountability and include many published disclosures that underpin the new measures. One of these disclosures relates to the state of internal control over financial reporting. Controls are a response to risks that impact business objectives, including the risk that disclosure requirements are not achieved. ERM is a basic necessity and part of the infrastructure that supports good internal controls. ERM means that objectives are set, and risks are identified and assessed and therefore controls may be designed to mitigate risk to an acceptable level. The development of governance processes and disclosures sits alongside the growth in ERM and it is possible to discuss these two matters together, to reflect their interdependency.

CASE STUDY

Changing Audit Approaches

An auditor in a large life assurance company had spent the best part of two years implementing a Control Self-Assessment (CSA) program in all the local offices located in many states, as well as a major head office program. The CAE provided regular updates on the progress made with CSA in each of the quarterly audit reports that were provided to the audit committee. On receiving praise from the audit-committee members for the success of the CSA program, the board considered including an item to ensure that management assertions regarding the systems of internal control were reliable. The board asked the CAE to feed into the quarterly control disclosures by providing an opinion on the reliability of management assertions and a formal perspective on the state of internal controls across the organization. The CAE reduced the level of CSA support work and asked the audit staff to focus on testing the reliability of controls and find out whether management control reviews were carried out in a meaningful manner. The annual audit plan was revised to include built-in reviews of all high-risk systems, consider how CSA was applied and if the results could be counted on by the top management.

IAP, EAP, and CAP

In the past, audit planning was pretty straightforward. The Internal Audit Plan (IAP) was prepared each year on the basis of the previous year's framework and simply contained a list of worthwhile audits that meant the audit resource was spread around parts of the organization over the ensuing twelve months. This format was normally accepted as a good enough way of discharging audit's role. Nowadays, this falls short of world-class practices, and most organizations today have a clear idea of the Expected Audit Product (EAP), as the top management and nonexecutives know what a good audit department should be providing, within the new governance context. Also, consulting work should be fitted into the plan:

> The chief audit executive should consider accepting proposed consulting engagements based on the engagement's potential to improve management of risks, add value, and improve the organization's operations. Those engagements that have been accepted should be included in the plan.[12]

The final factor relates to the Competitors' Audit Promises (CAP) in the form of representations from external providers of internal audit services. This means the in-house audit plans may well be compared to the types of services that other audit providers can supply, and again the audit committee will have a good idea of what is on offer. When the plan is ready, it should be formally released:

> The chief audit executive should communicate the internal audit activity's plans and resource requirements, including significant interim changes, to senior management and to the board for review and approval. The chief audit executive should also communicate the impact of resource limitations.[13]

The internal audit plan, in this scenario, becomes a crucial part of the CAE's agenda, as it needs to be focused, flexible, and well positioned to meet the needs of extremely demanding, regulatory and performance-driven organizations. In essence, the internal audit plan needs to be risk based to be of any real use in addressing the risks arising from possible external competition and enhanced expectations from executives and nonexecutives alike. The IIA's definition of an internal audit activity is in fact quite wide and incorporates different ways that audit work may be resourced:

> A department, division, team of consultants, or other practitioner(s) that provides independent, objective assurance and consulting services designed to add value and improve an organization's operations. The internal audit activity helps an organization accomplish its objectives by bringing a systematic, disciplined approach to evaluate and improve the effectiveness of risk management, control, and governance processes.[14]

The best audit plan is one that provides the results that are expected by stakeholders:

> Senior management and the board normally expect that the chief audit executive (CAE) will perform sufficient audit work and gather other available information during the year so as to form a judgment about the adequacy and effectiveness of the risk management and control processes. The CAE should communicate that overall judgment about the organization's risk management process and system of controls to senior management and the audit committee. A growing number of organizations have included a management's report on the risk management process and system of internal controls in their annual or periodic reports to external stakeholders.[15]

It is always a good idea for the CAE to work toward the best audit plan and, therefore, the best audit result possible.

RISK-BASED AUDIT-PLANNING MODEL: PHASE TWO

So far our model has been built on the framework that represents the change in audit's role, in response to the development of ERM from the changing role. Our model is further enhanced in Figure 1.2 in recognition of this fact.

Each new aspect of the model is described in the following paragraphs.

Context

Now, more than at any other time, the context in which audit planning occurs is extremely important. SOX results in a great deal of focus on corporate social responsibilities and ethical values. Risks that arise from poor codes of ethics or codes that have not been properly embedded within the business may not sit on the board agenda but can cause tremendous problems if not managed effectively. Robert Moeller and Herbert Witt have discussed the impact of SOX:

> Internal audit functions need to accept this new challenge. The designated accounting and financial expert on the audit committee needs the help of internal audit to explain internal control issues within the organization, to better assess audit risks, and to plan and perform effective internal audits. Internal audit now typically has a level of responsibility to SOX Section 404 reviews of internal controls in the organization...[16]

Figure 1.2 Risk-Based Audit-Planning Model: Phase Two

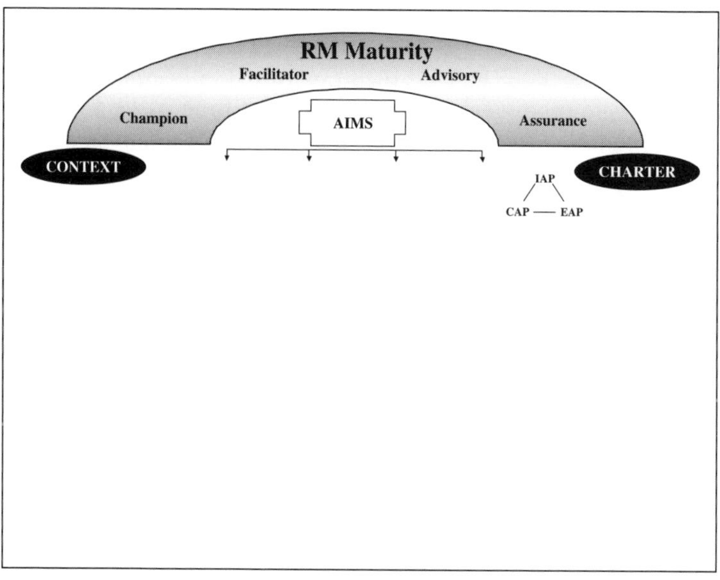

SOX not only creates formal responsibilities for the CEO, board, and audit committee but it also creates additional responsibilities for the CAE. These additional responsibilities in turn create a new context for the audit plan, and one commentator has documented this trend:

> Corporate Governance Committee demands will be incorporated into the plan as this committee take on more specific roles and require validation and verification.[17]

Internal audit may plan to bring to bear an impressive array of tools to assist the organization as it grapples with the new SOX requirements, including the following:

- *Flowcharting.* Many companies are responding to SOX by documenting their financial systems and ensuring that these systems are properly understood and acted upon throughout the organization. Auditors have quite a track record in both documenting systems and testing that they are actually working as intended.
- *Risk database.* Another development is the compilation of a detailed risk register or database that records major risks and where they fall across the organization. This is another area where audit have some expertise in that many audits involve tracking risks and assessing which ones need to be mitigated.

- *Employee surveys.* There is a growing use of surveys to check on issues such as the state of control awareness, understanding of risk, degree of control compliance, and perceptions of ethical behavior. These issues all contribute to the development of a good control environment, and many audit teams have spent time using such surveys to check where the organization stands in risk and control practices.
- *Corporate compliance checks.* SOX and other regulatory guidance require that organizations get a grip on their internal controls and ensure that the workforce properly observe the risk management arrangements. The importance of compliance reviews is pretty much ingrained in many audit departments and there is a great deal of help that auditing can provide in teaching the management the ways of promoting and monitoring compliance with control routines.
- *Data interrogation.* Control standards are based on high levels of success in business and support systems and processes. Rogue transactions can creep into any system where human error, system failures, and unforeseen circumstances kick in to cause problems for the organization. Attention to the integrity of systems throughout the organization can be checked through interrogating the data and ensuring that incorrect or inappropriate transactions are quickly identified and corrected. Powerful data interrogation tools have been used by auditors for many years and are an important part of the measures to help achieve well-controlled systems:

  In exercising due professional care the internal auditor should consider the use of computer-assisted audit tools and other data analysis techniques.[18]

- *Risk profiling.* Internal control is based on tackling risks before they harm the business. It is this understanding of risk that enables the management to ensure that there is good control. Risk profiling is essential in helping ascertain where the risks are and how they impact the organization. Again, auditors have a lot to offer in helping this happen.
- *Fraud detection.* The final example of audit tools relates to fraud detection. Many of the problems that led to the emergence of SOX resulted from corporate fraud and a generally lax attitude to accounting policies and practices. Each organization needs to have in place a sound antifraud policy, including a fraud detection strategy, if it is to report that controls are generally sound. The auditors, while not specialist fraud investigators, can help create the type of culture

where the risk of fraud is appreciated and addressed at all levels in the organization:

> The internal auditor should have sufficient knowledge to identify the indicators of fraud but is not expected to have the expertise of a person whose primary responsibility is detecting and training update specialist skills.[19]

The question then arises as to how to best build the use of these tools into the audit-planning process. Tools that used to be applied to individual audits may now be applied across the business to promote a corporate wide initiative to get financial and disclosure controls documented, tested, and improved. It is difficult to see how the audit team can prepare a long-term plan without taking on board the pressing need to respond to challenging new demands on the business.

CASE STUDY

Using ERM as the Driver

One audit department consisting of seven audit staff reporting to the CAE was asked to present a paper on ERM to their audit committee. The paper covered the implications of establishing an ERM process throughout the organization and the need to set up a suitable infrastructure based on the risk policy. The audit committee asked the CAE to take the lead on this task and redirect at least two audit staff to work over the next six months to provide ways for taking the ERM process forward. The current annual audit plan was redrafted with this in mind and the work undertaken by the two auditors was described as an audit-consulting project. The audit committee defined the failure to install ERM as one of their biggest risks and accepted cuts in other parts of the audit plan to fund this new work.

Charter

The right-hand side of Figure 1.2 brings the audit charter into the audit-planning process. In the past, this consideration was straightforward, as most charters would simply state that internal audit would seek to add value to the organization in line with the formal definition of the audit function. Before we explore this idea further, it is appropriate to define the charter:

> The charter of the internal audit activity is a formal written document that defines the activity's purpose, authority, and responsibility. The charter should (a) establish the internal audit activity's position within

> the organization; (b) authorize access to records, personnel, and physical properties relevant to the performance of engagements; and (c) define the scope of internal audit activities.[20]

We have suggested that the audit role adopted must be aligned to the position that the organization has achieved in terms of designing and implementing an effective response to SOX/ERM requirements.

CASE STUDY

Internal and External Audit Roles

The audit charter of a small private sector audit team made a clear distinction between the work of the external auditor as compared to the work of the internal auditor. The internal auditor's work was related to nonfinancial systems so as to keep clear of the external auditor's verification of financial statements. The Audit Committee (AC) asked the CAE to include accounting systems within the scope of IA work, particularly relating to the application of accounting policies and practices that impacted the financial statements. The audit charter was changed to reflect this measure and made mention of IA supporting the board in the way it formulated its corporate disclosures regarding internal controls over financial reporting.

IIA Standard 1000 makes it clear that internal audit's role should be defined in a charter, consistent with the standards, and approved by the board. Note that when a standard indicates that something should happen, this means, according to the IIA's glossary of terms, it is a mandatory obligation. Before we can talk about audit planning, we need to work out where our responsibilities lie. There is help at hand in the form of IIA guidance:

> Risk management is a key responsibility of management. To achieve its business objectives, management should ensure that sound risk management processes are in place and functioning. Boards and audit committees have an oversight role to determine that appropriate risk management processes are in place and that these processes are adequate and effective. Internal auditors should assist both management and the audit committee by examining, evaluating, reporting, and recommending improvements on the adequacy and effectiveness of management's risk processes. Management and the board are responsible for their organization's risk management and control processes. However, internal auditors acting in a consulting role can assist the organization in identifying, evaluating, and implementing risk management methodologies and controls to address those risks.[21]

Each audit charter should reflect the emerging role of audit in improving corporate governance, and IIA guidance creates a challenge in this respect:

> Section 404 of Sarbanes-Oxley requires management's development and monitoring of procedures and controls for making their required assertion regarding the adequacy of internal controls over financial reporting, as well as the required attestation by an external auditor, regarding management's assertion. Section 302 deals with managements' quarterly certification of not only financial reporting controls, but also disclosure controls and procedures. The requirements of Sarbanes-Oxley place responsibilities on both management and independent accountants. The Standards require that the internal audit activity evaluate and contribute to the improvement of the organization's risk management, control, and governance processes through consulting and assurance activities.[22]

Aims

Our model includes the aims of the audit department as a fundamental aspect of the planning process. In one sense, planning is about taking steps to ensure that the aims set are achieved and these aims need to be fully clarified before we can move on. Moreover, the actual aims of the audit process must be set against the context outlined earlier. We can turn to authoritative guidance to start our discussion:

> Internal audit functions typically provide an assessment of risks and control activities of a business unit, process, or department. These assessments provide an objective perspective on any or all elements of enterprise risk management, from the company's internal environment through monitoring. In some cases particular attention is given to risk identification, analysis of likelihood and impact, risk response, control activities, and information and communication. Internal audit, based on its knowledge of the business, may be positioned to consider how new company initiatives and circumstances might affect application of enterprise risk management, and to take that into account in its review and testing of relevant information.[23]

This viewpoint is reinforced in the New York Stock Exchange Rules that require every listed company to have an internal audit function to provide management with an ongoing assessment of the company's risk management process and systems of internal control. In terms of SOX compliance, most experts agree that internal audit should offer a significant amount of support and guidance. Most listed companies are establishing formal projects to design and implement a suitable response to SOX, and internal audit will need to sort out how it can best assist this task. One auditor has commented on the impact of disclosure requirements:

> There will be a SOX component in every audit program we execute, as an independent verification that management is performing work for their quarterly sub-certifications.[24]

When defining aims, the CAE needs to be aware of overall responsibilities for managing the audit team:

> The chief audit executive is responsible for properly managing the internal audit activity so that:
>
> Audit work fulfills the general purposes and responsibilities described in the charter, approved by the board and senior management as appropriate.
>
> Resources of the internal audit activity are efficiently and effectively employed.
>
> Audit work conforms to the International Standards for the Professional Practice of Internal Auditing (Standards).[25]

Using the IIA standards as a framework, the CAE will need to set out the audit objectives, which may include the following:

1. **Objective.** Provides independent, objective assurance and consulting services. The IIA defines objectivity as:

   > An unbiased mental attitude that *allows* internal auditors to perform engagements in such a manner that they have an honest belief in their work product and that no significant quality compromises are made. Objectivity requires internal auditors not to subordinate their judgment on audit matters to that of others.[26]

2. **Adds value.** Designed to add value and improve an organization's operations. The IIA defines value add as:

   > Value is provided by improving opportunities to achieve organizational objectives, identifying operational improvement, and/or reducing risk exposure through both assurance and consulting services.[27]

3. **Achieves objectives.** Helps an organization accomplish its objectives. The auditors need a good understanding of what the management is seeking to achieve. Management's role is set out by the IIA:

Management plans, organizes, and directs the performance of sufficient actions to provide reasonable assurance that objectives and goals will be achieved. Management periodically reviews its objectives and goals and modifies its processes to accommodate changes in internal and external conditions. Management also establishes and maintains an organizational culture, including an ethical climate that understands risk exposures and implements effective risk strategies for managing them.[28]

4. **Professional.** Brings a systematic, disciplined approach to evaluate and improve the effectiveness of risk management, control, and governance processes. Audit plans will need to demonstrate exactly how this objective will be achieved. Conversely, published plans that are not linked to this task may well be substandard.

RISK-BASED AUDIT-PLANNING MODEL: PHASE THREE

Our model is continued in Figure 1.3.

Figure 1.3 Risk Management Framework Model: Phase Three

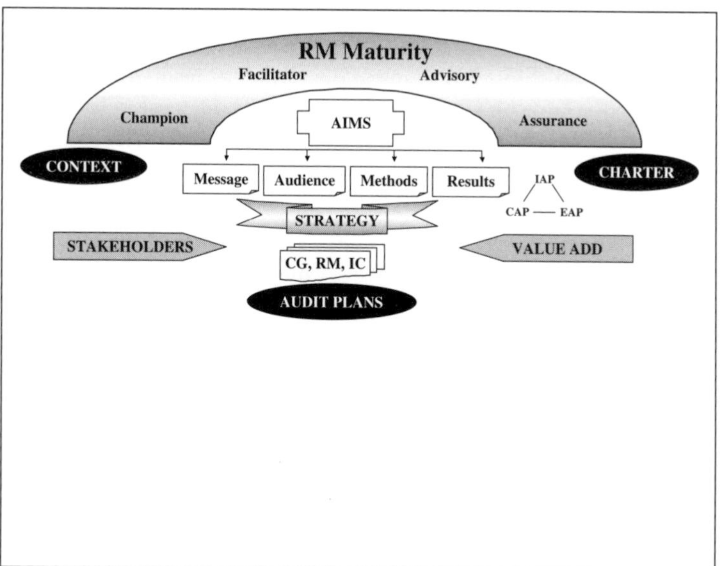

Each new aspect of the model is described in the following paragraphs.

Stakeholders

The concept of stakeholders has grown over the years to have a huge impact on all types of organizations. Commercial companies can no longer just make large profits to be successful—they need to take on board the needs and expectations of all key stakeholders who are affected by the way they work. Public service stakeholders means that federal and state government officials cannot simply aim at a range of targets, but must also judge the way their services impact the client groups and the general public. Likewise, auditors need to build the concept of stakeholders into the planning process in terms of who will lose out if the audit process is flawed or simply inefficient. There are many groups who are affected by the services that are being delivered, or for that matter, audit services that are not being properly delivered, including:

- *The audit committee.* The audit committee will need to review and approve all audit plans and will want these plans to demonstrate that they make good use of scarce audit resources.
- *The board.* The board will be concerned that audit plans feed into the corporate agenda to improve governance, risk management, and internal control—and ensure that they receive an objective opinion on whether enough is being done in this respect.
- *The CEO and PFO.* The Chief Executive Officer (CEO) and Principal Finance Officer (PFO) assume personal liability for many governance disclosures and they will want audit plans to do as much as possible to ensure there are no slip-ups that damage the corporate reputation.
- *Senior management.* Top management will look to the audit plans for help in getting ERM in place.
- *The external auditor.* Internal audit plans should feed into the work that is carried out by the external auditor to form a comprehensive "audit process." The external auditor will want the internal audit plans to enrich this concept and provide a platform for solid audit work for the year to come.
- *The customer.* So far, not many audit shops acknowledge the fact that their services reach out beyond the corporate boundary and help give credibility to the products that end up with the customer. As such, the customer may be seen as a stakeholder for the auditor and has a stake in the audit plans that are prepared and implemented within the organization. Customers may rest easy if they feel that

the organizations they subscribe to are well run, perform well, and adhere to all relevant rules and regulations.

- *The corporate investor.* Many corporate scandals have left scars on investors who have lost money. CAEs may do well to think through the expectations of corporate investors and the way in which they might benefit from a high-impact risk-based audit plan that tackles important parts of the organization.

The main expectation of stakeholders is that the audit process is planned and performed with professional proficiency:

> Professional proficiency is the responsibility of the chief audit executive (CAE) and each internal auditor. The CAE should ensure that persons assigned to each engagement collectively possess the necessary knowledge, skills, and other competencies to conduct the engagement properly.[29]

Value Add

We have already mentioned that added value sets an important challenge for the CAE, but there is a word of warning from WorldCom at spending too much time chasing the "golden goose" of value add:

> At WorldCom, risk analysis was instead performed with the goal of selecting audits that could add "value" to the Company by emphasizing revenue enhancements and cost reductions. Moreover, the lack of any consultation with Arthur Andersen resulted in gaps in audit coverage. Given the absence of a comprehensive risk-based internal audit plan, there was no apparent relationship between the audits scheduled annually and the risk and the effectiveness of internal controls associated with these audit areas.[30]

The concept of value is nonetheless important as each part of the organization has to have some form of value proposition:

> The value proposition of the internal audit activity is realized within every organization that employs internal auditors in a manner that suits the culture and resources of that organization. That value proposition is captured in the definition of internal auditing and includes assurance and consulting activities designed to add value to the organization by bringing a systematic, disciplined approach to the areas of governance, risk, and control.[31]

One issue that supports the value add concept is the type of services that audit provides in helping improve the organization's risk management process. Research funded by the IIA Research Foundation considered the question: *To what extent is internal auditing involved in these ERM activities?* [32] The results are shown in Figure 1.4.

We would expect that the value added by the auditors is maximized by the use of risk-based audit planning, which means the CAE will need to consider:

- Clarifying audit's role in risk management.
- Ensuring how it can help ensure that ERM itself adds value to the organization.
- Resourcing ERM training and development programs for the workforce.
- How to help the organization progress through the stages of ERM maturity.

Figure 1.4 To What Extent Is Internal Audit Involved in ERM Activities?

Scale ranging from 1–5:

1: No internal audit activity

5: Extensive internal audit activity

Internal Auditing is involved in:	**Response**
Coordinating ERM efforts among internal auditing and others	3.8
Assisting with risk identification in ERM (establishing list of possible risks)	3.7
Suggesting control activities to ensure risk response is in place	3.7
Monitoring the ERM process	3.7
Providing ERM leadership in the organization	3.6
Providing ERM education in the organization	3.5
Performing risk assessments in ERM (considering likelihood and impact)	3.5
Assisting with identifying risk responses (deciding how to respond to risks)	3.0

Source: Internal Auditing Journal, February 05, page 71, ERM: A Status Report, survey funded by the IIA Research Foundation, 2004.

- Producing audit plans that are driven by the strategic risks facing the organization.
- The extent to which the audit plans to incorporate an understanding of risk dependencies and interdependencies.
- The way that ERM is being used to employ a holistic approach to risk management within the business.
- Moving away from silo audit plans to holistic enterprise wide risk-based plans.
- Focusing on the business, business processes, risks, and internal controls.
- Using the corporate risk database and the expertise of corporate risk specialists
- Using the audit process to provide a health check on the state of ERM within the organization.

It is only after considering items such as those listed above that we can really start talking about achieving top value from the audit process.

Message, Audience, Methods, and Results

The next item on our Model relates to the need to ensure that audit planning takes on board the need to get the audit mission into the organization by focusing on four main matters:

1. **Message.** The audit plan sets out what audit will be doing in the future and in this way communicates important messages about what audits see as important and what does not make it to the table. If these messages are out of step with perceptions of importance in the business itself, then they may convey a view that audits are not aligned with the corporate agenda.
2. **Audience.** Another issue that has to be addressed when formulating the audit plan relates to the target audience. Stakeholders were discussed earlier and these groups are directly or indirectly the audience for audit services. The audit-planning process should be based on a careful consideration of who receives drafts and final versions of the plans. It should also consider ways to generate interest among the target audience so that people are encouraged to look forward to the planning documents and can appreciate how the work will benefit them.

3. **Methods.** Audit planning must adhere to an agreed methodology for it to make any sense. The adopted methodology will be one that suits the organization and satisfies the CAE, audit committee, and board. Methodology should be based on risks to the business, whatever be the detailed model in use.
4. **Results.** It is important to return to first principles to work out why we plan and what results we expect from risk-based audit plans. Good plans should lead to excellent work, well-informed managers who know when an audit will occur, and well-motivated auditors who can see how they will be contributing to the organization over the ensuing months and years.

The four-pronged approach is necessary to drive the audit process through the organization in a way that is understood and appreciated. Paul Sobel has defined an important aspect of the audit-planning process by suggesting that auditors must:

> Plan their audit activities to periodically reassess the design and operation of key risk management processes.
>
> Make periodic evaluations of the ongoing accuracy and effectiveness of the communications from risk owners to senior management, and from senior management to the board.[33]

This essential task must not only be carried out but should be carried out in such a way that the value is fully appreciated in the organization. SOX has caused some concern among both executives and nonexecutives and the auditors are, in a sense, rushing to the rescue. The new audit-planning approach has come on board to address this issue as described below:

> Assessing risks in real-time means that identifying and evaluating risks is an ongoing, infinite process that cannot be accomplished in a once a year, weeklong exercise. Organizations, their markets, and the general business environment are constantly changing, and the risks affecting the organization change right along with them. To stay on top of an entity's dynamic risk environment, internal auditing's processes for assessing risk must include mechanisms for continually acquiring new risk information.[34]

The approach to auditing risk management in one organization will differ from what is used in other organizations. This point is fully recognized in auditing standards, which means a rigid checklist approach can be useful but must be used with care.

> Internal auditors should recognize that there could be significant variations in the techniques used by various organizations for their risk management practices. Risk management processes should be designed for the nature of an organization. Depending on the size and complexity of the organization's business activities, risk management processes can be:
>
> Formal or informal.
>
> Quantitative or subjective.
>
> Embedded in the business units or centralized at a corporate level.[35]

Strategy

The next item to be addressed is strategy, which appears as the central component of our model. The context has been set in terms of the ongoing development of ERM that appears in most organizations. But, before getting to the more detailed aspects of the audit-planning process, there needs to be a clear strategy in place that drives the audit department. Strategy is about setting a long-term direction for ensuring that we know how we are currently positioned with an organization, and working through where we want to be and how we can progress toward the aspired position. In formulating strategy, there are five fundamental questions to be addressed:

1. Where do we currently stand in the organization and where do we want to be in one-, two-, or three-years' time?
2. What services do we currently provide to the organization and what do we want to provide in one-, two-, or three-years' time?
3. How are we currently perceived by our stakeholders and how do we want to be perceived in one-, two-, or three-years' time?
4. How does our audit team currently perform in terms of efficiency and effectiveness and how do we want them to perform in one-, two-, or three-years' time?
5. To what extent do we currently add value to the organization and to what extent do we want to add value in one-, two-, or three-year's time?

These five questions could be addressed by the audit team if it carried out a risk assessment, and considered threats and opportunities to the set audit objectives, using the five items as a platform for this task. If the auditors recommend risk management throughout the business by calling it ERM, there is really no good reason why this technique could not be used by the auditors themselves. Paul Sobel has given a clue as to the drivers that may be used to support a change in audit strategy, as we move into the new ERM dimension by considering four levels of change in the approach to audit work:

1. Control-based auditing
2. Process-based auditing
3. Risk-based auditing
4. Risk-management-based auditing[36]

As audit teams move into risk-management-based auditing, the audit strategy will need to change to reflect the new challenges, and Sobel goes on to suggest that risk-management-based auditing is a key part of a successful ERM program. In fact, we may well be moving into ERM-based auditing, where the audit process is determined by the risks facing the organization and the way risk is being managed as suggested in the following case study.

CASE STUDY

Focusing on Disclosure Risk

One organization assumed a wide concept of risk management that addressed the risk of poor business performance but also incorporated the risk of:

- Poor SOX compliance.
- Failure to document, evaluate, test, and operate effective controls.
- Poor understanding among management of their responsibilities for internal control over business operations and financial reporting.
- Failure to identify and report "material weaknesses" in internal control over financial reporting.
- Inability to track changing risks and ensure that they are mitigated if they result in exposures outside the corporate risk appetite.
- Lack of appreciation of the importance of corporate social responsibilities and codes of conduct.
- Poor coordination of assessment work that support Sections 301, 302, and 404 that result in duplication of effort.

The audit department was asked to take into account these risks when setting their annual audit plan and help review and monitor these risks, as well as test for compliance, in almost all audit work that was carried out across the organization. One spin-off was a turnaround in audit staff where facilitation skills were prioritized and auditors received detailed training in ERM and governance.

Audit strategy feeds into audit plans, while audit plans determine the types of audit products to be delivered. If this equation is ignored, the final result may well be an audit service that is substandard and poorly thought out. The audit strategy also provides a framework that defines the auditors' input into the risk management process, and the balance between audit assurance and consulting services will have to be carefully planned against the risk maturity concept discussed earlier.

CG, RM, and IC

The next item in our model, which appears before we get to the actual audit plans, includes Corporate Governance (CG), Risk Management (RM) and Internal Control (IC) dimensions. These are defined as follows:

Corporate Governance:

The combination of processes and structures implemented by the board in order to inform, direct, manage and monitor the activities of the organization toward the achievement of its objectives.[37]

Risk Management:

A process to identify, assess, manage, and control potential events or situations, to provide reasonable assurance regarding the achievement of the organization's objectives.[38]

Control:

Any action taken by the management, the board, and other parties *to manage* risk and increase the likelihood that established objectives and goals will be achieved. The management plans, organizes, and directs the performance of sufficient actions to provide reasonable assurance that objectives and goals will be achieved.[39]

It is a good idea not to forget the three components of audit work when setting the audit plans. The audit plans will focus on how auditors can make a positive contribution to improving governance, risk management, and controls within the organization by addressing several important questions:

- How can audit contribute to better governance?
- What is the state of play with ERM and how can audit stimulate progress?

- How effective are internal controls and does the current control framework deliver results?

It is also important to keep in mind the formal scope of audit work when considering audit's role in risk management:

> Based on the results of the risk assessment, the internal audit activity should evaluate the adequacy and effectiveness of controls encompassing the organization's governance, operations, and information systems. This should include:
>
> Reliability and integrity of financial and operational information.
>
> Effectiveness and efficiency of operations.
>
> Safeguarding of assets.
>
> Compliance with laws, regulations, and contracts.[40]

Audit Plan

The final part of this stage of the model is the actual audit plan. A good starting place is the IIA standard that tackles audit planning:

> The chief audit executive should establish risk-based plans to determine the priorities of the internal audit activity, consistent with the organization's goals.[41]

Good audit plans have the following attributes:

- Promote shareholder confidence.
- Represent a good use of the audit budget.
- Enhance corporate reputation.
- Reflect organizational values, goals, and conduct.
- Increase auditors' motivation.
- Ensure that the delivery of audit services has a major impact on the organization.
- Keep the regulators happy.
- Make life easier for the external auditors.

Another way of viewing risk-based audit plans is to suggest that good plans guard against the risk of not achieving the above mentioned attributes. The audit plan should be risk assessed and inclusive in the way it is developed:

> The internal audit activity's plan of engagements should be based on a risk assessment, undertaken at least annually. The input of senior management and the board should be considered in this process.[42]

A short case study follows.

CASE STUDY

Scoring Audit Units

An audit team established a risk assessment model based on the format shown in Figure 1.5.

Figure 1.5 Scoring Audit Units

Audit Area	Risk Factor 1 Materiality	Risk Factors 2 Importance to the Business	Risk Factor 3 Audit Committee Requests	Rating
Xxx				
Yyy				
Zzz				

Having assigned a score where each audit area is scored high, medium or low risk the following audit cycle length is set:

High risk areas:	Audited every year
Medium risk areas:	Audited every two years
Low risk areas:	Audited every three years

RISK-BASED AUDIT-PLANNING MODEL: PHASE FOUR

Our model continues in Figure 1.6.

Figure 1.6 Risk-Based Audit-Planning Model: Phase Four

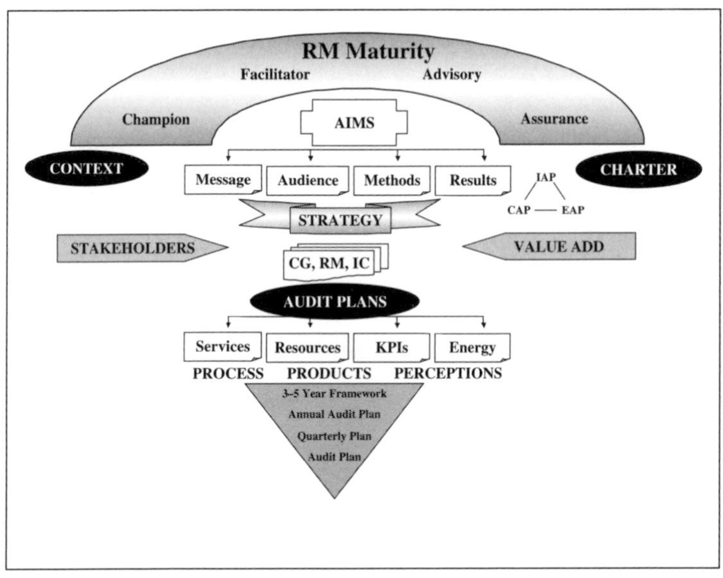

Each new aspect of the model is described in the following paragraphs.

Services

The next item that should be considered during audit planning is the types of services that audit perform. There are several aspects of audit work to be noted:

Review operations:

Internal auditors should consider all parts of the business and not just the financial systems:

> Internal auditors should review operations and programs to ascertain the extent to which results are consistent with established goals and objectives to determine whether operations and programs are being implemented or performed as intended.[43]

Compliance:

Internal auditors should be concerned about the degree to which the organization is in compliance with all relevant laws, rules, regulations, and procedures. Audit work may focus on checking compliance or concentrate on reviewing the arrangements that are designed to promote compliance with procedures.

Consulting projects:

Auditors may engage in consulting projects where they work primarily for the manager who has requested the work. These consulting engagements should be built into the plan as far as possible, or resourced from a contingency allowance for additional work. Larger projects may mean that a revised plan will have to be submitted by the CAE to the audit committee during the year.

Assurances on internal control:

An important audit service, based on much of the existing audit work, is formal assurance on the internal controls applied by the organization. This opinion may be the culmination of the individual audits performed during the year or may be derived from special reviews of the internal control environment and the controls reporting arrangements.

Corporate governance arrangements:

Most audit shops are starting to advise top management about any failings in the governance arrangements that are in place within the organization. These failings may result from a lack of proper observance of corporate policies such as those relating to conflict of interests not being declared by board members. Failings may also be about not living up to the best practice guidance issued by regulatory bodies and authoritative sources.

ERM:

Internal audits must be prepared to formulate an opinion on ERM. This means commenting on whether the organization has developed suitable arrangements for identifying and dealing with risks to the business and taking on board guidance such as that found in the COSO ERM document. Audit plans need to reflect this growing dimension of audit work for it to be of real value to an organization.

Facilitation and awareness training:

Many audit shops are making space in the audit plan for helping to kick-start or implement risk management programs and risk/control awareness training across the organization. As such, allowance has to be made in audit plans for time to be spent on these projects, as they form part of many audit teams' core services.

Advice and information:

Rather than engage on large projects to help implement risk management within an organization, many audit teams are providing a low-key support role. This support may consist of general advice or information made available to managers, supervisors, and work teams as and when required. This all-important aspect of audit work needs to be resourced, and again, audit plans have to be adjusted to allow for time spent on this aspect of audit work.

Others:

This category is included here to reflect the need for a flexible approach to audit planning when new issues may appear on the board agenda that are sent down to the auditors. If the board feels it is important and if this view is endorsed by the audit committee and falls in line with audit standards, then the work may be reflected in audit plans. This open door policy moves audit into the real world outside the audit offices, where problems occur and everyone is asked to rally round the agreed solutions. Audit independence should nonetheless be preserved:

> Impairments to individual objectivity and organizational independence may include personal conflicts of interest, scope limitations, restrictions on access to records, personnel, and properties, and resource limitations (funding).[44]

Where such impairments are not apparent from the request for audit coverage, the CAE may well get involved in other noncore audit services. Using audit's role to focus audit plans is often the best way forward, and a case study illustrates this approach:

CASE STUDY

Helping the Audit Committee

A small audit team based in a manufacturing company focused their audit plans around the services that they were asked to provide by the audit committee. The terms of reference for the audit team were defined as:

- Compliance
- Information systems
- Value for money

Helping the Audit Committee *(continued)*

Using these three main headings the planning categories were then further refined in terms of corporate risk as:

1. **Compliance**—Key risks:
   a. Breach of control disclosure regulations
   b. Breach of local state laws
   c. Breach of industry specific provisions
   d. Breach of operational procedures
2. **Information systems**—Key risks:
   a. Failure of systems security
   b. Incorrect data processing
   c. Poor contingency arrangements
   d. Substandard systems coming on line
3. **Value for money**—Key risks:
   a. Inefficient operations
   b. Overstocking
   c. Poor business performance
   d. Poor financial management

The audit-planning template involved setting risk scores against each of the risk categories across the organization as shown in Figure 1.7:

Figure 1.7 Audit Planning Template

Audit Topic	1a–d 1–10	2a–d 1–10	3a–d 1–10	Score 3–30

High scoring parts of the organization were then placed into the annual audit plan up to the level that could be handled by the audit team in post. Each year the audits would be rescored to arrive as a new audit plan for the following year.

Resources

Another planning consideration relates to the type of resources that need to be in place to support audit plans. There is much guidance on the best way to consider resources for the audit plan, and IIA standards set the primary challenge:

> The chief audit executive should ensure that internal audit resources are appropriate, sufficient, and effectively deployed to achieve the approved plan.[45]

Where the audit team is too small to deliver the audit plan, steps should be taken to fill this gap through secondment, recruitment, use of temporary and contract staff, and co-sourcing arrangement. Where the audit plan calls for specialist expertise that does not reside with the audit team, help may be secured from an external service provider, which is defined as:

> A person or firm, outside of the organization, who has special knowledge, skill, and experience in a particular discipline.[46]

These external specialists may be used for a variety of jobs as suggested below:

> Information technology, statistics, taxes, language translations, or to achieve the objectives in the engagement work schedule.
>
> Valuations of assets such as land and buildings, works of art, precious gems, investments, and complex financial instruments.
>
> Determination of quantities or physical condition of certain assets such as mineral and petroleum reserves.
>
> Measuring the work completed and to be completed on contracts in progress.
>
> Fraud and security investigations.[47]

Key Performance Indicators

We turn next to Key Performance Indicators (KPIs) as an important part of performance management. Good plans, when achieved, lead to good results. The problem is that these plans need to be monitored to ensure that they are carried out as intended, and this is where KPIs come into play. Audit plans should lead to the development of targets that can be tracked by audit management in line with an overall mission:

> The internal audit activity should evaluate and contribute to the improvement of risk management, control, and governance processes using a systematic and disciplined approach.[48]

The results may also be reported to the audit committee to satisfy their need to oversee the efficiency and effectiveness of the audit service. There is a whole range of KPIs that can be used to keep the audit service on track, but in terms of delivering the audit plan, these may include the following items:

- Preparation of a risk-based audit plan that meets the needs of key stakeholders.
- Approval of an annual audit plan by the audit committee in time for the New Year.
- Completion of the annual quarterly audit plan.
- Development of quarterly audit plans that fit in with the logistical issues facing the areas that are being audited.
- Engagement plans that focus on terms of reference that represent the best use of audit resources in conjunction with the type of risks that face the area under review.
- An audit-planning process that is in line with existing best practice in the audit world.

It is quite easy to set out a list of aspirations, but it is much more difficult to turn these into specific, measurable, achievable, result-oriented, and time-based targets that together lead to a good use of the available audit staff.

CASE STUDY

Using the Audit Opinion

In one audit department, the annual audit plan was developed using the categories of work that the audit committee had decided were needed to form the audit reports that they received each year and each quarter from internal audit. They asked for an audit opinion on:

- The governance arrangements.
- The development of an ERM framework and process.
- Internal controls reporting systems, particularly relating to financial systems.
- The overall state of compliance, antifraud arrangements, and ethical conduct within the organization.
- Whether operational procedures in each of the business lines were addressing risk in an appropriate manner.

Using the Audit Opinion *(continued)*

The audit plan contained targets for each of the above and the main driver was that sufficient work needed to be completed by the auditors each year to allow a formal view of the listed items. Moreover, at least one consulting project was required during the year that helped address the way the organization had improved in these areas. The audit committee monitored these targets and was particularly concerned about the overall state of the control culture within the organization as reported through annual surveys and management reports. The CAE was meant to help improve the workforce's basic understanding of governance, risk management, and internal controls and the way these matters were built into the business units, partners, corporate planning, and support services.

Energy

We have placed the idea of "energy" within the model to bring out the importance of using plans to drive the motives and focus of the auditors. Stagnation is extremely dangerous to the audit process if the previous year's plans are updated and rolled forward with minor changes. Stagnation could also occur if a cycle of audits is rolled out, where every part of the organization is visited on a one-, two-, or three-year basis. More now than ever before, audits have been placed in the spotlight where legislators, regulators, and top executives in all types of businesses have been made aware of the importance of auditors in the governance and performance equation. This heightening of expectations has put audit right up front with the top agenda issues that are crucial to organizational success. But at the same time, the enhanced expectations place a burden on the CAE to define, design, and deliver a top-class audit service. The best-set plans have little impact if these plans are not delivered with gusto and some urgency. It is this urgency that makes the difference between an adequate audit service and a world-class one. The CAE can inject energy into the audit team by using the following guidelines:

- Involve the entire audit team in the planning process by getting them to input ideas, do research, and make sure they understand how the plan is developed and approved.
- Make audit managers responsible for defined aspects of the plan under the overall direction of the CAE. Getting the audit managers

to buy into the plans is the best way to motivate them. They in turn will motivate their junior audit staff.

- Let people know what they will be doing over the next quarter so that they can look forward to the work. At the same time, there must be some flexibility built into the process so that the CAE can make changes wherever necessary.
- Take into account career development aspects of the audit team; it may also be possible to incorporate individual preferences in the plan.
- Discuss the plan and any proposed changes in audit manager meetings and audit department meetings and conferences. Listen to views where it makes sense and use draft plans to ensure it is possible to make changes where there is strong feedback.
- Make sure the plan itself is sensible and meets the needs and expectations of key stakeholders.
- Try to move away from the cyclical approach that suggests the auditor does each audit periodically and performs much the same basic tasks on an annual basis. Even where the same audit that was completed last year is being performed this year, the preliminary survey should ensure that the terms of reference reflect current risk profiles.
- Make clear that planning is an important task and leads to professional work that enhances the reputation of the auditors and leads to a better-managed organization.
- Finally, make sure the planning methodology is well defined and understood by the audit team. If done well, a three-year audit strategy should mean that each individual audit and audit task represents a valuable piece of work.

High levels of energy applied by the audit team are great if directed at the right issues and if they produce the right results, as was achieved by one audit department.

CASE STUDY

Dropping the Cyclical Approach

One head office–based audit team for a pharmaceutical group, with over 50 overseas operating companies had operated a cycle of routine audits for many years and managed to review each part of the business once every two years.

Dropping the Cyclical Approach *(continued)*

The audit team was quite used to working through a set audit program in an audit area that it had worked in many times before, and the CAE noticed that many audit staff were demotivated and bored. The CAE moved away from the cyclical audits and adopted a risk-based approach where she completely reformatted the audit plans each year having regard to the corporate risk register and what was deemed important to the organization for the period in question. The outcome was a series of high-level audits that concentrated on key corporate issues and resulted in a marked increase in energy, motivation, and enjoyment from the audit team.

Products

If the audit-planning process is dynamic and takes on board all the issues that have so far been discussed, it would be possible to deliver various significant audit products as described below:

- *An improved risk management process.* The auditor should benchmark where an organization stands in terms of the development of an effective risk management process and work toward improving the position.
- *Better secured IT systems.* Many boards do not have a place for IT security on their agenda as they feel it is a technical matter. If there is no real security officer in place, the auditors will need to make sure that the risk to corporate systems is properly understood and mitigated by management. Corporate governance has as a subset IT governance through which business systems are protected and suitable contingency arrangements are made in the event of an attack, disaster, or systems failure. IT controls are important to all systems, including financial ones, and fraud, error, and breach of regulations can arise where these systems are not properly protected.
- *Corporate social responsibility.* This is another important issue that audit may have to lead on, if it is not already being championed elsewhere in the organization.
- *Help for the external auditors.* External auditors may be helped, based on their evaluation of internal audit's plans and ways suggested to reduce their coverage in respect of areas already addressed by internal audit.

Some audit products are not in fact part of audit's proper workload. These products represent non–audit work where auditing involvement has been requested. Where this happens, due regard should be given to Practice Advisory 1130.A1-2.

> When the internal audit activity or individual internal auditor is responsible for, or management is considering assigning, an operation that it might audit, the internal auditor's independence and objectivity may be impaired. The internal auditor should consider the following factors in assessing the impact on independence and objectivity: International Standards for the Professional Practice of Internal Auditing (Standards); The requirements of The IIA s Code of Ethics; Expectations of stakeholders that may include the shareholders, board of directors, audit committee, management, legislative bodies, public entities, regulatory bodies, and public interest groups; Allowances and/or restrictions contained in the internal audit activity charter; Disclosures required by the Standards; and Subsequent audit coverage of the activities or responsibilities accepted by the internal auditor...If on occasion management directs internal auditors to perform non-audit work, it should be understood that they are not functioning as internal auditors.[49]

Process

One aspect of the planning system that needs to be considered is the way planned audit is actually performed. Audit standards set a basic requirement on this topic:

> The chief audit executive should establish policies and procedures to guide the internal audit activity.[50]

Good plans using good auditors will deliver good results, but only if there is a sound process in place, which means effort gets properly translated into professional work.

CASE STUDY

Engaging Stakeholders

In one audit shop, risk-based audit planning was an important part of the overall audit process, which was as follows:

- Engage with key stakeholders about their objectives and expectations.
- Determine the risk universe that relates to the entire organization, broken down into auditable units.

Engaging Stakeholders *(continued)*

- Formulate a three-year audit strategy based on improving the governance, risk management, and control environment.
- Establish risk-based audit plans that balance consulting work to improve risk management and controls, with assurance work that reports on areas where there are unacceptable levels of risk.
- Construct quarterly audit plans that make a final allocation of audit resources to the planned work areas with a contingency for additional work that may need to be covered.
- Prepare monthly work plans for each member of audit staff and ensure there are briefings and staff meetings that help energize the audit teams.
- Assign a lead auditor to each audit and perform a preliminary survey to refocus the terms of reference for the audit in question.
- Using the set terms of reference, perform fieldwork to perform the audit.
- Discuss findings and talk about ways forward with the line management in question.
- Issue and draft the final report that seeks to improve risk management arrangements and determines the status of the existing conditions.
- Follow up the audit after a suitable time frame to ensure agreed recommendations are implemented.
- Ensure that the cumulative results of audit work can be reported to the audit committee and board in a way that supports control disclosures made by the CEO.
- Ensure that the above is conducted in line with professional audit standards.

Perception

Planning should take on board the image that audit has throughout the organization: that is, how audit is perceived by its principal stakeholders. IIA standard 1220 covers "Due Professional Care":

> Internal auditors should apply the care and skill expected of a reasonably prudent and competent internal auditor. Due professional care does not imply infallibility.[51]

A second audit standard also comes into play:

> The internal audit activity should be free from interference in determining the scope of internal auditing, performing work, and communicating results.[52]

CASE STUDY

Communicating Aims

A small audit team developed a clear customer focus strategy based on delivering high-impact risk-based audits that kept the clients in close touch with audit plans, engagement dates, fieldwork, and draft audit reports. Much use was made of briefings with the client and electronic files to ensure the company management understood:

- The role of internal audit.
- The way the annual audit plan was put together to focus audit resources on high-risk elements of the organization.
- The timing of audits and the aim to help managers improve the way they assess risk and install controls to guard against them.
- The positive way that controls could be applied to ensure opportunities can be grasped as well as threats contained.
- Feedback surveys are used to secure information regarding the audit service and all information received is acted on by the CAE.

There are several basic steps that the CAE could take to improve the perceived standing of the audit function:

- Work through audit's stakeholders and find out what they know about the audit service and what they expect from their auditors.
- Line up the current audit services against the above and also benchmark them against professional auditing standards and guidance issued by the IIA.
- Include an improvement plan within the audit strategy to grow and improve the audit process.

It is a good idea to continually reassess the views of internal audit's key stakeholders and judge whether this viewpoint can be improved on. Plans that set targets on this matter may be made an important part of the overall audit planning process. There is no short cut and Practice Advisory 2100-3 sets a real challenge for the auditor in suggesting that:

> The chief audit executive should obtain an understanding of management's and the board expectations of the internal audit activity in the organization's risk management process. This understanding should be codified in the charters of the internal audit activity and audit committee.[53]

Three- to Five-Year Framework

The next element of the basic planning model consists of a funnel that starts with the long-term plan and ends with the actual audit. If this link between the different planning horizons is well structured, then high-level aspirations can get translated into actual audit work. Meanwhile, high-level strategic risks can become focused at the detailed operations level, again in actual audit work. Audit standards can be used as a good start place:

> The chief audit executive should establish risk-based plans to determine the priorities of the internal audit activity, consistent with the organization's goals.[54]

Practice Advisory 2010-1 makes clear that long-term plans need to fit with the overall direction of the organization and the way the audit process is meant to help promote this direction:

> Planning for the internal audit activity should be consistent with its charter and with the goals of the organization.[55]

Most audit departments create a three- to five-year plan, although many are now scaling down the planning time frame to shorter periods to reflect that risk change can be so rapid that any plans that seek to reach out over a year may not be worth the effort. Much depends on the type of organization and business sector in question. An oil company may well have a 15-year plan of exploration and penetration, while a software company may predict a product life span in months rather than in years. In the past, audit teams tended to resource a cycle of audits that ensured each part of the organization was audited over, say, a three-year period. Many argue that the audit approach has been developing over the years to move the definition of risk from:

> The chance that audit will not visit parts of the organization where non-compliance and poor performance is happening unbeknown to head office management.

to a newer interpretation of risk:

> The chance that audit will not help the organization optimize its enterprise risk management process and so undermine its governance arrangements and its overall system of internal control, through the provision of effective assurance and consulting services.

The leap from the first to the second levels of audit planning can be tremendous and this forms the basis for most of this book. Superimposed over the move to risk-based auditing is the view that each year the audit function should plan to move forward and progress toward world-class professionalism. Note that the annual audit plan is discussed in some detail later on in the book.

Quarterly Audit Plan

The longer-term plans set out what may be seen as a set of aspirations that audit promises to accomplish rather than as concrete targets. Many view the quarterly planning process as the ideal time frame for firming up these aspirations and formulating clear plans, with dates, targets, and resource allocations. IIA guidance suggests that:

> The planning process involves establishing:
>
> Goals
>
> Engagement work schedules
>
> Staffing plans and financial budgets
>
> Activity reports.[56]

A great deal of this activity may be carried out during the quarterly planning and review process. The audit team may focus on work schedules, assigning work to audit staff and setting targets for the work. Once targets have been set, audit management needs to take steps to ensure that these targets are achieved as suggested by IIA guidance:

> The goals of the internal audit activity should be capable of being accomplished within specified operating plans and budgets and, to the extent possible, should be measurable. They should be accompanied by measurement criteria and targeted dates of accomplishment.[57]

There are some audit teams that have taken the quarterly planning period to the heart of the audit process and restrike the plan every three months as described in the case study:

CASE STUDY

Flexing the Plan

An audit team established a rapid review system where the audit plan was reformulated each quarter, in conjunction with its audit committee. While the

Flexing the Plan *(continued)*

annual plan contained an overall framework for the year's audit work, because of the fast changing environment within which the organization operated, the real planning period was set as a quarterly exercise. For many years, the CAE could not give an assurance that the audits set out in the annual plan at the start of the year were the best use of resources as the year progressed. This situation existed for some time before the audit committee agreed that the quarterly revised plan contained a much more realistic view of the best audit coverage for the organization.

Audit Plan

The audit-planning process concludes with planning the actual engagement. If the entire planning process is robust and properly designed, it may start with a high-level aspiration to, for example:

> Formulate an opinion on the state of ERM and internal controls with a view to helping management make suitable improvements.

This may be applied throughout the auditors' work so that an audit engagement may have as its terms of reference words along the lines of:

> Review the adequacy of risk management and internal control in the application of security vetting for senior operations personnel in the Florida Area Office.

While a consulting engagement may appear as:

> Assist the project manager with designing a rapid response based risk assessment system to support the implementation of Project X.

The problem arises when audit engagements are planned with no reference to the long-term planning framework. In this instance, audit work can become fragmented and lead to no long-term advances for the organization. Moreover, the audits themselves can be demotivating for audit staff who have no overall sense of direction to help energize their performance. The CAE should evaluate the coverage of the proposed plan from two viewpoints:

Adequacy across organizational entities and

Inclusion of a variety of transaction and business-process types.

If the scope of the proposed audit plan is insufficient to enable the expression of assurance about the organization's risk management and control processes, the CAE should inform senior management and the board of the expected deficiency, its causes, and the probable consequences.[58]

RISK-BASED AUDIT PLANNING MODEL: FINAL

Our complete model is presented in Figure 1.8.

Each new aspect of the final model is described in the following paragraphs.

Visits, Checks, and Fraud

One element of our model relates to the dynamic nature of audit planning. Planning is not just about deciding which staff to assign to which audit. It is more about directing and motivating the audit resource through a jour-

Figure 1.8 The Complete Model

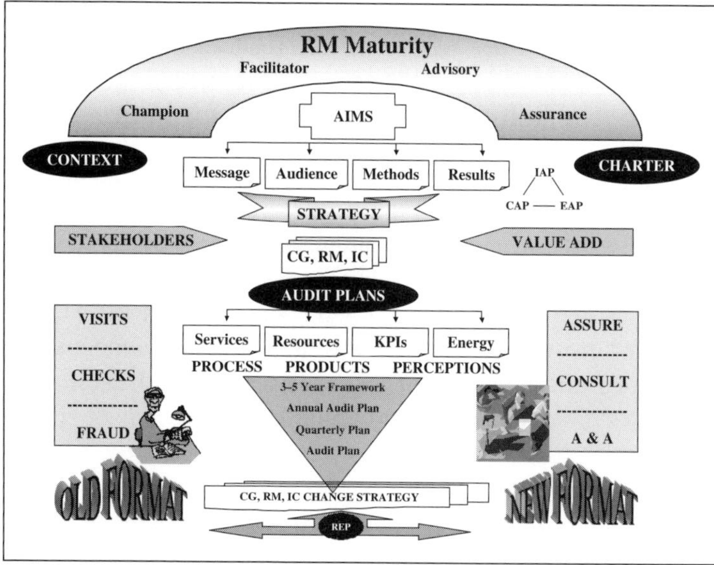

ney from where they are to where they need to be. It is about encouraging positive change for the better where the CAE has a vision for the future that becomes the force that binds the work team together around a common theme. One way to make progress is to focus on the new horizons for auditing and work out how to get closer to this horizon. Audit work used to comprise mostly of visiting remote establishments on behalf of head office management so as to judge whether the locals were behaving well and following head office procedures, the aim being to minimize fraud, abuse, errors, and general out-of-step work practices. This is what we have called the "Old Format" in our model.

CASE STUDY

Basic Risk Assessment

An old-fashioned audit team used a basic risk assessment to assign audit resources to the many local offices that were operated by the organization. The risk criteria applied to each local office were listed as follows:

- Size of workforce.
- Level of attractive portable stock items that could be pilfered by staff.
- Number of complaints from customers.
- Number of reported frauds and thefts.
- Level of errors in head office returns.
- Number of concerns raised by the head office finance department.

Offices that scored high using the above items were visited by the auditors each year, while the lower-scoring offices were seen less frequently.

Assure, Consult, Give Advice and Information (A&I)

Our model suggests that there is a "New Format" of audit work that revolves more around providing high-level assurance and consulting services to the board and audit committee, and across the organization. In this scenario, the members of the audit team are seen as the experts in governance, ERM, and internal control and spend some of their time giving advice and information (A&I) wherever this is needed within the organization. Risk-based audit planning supports risk-based audit work, and Paul Sobel has provided an idea of the most effective way of approaching audit work:

> A risk management based audit approach is the best, most comprehensive means of providing management with the assurances they desire;

that is that the key barriers to business success can be managed to an acceptable level.[59]

A case study brings home the main features of risk-management-based auditing.

CASE STUDY

Using Risk Issues

A forward-looking audit team developed a "risk issues" criteria for planning audit work. Using the corporate risk register, board risk management strategy, and discussions with top management, an issues document was published each year to set out the audit priorities for the ensuing year. The annual audit plan was derived from these discussions and made for a common sense approach to risk-based audit planning.

Old and New Formats

The move from the old format to the new format for audit work is built into our planning model and changes the auditor from being an inspector to an in-house governance, risk, and control expert. The differences in these two dimensions of style are summarized in Figure 1.9.

Figure 1.9 Old versus New Format

Old Style	New Style
Low-level audit process	Efficient risk focus to planning
Inflexible plans	Collaboration and change
Long-winded reviews	Embedded quality assurance
Many missed areas	Customer focus
Negative connotations	Positive value driven
Fragmented audit teams	Common themes driving audit work
Detailed reports	Automated executive reporting
CFO reporting line	Wider reporting line (to the audit committee)

CG, RM, and IC Change Strategy

We have already mentioned corporate governance (CG), risk management (RM), and internal control (IC) several times in the sense that these three concepts define the new-look auditor. We have suggested that a change strategy is embedded within the audit-planning process since most types of larger organizations are embarking on a journey to improve their governance arrangements to ensure they fit the heightened expectations from all parties who have a stake in the way an organization performs and behaves. Planning has little use if it is not based on setting clear goals and directing one's efforts toward these goals. Audit planning has little use if it does not revolve around a change strategy for encouraging better governance, robust risk management, and more reliable internal controls.

CASE STUDY

Using a Planning Forum

An audit team developed a current risk planning forum. Here, audit plans were completely reappraised each quarter to take on board all developments in the previous quarter. The audits that were completed during the year bore little resemblance to the annual audit plan set at the start of the year. The audit committee had agreed to a dynamic review mechanism whereby the annual audit plan was reapproved each quarter to reflect the various changes that would invariably have been put forward by the CAE. Most of these changes were in response to adjustments to the corporate risk register from new strategies, takeovers, and changes to operations and systems that were a feature of the way the organization worked. The above plans were held together by several common themes that incorporated the need to review and help improve the organization's ERM process and control disclosures infrastructure. Each proposed change to the audit plan was assessed against these criteria before being formally adopted.

Report

The final component of our first audit-planning model is reporting. Planning sets out what should be done and by whom, while after the work has been performed, it needs to be reported. It is always a good idea to build reporting into planning models as it is then possible to work backward, by defining what needs to be reported on by the audit department, and therefore what needs to be planned and performed to ensure that these reports can be delivered. Planning systems that do not incorporate the reporting process tend to be flawed. Management, the board, and/or the audit committee may well want to see several reports from the auditors, covering, for example:

- Assurances to the board regarding the adequacy and effectiveness of risk management arrangements and internal controls across the business.
- An account of the consulting work and ways in which the auditors have supported the development of governance, risk management, and controls.
- Information on high-risk aspects of the business where there is actual or potential for the corporate risk appetite to be exceeded.
- Information that can be used to gauge the success of internal audit in conjunction with the expectations of the audit committee and demands of professional auditing standards.
- Details of special investigations, systems failure, and breach of procedure that should be brought to the attention of the audit committee.
- Ways in which internal and external audit have cooperated to ensure best use of available resources.
- Any other information requested by the audit committee.

Another way to view audit reports is to consider what the CEO and board are obliged to report and how the auditors can input into these demands. IIA standards reinforce two main features of a good audit report:

> The CAE should evaluate the coverage of the proposed plan from two viewpoints: adequacy across organizational entities and inclusion of a variety of transaction and business-process types. If the scope of the proposed audit plan is insufficient to enable the expression of assurance about the organization's risk management and control processes, the CAE should inform senior management and the board of the expected deficiency, its causes, and the probable consequences.[60]

CASE STUDY

Controls Assurance Reporting

A firm of internal auditors won several audit contracts in the highly regulated heath service sector by focusing on assurance risk. The winning audit strategy presented to the audit committee was based on the following formula:

- Determine the exact regulatory disclosure requirement for the organizations in question.

Controls Assurance Reporting *(continued)*

- Isolate the assurance framework from various internal review teams and processes, along with control certifications from the management divisions that support the board's internal control disclosures.
- Review the assurance framework and determine which aspects were inadequate and in need of improvement.
- Place the above in an improvement program involving staff development, training programs, reporting tools, and self-assessment workshops.
- Indicate where the audit resource will be focused over the next year in terms of high-risk aspects of assurance reporting and areas where there is a need for further independent assurances to support the board's statements on internal control.

The above was then incorporated in an audit strategy that formed the basis of the successful bids for the contract for internal audit coverage of the organizations in question.

SUMMARY

It takes some effort to formulate good risk-based audit plans, and some audit teams are tempted to take short cuts in getting around planning so that audit staff can spend much more time on actual audit engagements. In our view, risk-based audit planning should be properly resourced, as it is a crucial part of auditors' work. One way to realize the benefits from risk-based audit planning is to go through the following five steps:

1. Understand the resources it takes to formulate a good, risk-based audit plan and make sure that audit managements are convinced of the benefits, including the need to tackle the risk of poorly focused plans.
2. Develop a clear policy on assurance and consulting work in the context of the state of maturity of ERM within the organization.
3. Understand and build in the concerns and views of key stakeholders when developing a risk-based planning process.
4. Ensure there is a strategy that sets a framework for risk-based audit planning designed to add value to the organization through the best application of audit resources.

5. Use risk-based audit planning to help drive new interpretations of audit's role, moving from traditional approaches to a balanced assurance and consulting service.

Note that Appendix A contains a checklist that can be used to assess the overall quality of risk-based audit planning.

NOTES

1. United States Bankruptcy Court, Southern District of New York, Re: WorldCom, Inc et al, Chapter 11 Case No. 02-15533 (AJG), Jointly Administered, Second Interim Report of Dick Thornburgh, Bankruptcy Court Examiner, June 9, 2003, page 193.
2. Institute of Internal Auditors, Professional Practices Framework.
3. Internal Auditing's Role in Sections 302 and 404 of the U.S. Sarbanes-Oxley Act of 2002, May 26, 2004, Section D. The Institute of Internal Auditors.
4. Internal Audit and Business Risk Journal, February 2005, pages 19–21, 2004, Oversight Systems Financial Executive Report on Sarbanes-Oxley Compliance. (www.oversightsystems.com)
5. Institute of Internal Auditors, Practice Advisory 1000.C1-2.
6. Institute of Internal Auditors, Practice Advisory 1000.C1-2.
7. Institute of Internal Auditors Global Auditing Information Network—GAIN Flash Survey March 2005—on audit planning—Workplan completion Rates.
8. United States Bankruptcy Court, Southern District of New York, Re: WorldCom, Inc et al, Chapter 11 Case No. 02-15533 (AJG), Jointly Administered, Second Interim Report of Dick Thornburgh, Bankruptcy Court Examiner, June 9, 2003, Page 193—Deficiencies in the Annual Internal Audit Planning Process (extracts).
9. Institute of Internal Auditors, Glossary of Terms.
10. Institute of Internal Auditors, Practice Advisory 1130.A1-1.
11. Institute of Internal Auditors, Practice Advisory 1110-2.
12. Institute of Internal Auditors, Standard 2010.C1.
13. Institute of Internal Auditors, Standard 2020.
14. Institute of Internal Auditors, Glossary of Terms.
15. Institute of Internal Auditors, Practice Advisory 2120.A1-1.
16. Moeller, Robert and Witt, Herbert (1999), *Brink's Modern Internal Auditing*, 5th edition, New York: John Wiley & Sons, page 314.
17. Institute of Internal Auditors Survey, March 2005, IIA's Global Auditing Information Network—Gain, SOX Impact on Audit Plan.
18. Institute of Internal Auditors, Standard 1220.A2.
19. Institute of Internal Auditors, Standard 1210.A2.
20. Institute of Internal Auditors, Glossary of Terms.
21. Institute of Internal Auditors, Practice Advisory 2100-3.
22. Internal Auditing's Role in Sections 302 and 404 of the U.S. Sarbanes-Oxley Act of 2002, May 26, 2004, Institute of Internal Auditors.
23. Committee of Sponsoring Organizations, Enterprise Risk Management, Application of Techniques, September 2004, page 87.

24. Institute of Internal Auditors Survey, March 2005, Institute of Internal Auditors Global Auditing Information Network—Gain, SOX Impact on Audit Plan.
25. Institute of Internal Auditors, Practice Advisory 2000-1.
26. Institute of Internal Auditors, Glossary of Terms.
27. Institute of Internal Auditors, Glossary of Terms.
28. Institute of Internal Auditors, Practice Advisory 2100-1.
29.. Institute of Internal Auditors, Practice Advisory 1200-1: Proficiency and Due Professional Care.
30. Southern District of New York, Re: WorldCom, Inc et al, Chapter 11 Case No. 02-15533 (AJG), Jointly Administered, Second Interim Report of Dick Thornburgh, Bankruptcy Court Examiner, June 9, 2003, Page 193—Deficiencies in the Annual Internal Audit Planning Process (extracts) United States Bankruptcy Court.
31. Institute of Internal Auditors, Practice Advisory 1000.C1-1.
32. Internal Auditing Journal, February 05, page 71, ERM: A Status Report, Survey funded by the IIA Research Foundation, 2004.
33. Auditors Risk Management Guide, Integrating Risk Management and ERM, Paul J Sobel, CCH Incorporated (Chicago) 2004, page 1.12.
34. Anderson, Urton and Chapman, Christy (2002), "The IIA Handbook Series" in *Implementing The Professional Practices Framework*, IIA, p.93.
35. Institute of Internal Auditors, Practice Advisory 2110-1.
36. Auditors Risk Management Guide, Integrating Risk Management and ERM, Paul J Sobel, CCH Incorporated (Chicago) 2004, pages 3.03–3.10.
37. Institute of Internal Auditors, Glossary of Terms.
38. Institute of Internal Auditors, Glossary of Terms.
39. Institute of Internal Auditors, Glossary of Terms.
40. Institute of Internal Auditors, Standard 2120.A1.
41. Institute of Internal Auditors, Standard 2010.
42. Institute of Internal Auditors, Standard 2010.A1.
43. Institute of Internal Auditors, Standard 2120.A3.
44. Institute of Internal Auditors, Glossary of Terms.
45. Institute of Internal Auditors, Standard 2030.
46. Institute of Internal Auditors, Glossary of Terms.
47. Institute of Internal Auditors, Practice Advisory 1210.A1-1.
48. Institute of Internal Auditors, Standard 2100.
49. Institute of Internal Auditors, Practice Advisory 1130.A1-2.
50. Institute of Internal Auditors, Standard 2040.
51. Institute of Internal Auditors, Standards 1220.
52. Institute of Internal Auditors, Standard 1110.A1.
53. Institute of Internal Auditors, Practice Advisory 2100-3.
54. Institute of Internal Auditors, Standard 2010.
55. Institute of Internal Auditors, Practice Advisory 2010-1.
56. Institute of Internal Auditors, Practice Advisory 2010-1.
57. Institute of Internal Auditors, Practice Advisory 2010-1.
58. Institute of Internal Auditors, Practice Advisory 2120.A1-1.
59. Auditors Risk Management Guide, Integrating Risk Management and ERM, Paul J Sobel, CCH Incorporated (Chicago) 2004, 3.10.
60. Institute of Internal Auditors Practice Advisory 2120.A1-1.

2

BASIC PLANNING TECHNIQUES

> The chief audit executive should effectively manage the internal audit activity to ensure it adds value to the organization.
>
> —IIA Standard 2000

INTRODUCTION

In Chapter One, we have shown the benefits of using risk-based planning along with providing a description of some of the elements that underpin the auditors' approach to developing suitable plans. Chapter Two aims to stand back from the audit context and outline some of the basic concepts that relate to planning. Planning is about defining expectations and focusing resources in a way that is designed to achieve more effective results. For auditors, planning should be flexible enough to achieve several objectives including to:

- Establish good relations with clients.
- Develop a better control environment in the organization.
- Secure a culture that encourages compliance with the procedure within the organization.
- Generally help promote processes that respond effectively to risks that impact the organization's objectives.

Simple models are used to illustrate the factors that support good planning.

BASIC PLANNING MODEL: PHASE ONE

Our first model appears in Figure 2.1.

Figure 2.1 Basic Planning Model: Phase One

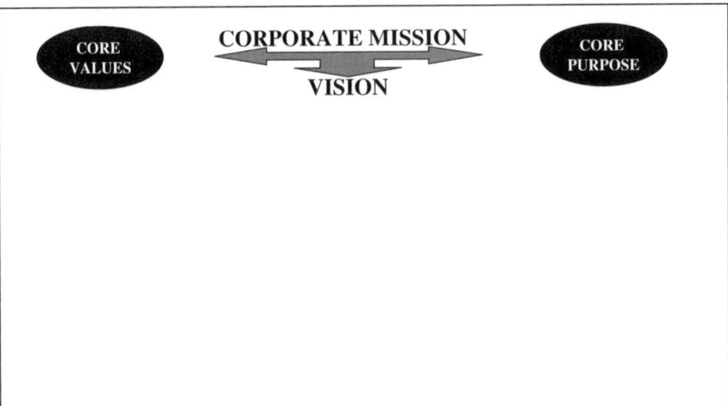

Each aspect of the model is described in the following paragraphs.

Corporate Mission

All plans should start with the mission that has been adopted by the entity in question. For auditors, the mission may revolve around the formal definition of adding value from internal auditing and incorporate the set components of this ideal:

> Improving opportunities to achieve organizational objectives, identifying operational improvement, and/or reducing risk exposure through both assurance and consulting services.[1]

CASE STUDY

The Audit Mission

In one organization, the auditors were asked to develop a mission that was based on improving the control environment within the organization. The audit plan was broken down into the following components:

The Audit Mission *(continued)*

1. Control awareness training.
2. Compliance reviews.
3. Key control reviews.
4. Control failure investigations.

The auditors were asked to help prepare control frameworks, based on the COSO model, and assess parts of the organization on a quarterly basis using a set benchmark. The audit team recently rescoped the plan to focus on the development of ERM within the organization. The new annual audit plan is broken down into:

1. ERM awareness training.
2. Compliance with risk policy reviews.
3. Facilitated risk workshops.
4. Consulting projects on helping management implement the ERM assessment, recording, and reporting infrastructure.

The mission should revolve around set responsibilities, and IIA standards suggest that risk assessment should be used to drive the auditors' work:

> Based on the results of the risk assessment, the internal audit activity should evaluate the adequacy and effectiveness of controls encompassing the organization's governance, operations, and information systems. This should include:
>
> Reliability and integrity of financial and operational information.
>
> Effectiveness and efficiency of operations.
>
> Safeguarding of assets.
>
> Compliance with laws, regulations, and contracts.[2]

For audit, the scope of work provides a framework within which the mission can operate. The mission should come from the chief audit executive, who is defined as holding the:

> Top position within the organization responsible for internal audit activities. *Normally*, this would be the internal audit director. In the case where internal audit activities are obtained from outside service providers, the

> chief audit executive is the person responsible for overseeing the service contract and the overall quality assurance of these activities, reporting to senior management and the board regarding internal audit activities, and follow–up of engagement results. The term also includes such titles as general auditor, chief internal auditor, and inspector general.[3]

Vision

The set mission is important because it tells everyone what is currently being done. The vision on the other hand is less tangible and tells everyone what we would like to be in the future. This vision creates a mental picture about the future in the minds of those working for the entity. Vision is important because it can help define strategy, in the sense that one can draw a map of how to arrive at the end result—or at least move forward toward this result. There is a great deal of guidance that is available to help the CAE work with the audit team in defining a shared vision that reaches out and extends the audit process into important new areas of work. One such reference is found in IIA standards:

> The internal audit activity should assess and make appropriate recommendations for improving the governance process in its accomplishment of the following objectives:
>
> Promoting appropriate ethics and values within the organization.
>
> Ensuring effective organizational performance management and accountability.
>
> Effectively communicating risk and control information to appropriate areas of the organization.
>
> Effectively coordinating the activities of and communicating information among the board, external and internal auditors and management.[4]

The question that confronts the CAE is, if this is not already happening, how can it be planned? Sarbanes-Oxley is one development that should be fed into the visioning exercise that audit teams should embark on from time to time. The IIA have set out their vision of the audit's role in Sarbanes-Oxley:

> The Institute of Internal Auditors (IIA) definition of internal auditing is: Internal auditing is an independent, objective assurance and consulting activity designed to add value and improve an organization's operations. It helps an organization accomplish its objectives by bringing a systematic, disciplined approach to evaluate and improve the effectiveness of

risk management, control, and governance processes. The IIA's International Standards for the Professional Practice of Internal Auditing (Standards) specifies that the chief audit executive (CAE) establish risk-based plans to determine the priorities of the internal audit activity, consistent with the organization's goals. Internal auditors should consider Sarbanes-Oxley noncompliance as a risk to the organization, along with all other risks, in their risk assessment process for determining internal audit plans and focus of their efforts. This audit risk assessment should also be reevaluated each year and audits assessment results should be disclosed to and discussed with the audit committee.[5]

CASE STUDY

Chasing the Vision

An engineering company had a history of poor systems, which meant regular complaints from clients whose products were often late, incomplete, and at times poorly conceived. The board had developed many operational procedures to get quality products out to clients, but these were often bypassed by the work teams, who were driven by several key performance targets. As a result, the board asked internal audit to concentrate their resource on a single vision of helping to achieve a well-trained, risk-aware, and compliant workforce who operated good procedures that were properly observed. This vision drove audit's plans, and measures were established to assess the extent to which the vision was being achieved. The main risk to the organization was seen as a failure to achieve the set vision.

It is a good idea to hold visioning workshops every few years to gauge the current impacts on the audit function and how these might alter in the future—or more precisely, how audit can take hold of its future and ensure it is in control. Some of the ways that the visioning workshops may be used include the following:

- To help focus the mission as a way of making the vision a reality.
- As part of the review of corporate objectives.
- To underpin a 3–5 year strategy and corporate annual plan.
- To help ensure that set benchmarks can be developed to assess the adequacy of results.
- To help define poor performance.
- To ensure limited resources are utilized efficiently.
- To underpin short- and long-term goals.

- To help define good performance and key performance areas.
- To give direction to process models used to target resources.
- To provide a compelling statement that can be driven down into the business.
- To ensure tools and systems lead the organization in the right direction.
- To support the desired work environment.
- To help define which products lead to a more successful future.
- To help management rise above the day-to-day detail and initiative overload.
- To help define a road map to success.
- To deter crisis management where unclear ideas lead to poor decisions.
- To support good leadership and stimulate a desire to act among staff.
- To provide direction to customer relations management.
- To help define core competencies needed from the workforce.

Where the organization has set a clear vision for the future, the onus is on the auditors to assess how that may be part of the effort to achieve this vision. The audit portfolio and resource allocation will determine which aspects of audit work will be prioritized and which will not be covered and signed off by the CAE. Audit's own mission statement, web site, and balance between assurance and consulting work will all reflect the input from the audit team toward the future direction of the organization.

Core Values

So far, our model suggests that the entity's chief officer, in our case the CAE, simply gets the audit team together and sets the mission and vision, or simply sits alone and conjures up a vision from blue-sky thinking. What is closer to the truth, and therefore built into our placing model, is that the mission is set within the context of the core values and core purpose of the audit function. For most back-office parts of an organization, the task of defining internal services, and making sure that these services are first class now and in the future, is quite straightforward. The task becomes one of discovering what these services are and then designing the most efficient way of delivering them. For auditors, it is not quite so simple. Auditors produce help and analysis that is reliable because it is carried out to professional standards and it is objective. Following this line, the audit services are objective because there is no conflict of interest that interferes with the ability to provide an impartial audit opinion. A conflict of interest is defined as:

> Any relationship that is or appears to be not in the best interest of the organization. A conflict of interest would prejudice an individual's ability to perform his or her duties and responsibilities objectively.[6]

Where there is a problem, it must be disclosed, as advice is available in the IIA's guidance for managing any impairment regarding audit's role in Sarbanes-Oxley:

> The CAE should ensure that the audit committee is kept up to date on the role and activities of internal audit in the organization's efforts to comply with Section 404. Instances where objectivity will be impaired by the role the internal audit activity assumes should be discussed with the audit committee prior to assuming this role. In addition, the implications as well as any impact to both current and future audit plans, because of devoting resources to assisting in Section 404 compliance efforts, should be discussed with the audit committee. Where the internal audit activity's objectivity is impaired, the CAE and the board need to consider how this impairment affects the ability to perform future internal audit engagements.[7]

A short case study illustrates one approach:

CASE STUDY

Audit-Committee Drivers

One CAE prepared a core service audit plan each year consisting of reviews of key systems relating to financial accounting, security, IT, and basic business operations. The audit committee would then nominate a series of high-level reviews to be completed each quarter and the remaining time was assigned to consulting projects requested by management. The annual plan therefore included the following:

1. Core systems cycle
2. Audit-committee topics
3. Consulting projects

Core Purpose

The mission and vision of the audit setup cannot simply be invented on the basis of what the management wants from its auditors. The audit shop must fulfill a core purpose for it to be of any real use. This core purpose is summed up in professional standards, legislation, and local regulations for the industry in question. For example, IIA guidance on the audit's role in risk management suggests the following:

> Internal auditors are expected to identify and evaluate significant risk exposures in the normal course of their duties. The internal audit activity's role in the risk management process of an organization can change over time and may be found at some point along a continuum that ranges from:
>
> No role, to
>
> Auditing the risk management process as part of the internal audit plan, to
>
> Active, continuous support and involvement in the risk management process such as participation on oversight committees, monitoring activities, and status reporting, to
>
> Managing and coordinating the risk management process.
>
> Ultimately, it is the role of executive management and the audit committee to determine the role of internal audit in the risk management process. Management's view on internal audit role is likely to be determined by factors such as the culture of the organization, ability of the internal auditing staff, and local conditions and customs of the country.[8]

Moreover, the auditors cannot simply embark on all work that comes their way without considering the implications. IIA guidance on the internal auditor's responsibility for other (nonaudit) functions states:

> Individual auditors with operational responsibility should not participate in the audit of the operation. If possible, auditors conducting the assessment should be supervised by, and report the results of the assessment to, those whose independence or objectivity is not impaired. Disclosure should be made regarding the operational responsibilities of the auditor for the function, the significance of the operation to the organization (in terms of revenue, expenses, or other pertinent information), and the relationship of those who audited the function to the auditor.[9]

The audit mission has therefore got to be set, having reference to what are acceptable and unacceptable working practices. The final point to note is that the scope of audit activities has been carefully considered by the profession and there are standards that cover the remit of audit work that need to be taken into consideration when determining the range of audit work that will be performed:

> Based on the results of the risk assessment, the internal audit activity should evaluate the adequacy and effectiveness of controls encompassing the organization's governance, operations, and information systems. This should include:
>
> Reliability and integrity of financial and operational information.
>
> Effectiveness and efficiency of operations.
>
> Safeguarding of assets.
>
> Compliance with laws, regulations, and contracts.[10]

The temptation to redefine audit's role without reference to external requirements can be overpowering as demonstrated in one case study:

CASE STUDY

The Lack of Strategy

In a large transport logistics company, the CAE felt that the demands on top management were all consuming and did what he could to help alleviate the pressures. He offered the entire audit staff to work in parts of the organization on "fire-fighting" duties. Where management and performance problems occurred, auditors were sent in to help them clear up the mess. Many problems arose from poorly conceived reactive systems and a lack of good risk management. This issue did not appear on the CAE's agenda as audit's role has been set as "helping prop up a poor management team." This policy reinforced the management team's approach and in fact meant that the deficiencies in management practices and policies were not addressed, as auditors plugged the gaps that appeared on a regular basis. The in-house audit team did not prepare any formal plans but assumed a policy of responding to requests from operational management across the business to help them deal with the day-to-day operational problems that resulted from dated and inefficient systems and poor working practices. A newly appointed CEO cleared out old-fashioned directors who had sat on the board for many years, set up a dynamic audit committee, got rid of over half of the senior and middle management and eventually outsourced the internal audit team. A new three-year improvement strategy aimed at core systems, better management, and staff training programs led to a greatly improved company.

BASIC PLANNING MODEL: PHASE TWO

So far, we discussed the overriding mission of the audit department and the way this has to be contained within a professional framework. Having arrived at a working model for the role and purpose of audit work, we can turn to more detailed aspects of the planning process, including objectives and how set targets may be used to drive performance. Our model is further enhanced in Figure 2.2.

Each new aspect of the model is described in the following paragraphs.

Strategic Analysis

Having established our role in the organization, the next stage in the basic planning model is developing a strategic analysis of issues and a possible response to the changing and dynamic environment that most organizations work within. Gap analysis may be used to determine where audit stands and how far it needs to progress to become world class. Strategic analysis should be inclusive and involve the audit team and stakeholders in setting a future direction. It should also result in clear decisions, ac-

Figure 2.2 Basic Planning Model: Phase Two

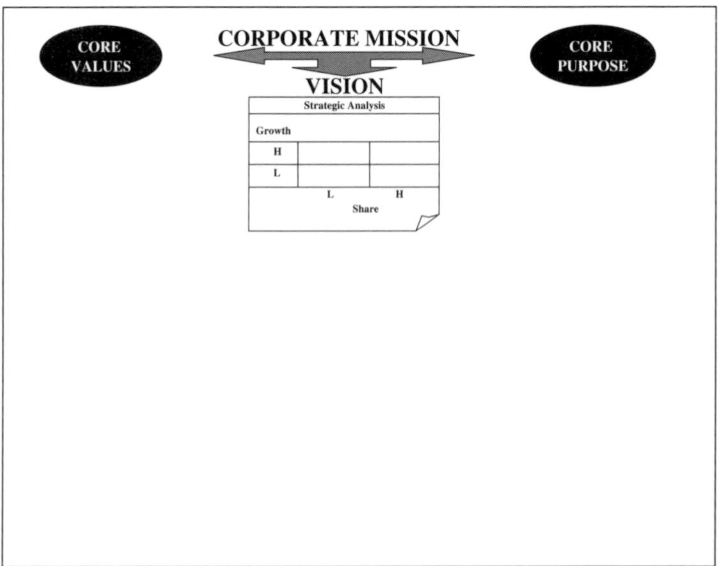

tions, and making a choice between alternative options, after weighing the pros and cons or, better still, the threats and opportunities that need to be managed. There is no reason why the audit team should not apply the standard environmental analysis that tends to be used in strategy setting. This analysis (many refer to it as PESTLE) will seek to isolate various important issues relating to:

- *Political.* The overall position on regulation, taxation, employment laws, and general level of political stability leads to an environment that either supports the audit process or calls for less review work. These political themes need to be closely monitored by the CAE to assess where the audit team stands and where it affects, for example, the balance between consulting and assurance work. Efforts to clamp down on rogue companies demand more assurance work from the auditors. A contrasting view that business and public interest organizations need to be encouraged to grow and innovate tends to promote more of a consulting basis for audit works.
- *Economic.* The economic situation facing different types of businesses should also be built into audit plans. Levels of growth in the economy, interests rates, exchange rates, and inflation levels all point to a need either to expand the audit department in line with a growing economy or to contain the audit budget because businesses needs to slow down to consolidate their period of growth. A CAE who gets this wrong will fall out of line with the rest of the business and either appear too expensive and top heavy or too light and superficial.
- *Social.* Factors such as health consciousness, population age and rates of growth, careers attitudes, and safety concerns impact audit as well as the rest of the organization. The strategic analysis will need to take on board these factors to ensure there is the right mix of audit staff and that compensation packages make sense.
- *Technological.* It is a brave CAE who ignores the growth in information and communications technology when establishing an audit strategy. The concept of the roving auditor has developed over the years over three levels.

    1. “I’m out of the office for a few weeks so I cannot be contacted.”
    2. “Have laptop; will travel.”
    3. “Not sure where I will be this week but I’m hooked into the corporate coms 24-7.”

- *Legal.* Auditors have a particular interest in compliance that is, in encouraging compliance, assessing compliance, and using compliance as a basis for assessing which key controls work well. Many compliance issues relate to corporate policies and local procedures, but many also relate to the legal and regulatory framework that impacts the business in question. The CAE will need to have a good handle on the legal framework that impacts the business in question as well as on issues that have a direct affect on audit work and the audit setup.
- *Environmental.* The final factor that most agree should be part of the external strategy analysis is the environmental issue. In some organizations, audit can operate as the conscience to counterbalance the constant struggle for profits or performance targets. Many environmental concerns relating to, say, overseas contracts or the treatment of low paid employees can affect the corporate reputation and eventually the bottom line if not addressed. The CAE will need to keep an eye on public perceptions and build the role of ethics advocate into the audit strategy where appropriate.

Moreover, after having isolated the external context, the usual SWOT analysis may also be applied to consider how the audit process is responding to these influences:

- *Strengths.* The audit department may well have a good reputation for top-quality performance, well-trained resources, and a network of experts that can be called on to support the audit service where required. All these matters should form the basis for a clearly defined maintenance and development strategy.
- *Weaknesses.* In contrast, issues such as poor branding, high costs, a lack of unimpaired access to corporate information, and a poor relationship with external audit may hold the audit team back. These and similar weaknesses should not be ignored, and it is a good idea to include steps to tackle known concerns within the audit strategy.
- *Opportunities.* Audit work is not stagnant and there is always room to develop new customers, promote less onerous controls, and expand audit work in new directions such as consulting projects and audit-committee support. These developments represent opportunities that may be grasped to expand the audit service and not allow it to stagnate.
- *Threats.* The final factor that needs to be built into the CAE's audit strategy is the recognition of threats to the continued viability of the audit service. This could range from an external firm, to an unimpressed audit committee through to out and out rebellion from

operations managers who see the auditors as mere intruders who interfere with their ability to get their jobs done.

Case Study

Developing Strategy

A large audit department was led by a CAE and four audit managers. As part of the strategy-setting exercise that is held every year, the CAE and managers met together at a hotel and were facilitated by a management consultant who took them through a formal strategy-setting workshop. The team analyzed their strengths, weaknesses, opportunities, and threats. They also assessed the PESTLE factors that impact their audit department. After discussing these issues for some time, the audit management team developed a clear strategy and action plans.

Growth

There are two major decisions that have to be made concerning the development of the audit process. One relates to a decision to expand the team (or not), while the other decision relates to the range of services that are being provided and, again, whether this should be expanded (or not). There are benefits in allowing, or encouraging, the audit team to grow and take on more staff:

- The audit team can get through much more work and cover a wide range of services across the organization.
- Extra consulting work that enhances the value derived from the audit process can be taken on.
- The CAE may assume a more senior profile in the organization as the command covers a larger resource.
- The audit function can take center stage as an important and well-resourced outfit.

However, there are also dangers that include:

- The cost of the audit service can become significant and appear as a burdensome overhead.
- More auditors may be needed and recruiting the right people could pose problems.
- The CAE may spend more time managing the service and less time with clients.

- The audit team may have to spend a great deal of time proving that the budget assigned to them is worthwhile.

It is a bad idea to simply allow the audit team to grow or shrink without having made a careful analysis of the strategic direction and how the resource base supports the current audit strategy.

CASE STUDY

When the Price Is Not Right

An ambitious chief auditor designed a rapid growth strategy where the audit plans contained many promises to help get risk management in place and provide assurances across a wide range of corporate and local office systems. The costs of the team spiraled in conjunction with a major recruitment program where many new people were taken on over a six-month period. After an eighteen-month period, the audit budget represented a major part of the entire corporate services budget. The CAE was under much pressure from the board during a budget-cutting exercise and the audit service was analyzed in some detail as measures were put in place to reduce corporate overheads and streamline the business. After a further six months, a firm of auditors was asked to present its proposals to the governance and risk agenda to the audit committee. After some deliberation, the in-house audit team was disbanded and the external firm appointed to provide a finely tuned internal audit service across the business. The CAE accepted a compensation package and now works as a stock checker.

Share

The growth of the audit team needs to be related to the share of the risk management services that is assumed by the CAE. In practice, the ERM process that operates within an organization will involve many different parties, each with a defined role and set of responsibilities. IIA guidance reinforces the need to coordinate these different groups:

> Responsibilities and activities should be coordinated between all groups and individuals with a role in the organization's risk management process. These responsibilities and activities should be appropriately documented in the organization's strategic plans, board policies, management directives, operating procedures, and other governance type instruments.[11]

The type of services that may be provided by the auditors will vary from organization to organization. Our model suggests that this needs to be planned as part of the overall strategy rather than simply developed by chance. The possible services may include the following:

- Financial systems reviews
- Corporate systems reviews
- Large consulting projects
- Compliance reviews
- Fraud-prevention work
- Risk management workshops
- Ad hoc advice and assistance.

The way audit services are defined can drive the way plans are formulated.

CASE STUDY

Service-Based Audits

In one audit team division, the products were broken down into audit services as follows:

- Risk-based audits
- Process audits
- Departmental reviews
- IT reviews
- Follow-up
- External audit assistance
- Continuous CAATs
- Preimplementation audits
- Consulting services, consisting of
  - Control self-assessments
  - Internal control education
  - Special projects
  - Ad hoc assistance

The annual audit plan was based on the following factors:

- Audit issues
- Problem areas
- Suspected fraud
- Potential for cost savings
- Potential for revenue increases
- Safeguard assets

CASE STUDY

Service-Based Audits *(continued)*

The audit plans were then broken down over different parts of the organization and resourced through the use of available audit staff and additional contract staff as and when required, as shown in Figure 2.3.

In Figure 2.3, hours are adjusted for training, vacation, and other absence and the work is monitored by using the following performance targets:

Output—number of planned audits completed

Outcomes—benefits resulting from audit service

Services—degree of customer satisfaction

Efficiency—cost per agreed audit recommendation

Figure 2.3 Audit Plan Breakdown

Audit Plans	**Audit Staff Hours**	**Contract Staff Hours**	**Total**
Hours charged to divisions:			
Human resource	x	x	
Finance	x	x	
Contracts	x	x	
Business operations	x	x	
Information systems	x	x	
Planning and development	x	x	
	x	x	x
Audit management:			
Planning audit work	x		
Administration	x		
Quality Assurance	x		
	x		A
Breakdown of audit hours:			
Assurance	x	x	
Consulting	x	x	
Special investigations	x	x	
Audit management	x		
	x	x	A

BASIC PLANNING MODEL: PHASE THREE

Our model continues in Figure 2.4.

Each new aspect of the model is described in the following paragraphs.

Figure 2.4 Basic Planning Model: Phase Three

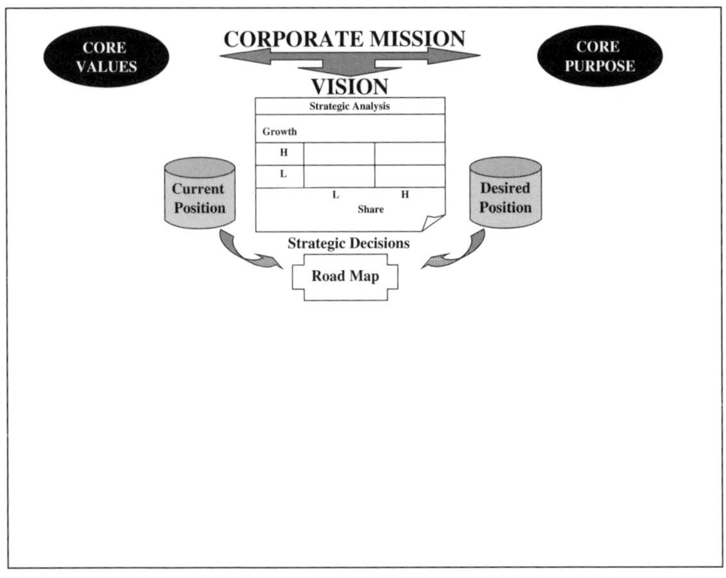

Strategic Decisions

Many strategies fail because, although they are well thought through and analyzed, they do not make it to the shop floor that is, sound decisions that result in constructive change are not made. To get strategy to work, several steps need to be taken:

Step 1. The strategy needs to be developed after a careful consideration of all relevant factors.

Step 2. It should be derived from clear objectives that move the audit service forward in a positive manner to benefit the organization.

Step 3. Strategic decisions should provide targets that are understood and supported by all members of the audit team.

Step 4. Audit management should set an example by taking a hands-on role for the more important matters that need to happen to ensure the goals of the audit department are achieved.

There is so much that the CAE can do to make audit work and work well. We have suggested that a great deal can be achieved by strategic analysis and good decision making that turns strategy into action into progress. But, it may not be as simple as this when other forces swing into action, as hinted at in audit guidance:

> Ultimately, it is the role of executive management and the audit committee to determine the role of internal audit in the risk management process. Management's view on internal audit role is likely to be determined by factors such as the culture of the organization, ability of the internal auditing staff, and local conditions and customs of the country.[12]

The final shape and form of the audit service is swayed by the organization as embodied in the CEO, the board, top management, and those nonexecutives on the audit committee.

Current and Desired Position

The next item on our model relates to the current positioning of the audit department, and the CAE should be able to assess its standing and impact on the organization. It is by comparing the current position with the desired position that we can move on to the next stage of our model, which is one of setting a road map for success. In assessing where audit stands as compared to an ideal scenario, several basic questions need to be addressed:

- Does the current audit strategy ensure the audit team is successful in light of any new circumstances that impact the organization?
- Do we do enough to provide suitable assurances to the organization's risk management process and state of internal control?
- Is auditing seen as delivering a world-class audit service?
- Does audit work to clear professional standards?
- Do the audit committee see the auditors as a key resource?
- Do the CEO and board members deem the auditors as reliable and competent?
- Does the audit team understand the strategic aims of the audit service?
- Are assurances on risk management and internal control formulated in a way that underpins the CEO's and CFO's attestations on internal control?
- Does the audit strategy result in key performance targets that help consolidate the efforts of the audit staff?
- Does the audit service provide marked improvements to governance arrangements, the risk management process, and internal controls?

- Are there good working relations between internal and external audit and other review teams?
- Does internal audit comply with professional standards and are they able to demonstrate this fact?
- Are there sufficient well-trained resources to achieve the audit plans?
- Do the auditors help create a better understanding of the control environment among the workforce?
- Are audit objectives based on defined organizational goals?
- Does the CAE spend sufficient time assessing options to improve the audit service?
- Is there an effective system in place to ensure that decisions made by audit management are properly implemented?
- Is the CAE able to evaluate the performance of audit staff in a way that is convenient, motivating, and reliable?
- Are audit plans based around the risks that face the organization?
- Does the audit strategy indicate what we are, what we need to do, and how we do it?

CASE STUDY

Long-Term Planning

One audit department established a formal strategy-setting process whereby the long-range operational plans were based on environmental scanning, forecasts, risk monitoring, evaluation, and ranking. The planning model used the present as a basis to predict the future and ensure that decisions made by the audit management were sensible and were implemented. The CAE set up a risk-scanning forum where her audit team was assigned aspects of the organizational systems and the team analyzed various internal and external factors using a set of criteria. Primary and secondary risks were evaluated along with causal links to prepare a list of existing and new products and a way of migrating the audit service to new elements. A two- to three-year planning platform was based on set goals, formal objectives, assumptions, and predictions focused around a core ideology based on a vision of a well run and controlled organization that sought out risk for suitable reward.

Road Map

After having gone through each aspect of our model so far, we are now in a position to prepare a road map for success, that is, a plan that signposts where we need to go to be seen as successful. One word of warning: audit work does not have to be delivered by a large and well-resourced in-house team. Audits can be outsourced or given to a small, underfunded unit that is tucked away from the real issues facing the organization. The road map consists of an ongoing journey of continuous improvement—a journey that ensures the audit team stays ahead of the competition and is able to command resources even where the overall budget is shrinking. If this road map is not in place, it is difficult to know how the audit process can develop, prosper, or even survive.

BASIC PLANNING MODEL: PHASE FOUR

Our model continues in Figure 2.5.

Each new aspect of the model is described in the following paragraphs.

Objectives and Accountabilities

Once a clear sense of direction has been agreed upon, along with a comprehensive strategy, most planning models will argue that formal objectives should then be formulated to bring about the strategic ambitions.

Figure 2.5 Basic Planning Model: Phase Four

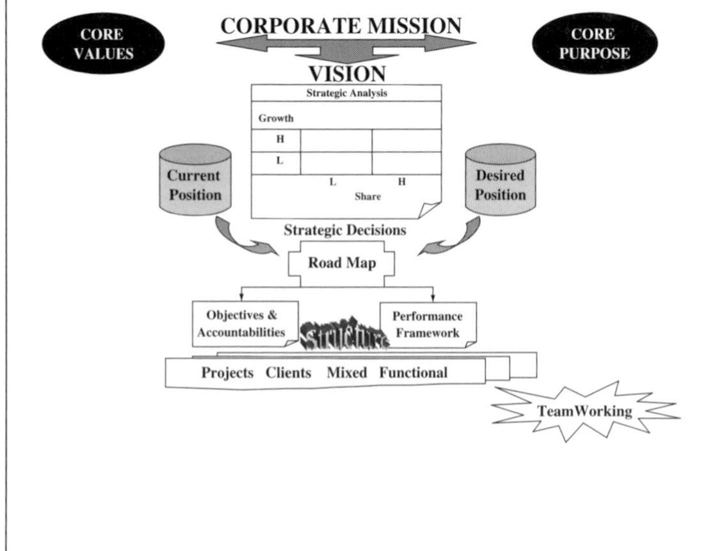

When defining operational objectives, the CAE will need to consider the following points:

- Expectations of the CEO, board, and senior management.
- Responsibilities of the audit committee.
- Requirements of the professional auditing standards.
- The roles and responsibilities set out in the formal audit charter.
- The need to provide assurances on the state of governance, risk management, and internal control.
- The need to provide consulting work to help improve the state of governance, risk management, and internal control.

In terms of accountability, it is a good idea to analyze the relevant stakeholders and work out what they want from the audit service. One way of performing this analysis is to determine the extent to which different stakeholder groups have a direct influence over the audit service in contrast to other stakeholders who simply have an interest in what audit does in the organization, as shown in Figure 2.6.

For the auditors, planning is not just an internal exercise that is carried out behind closed doors. Planning is an important mechanism for delivering assurance and consulting services across the organization, and resultant plans need to be properly communicated as suggested in audit guidance:

> The chief audit executive (CAE) should submit annually to the board for approval, and senior management as appropriate, a summary of the internal audit activity work schedule, staffing plan, and financial budget. The CAE should also submit all significant interim changes for approval and information. Engagement work schedules, staffing plans, and financial budgets should inform senior management and the board of the scope of internal auditing work and of any limitations placed on that scope.[13]

Figure 2.6 Working with Stakeholder Groups

LEVEL OF INFLUENCE	HIGH	Provide basic information	Nurture and consult
	LOW	Minimal intervention	Provide basic information
		LOW	**HIGH**
		LEVEL OF INTEREST	

The audit-planning process needs to incorporate formal accountabilities to prepare and deliver the plans in such a way as to meet the expectations of key stakeholders. Good plans will generate specific objectives that need to be achieved during the period covered by the plans in question, say on a quarterly basis.

Performance Framework

Performance is built into our basic planning model because it goes hand in hand with setting out objectives and accountabilities. There is little point in establishing detailed plans without working out how the implementation of these plans may be monitored. Such monitoring can be achieved by observing staff working hard and appearing well motivated, but there needs to be hard evidence to support general impressions. And one form of hard evidence is to set targets and review the extent to which they are being achieved. These targets should be set within a formal performance management framework, which is a wider concept than simply setting out a list of outcomes that have to be achieved. Many audit plans fail because they do not integrate the planning process with the performance management process or, worse still, there is no real way of measuring performance—apart from observing staff starting work early and staying on until the official end of the working day. It is possible to compare the attributes of poor audit performance management systems and good audit performance management systems, as shown in Figure 2.7.

Figure 2.7 Attributes of Poor Systems and Good Systems

Poor systems	Good systems
Vague targets	Smart targets
Unstructured process	Clear process
Informal feedback only	Formal documented feedback
Ignores special effort	Rewards special efforts
No link to audit services	Based on good audit services
No defined quality standards	Clear link with quality procedures
Based on personal factors	Derived from audit plans
Inflexible	Changes with new developments
Encourages risk averse behavior	Encourages active decisions
Targets unachievable in practice	Challenging but achievable
Causes resistance	Accepted by staff as sensible and balanced

Meanwhile, targets that can be set for the audit service may include some of the following:

- Views of audit-committee members.
- Percentage of agreed audit recommendations implemented.
- Level of trust in internal audit across the organization.
- Amount of training hours and CPE for audit staff.
- Level of customer satisfaction from audit clients.
- The time taken from fieldwork to draft audit report.
- The percentage of audit plans completed.
- Operational efficiency of the audit process.
- Overall reputation of the audit department.

One interesting concept is to plot the success of the audit function by assessing the success of risk management within the organization on the basis that:

> The internal audit activity should monitor and evaluate the effectiveness of the organization's risk management system.[14]

While the auditors are not responsible for ERM, they are responsible for helping review and improve the current arrangements. A solid audit team will have the right impact on ERM, and it is by plotting the progress of ERM, say on a scale of 1–5, that we can suggest the extent to which the auditors are making a difference. Risk may likewise be assessed by using a formal risk index that measures where the organization stands in respect of an efficient risk management process, from levels 1–5, as shown in Figure 2.8.

The idea is to build the progress an organization makes through levels 1–5 into the targets that are set for internal audit.

Structure—Projects, Clients, Mixed, and Functional

When the strategic analysis has been completed, and all the contextual matters that we have so far discussed in our model have been addressed, we can turn to the workings of the audit team. Good planning models suggest that the agreed strategy determines the way resources are employed to deliver the strategic objectives. The decision on organizing the audit team can have a fundamental affect on whether the resultant audit service is successful. We have identified four main groupings in our model:

Figure 2.8 Levels of ERM Progress

Level of Assessment	Control Environment	Business Exposure	Political Sensitivity	Compliance Requirements	Reporting Information Systems
1	High confidence	Low	No negative press interest	Very limited	Highly reliable
2	Good	Fairly low	Limited interest	Limited regulations	Fairly reliable
3	Fair	Moderate	Some interest	Moderate	Moderately reliable
4	Poor	Fairly high	Local interest only	Fairly high	Some reliability
5	No confidence	High	National interest	Very high	Unreliable

1. **Projects.** The audit team consists of a pool of staff who are assigned to audit projects as and when the projects come on line.
2. **Clients.** The audit team members are put into groups based on defined parts of the organization, and each group has a different range of clients that they get to know and work with over time.
3. **Functional.** The audit team is broken down into different audit services based on set competences ranging from financial systems, compliance visits, corporate services, risk management, fraud prevention, contracts and procurement, projects, and consulting services.
4. **Mixed.** A mix of the above structures.

Team Structures

A large audit team was broken down on a service basis ranging from IS/financial systems, compliance visits, corporate services, risk management, fraud prevention, contract/procurement/projects, and consulting services. The seven audit groups were each headed up by an audit manager who reported to the CAE. Audit staff members were assigned to a particular group but were moved around in line with various personal development programs. Periodically, large audit projects were run by using a mix of staff taken from the seven groups.

BASIC PLANNING MODEL: FINAL

Our complete model is presented in Figure 2.9.

Each new aspect of the final model is described in the following paragraphs.

Goals

All those issues that have appeared so far in our model need to result in clear goals that drive the audit staff on strategic, tactical, and operational levels. This is where many planning models fall apart—where the high-level assessments carried out by the CAE and audit management fail to break through to the daily work of the field auditor. The three-stage goal framework starts with overarching high-level goals, something along the lines of:

> Ensuring the audit process adds value to the development of governance, risk management and internal controls.

Figure 2.9 The Complete Model

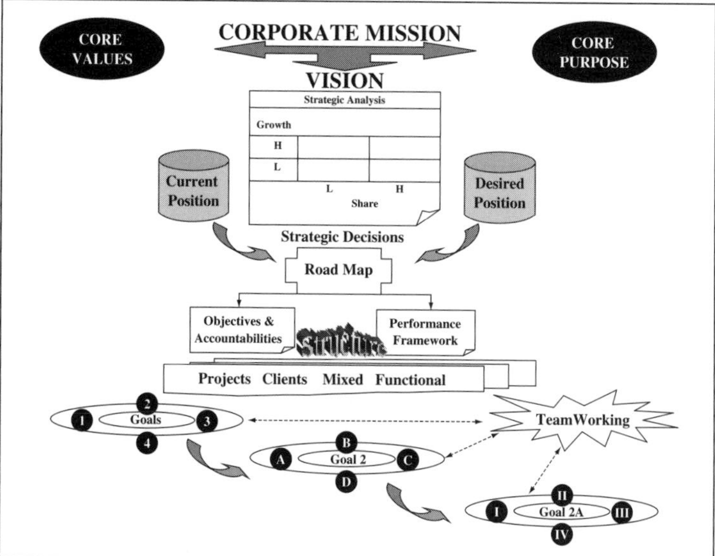

Goal 2

We can continue cascading the goals down into the audit team by breaking the main goals into a subset, for example:

> Ensuring that audit provides consulting services to help improve the risk management process.

Goal 2a

The next tier of goals will go into even greater detail on more specific engagements, for example:

> Ensuring that audit facilitates a series of CSA workshops to help embed risk management into the local front office services.

Teamworking

The final component of our model relates to teamwork. That is the way the audit staff relate to each other and come together to form teams, groups, and work-related associations. Audit work can be quite lonely as short sharp engagements are given out to auditors and they rush off to work through the set routines, returning in due course with a draft report and working paper file for review by the audit manager. Good planning makes good use of teamwork, either in getting people to work together in small teams or using people to provide inputs into engagements as and when appropriate.

CASE STUDY

Resourcing the Plan

In a large audit department, the results of formal risk assessments are fed into a planning forum consisting of the CAE, audit managers, and the Chair of the audit committee. High-scoring systems were identified and special projects of strategic importance were added to the plan if they were deemed important in terms of tackling high-risk aspects of the organization's business development. The output from the audit plan was a level of audit resource required to deliver the defined audits. This was compared with the available audit resource with the following options:

Resourcing the Plan *(continued)*

- *Plan matches resources.* Implement the plan and monitor the situation.
- *Insufficient resources.* Buy in more resource, cosource some of the work with external providers, or use consultants on one-off consulting projects.
- *Excessive resources.* Get rid of contract staff and transfer some audit staff to other parts of the business.

The audit resourcing strategy involves a flexible approach to temporary and short-term contract staff, who complement the core audit teams. Meanwhile a three-year strategy was developed that considered factors such as:

- Growth in different types of audit services.
- Refocus on different aspects of consulting and assurance services.
- Transfer of skills to the business in line with the CSA program.
- New audit competencies that need to be developed in conjunction with planned changes in audit services, methodologies, and software tools.
- Training and development programs, including qualification-based schemes.
- Future supply of auditors and surveys of satisfaction levels among the audit staff.
- Departure rates and retirement plans of current audit staff.
- Compensation packages and whether they are set to attract the right type of auditor.
- Performance reports and feedback on the quality of auditors in the post.

The planning forum consider the above factors and initiate a project to align the three-year staffing strategy with the three-year audit strategy to secure as best a fit as possible between the planned audit coverage and core audit team numbers, experience, and overall competence. The overriding consideration is that the resource profile has to fit the risk-based audit plans and not the other way round. Moreover, auditors who are too far from a good fit with the competence profile generated by the audit strategy are not retained. The audit managers provide a strong sense of continuity and are given a substantial budget for ongoing personal development through training, conferences, and involvement in various national working groups and specialist forums.

SUMMARY

Risk-based audit planning is the same as all planning systems in that it seeks to assign the right resources to the right tasks in a way that is motivating and sensible. One way to realize the benefits from the principles of basic planning is to go through the following five steps:

Step 1. Start the audit-planning process with a good understanding of the corporate mission, and as this changes, so should the general direction of the audit plans.

Step 2. Hold visioning workshops in internal audit every few years to get an agreed perspective on what the audit shop should look like in the future.

Step 3. Utilize the usual PESTLE and SWOT analysis used in most planning systems, which may be incorporated with the wider concept of risk management workshops.

Step 4. Develop a clear view on whether a growth strategy, retrenchment strategy, or maintenance strategy should be adopted on the basis of the need to provide a valuable audit service to the organization.

Step 5. Install a planning hierarchy that turns strategy into plans and into a structure of the audit shop that has clearly cascading goals and performance measures that make sense for each auditor and audit team.

Note that Appendix A contains a checklist that can be used to assess the overall quality of risk-based audit planning.

NOTES

1. Institute of Internal Auditors, Glossary of Terms.
2. Institute of Internal Auditors, Standard 2120.A1.
3. Institute of Internal Auditors, Glossary of Terms.
4. Institute of Internal Auditors, Standard 2130.
5. Internal Auditing's Role in Sections 302 and 404 of the U.S. Sarbanes-Oxley Act of 2002, May 26, 2004, IIA.
6. Institute of Internal Auditors, Glossary of Terms.
7. Internal Auditing's Role in Sections 302 and 404 of the U.S. Sarbanes-Oxley Act of 2002, May 26, 2004, IIA.
8. Institute of Internal Auditors, Practice Advisory 2100-3.
9. Institute of Internal Auditors, Practice Advisory 1130.A1-2.
10. Institute of Internal Auditors, Standard 2120.A1.
11. Institute of Internal Auditors, Practice Advisory 2100-3.
12. Institute of Internal Auditors, Practice Advisory 2100-3.
13. Institute of Internal Auditors, Practice Advisory 2020-1.
14. Institute of Internal Auditors, Standard 2110.A1.

3

USING THE CORPORATE RISK REGISTER

> Evaluating management's risk processes is different than the requirement that auditors use risk analysis to plan audits. However, information from a comprehensive risk management process, including the identification of management and board concerns, can assist the internal auditor in planning audit activities.
>
> —IIA Practice Advisory 2100-3

INTRODUCTION

This chapter addresses the important topic of the corporate risk register, otherwise known as the risk log/database. There is a growing school of thought that suggests that the audit universe is the risk universe. Moreover, the audit risk that drives audit's plans is primarily derived from risks that drive the organization's activities in managing threats and opportunities. Some commentators go so far as to argue that audit should simply adopt the corporate risk register into their plans and so align themselves entirely with what the entity views as the key risks to its continued success. The model developed here makes use of these ideas, developing them into a more well-rounded view of how and where the corporate risk register may be fed into the audit-planning process.

CORPORATE RISK REGISTER MODEL: PHASE ONE

Our first model looks at the main drivers that affect the audit's role in the organization in Figure 3.1.

Figure 3.1 Corporate Risk Register Model: Phase One

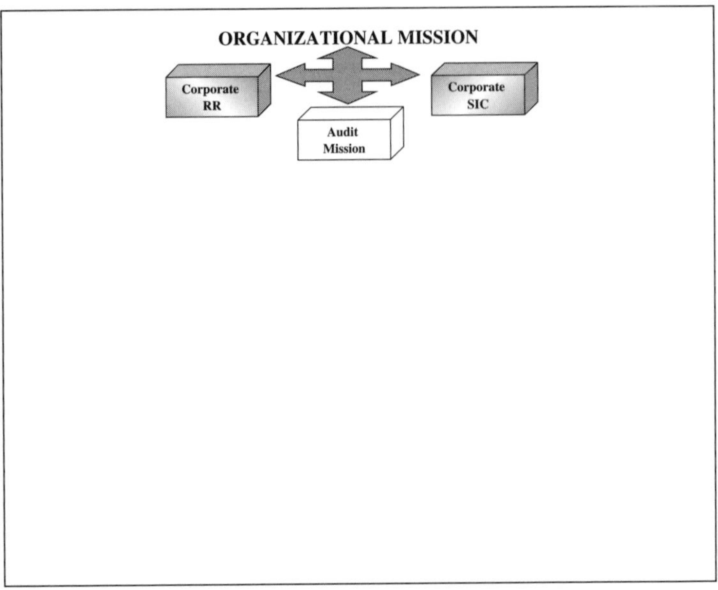

Each aspect of the model is described in the following paragraphs.

Organizational Mission

Our model suggests that the start place for audit plans is the organization's mission in life. This simple concept represents a leap in some of the more dated thinking where audit is seen as an isolated setup working to its mysterious goals pretty much by itself. In this scenario, much of the audit work was dressed up in technical jargon and a view of life that saw infringement in many of the practical working measures that were used in business, where strict rules cannot always be applied. The new-look approach asks the auditors to demonstrate how they contribute to the achievement of organizational goals.

> The approved engagement work schedule, staffing plan, and financial budget, along with all significant interim changes, should contain sufficient information to enable the board to ascertain whether the internal audit activity's objectives and plans support those of the organization and the board.[1]

Our model asks the CAE to be involved in the top management team's efforts to set a clear direction for the organization and firm up the mission to derive a strategy and precise objectives, as we discussed in the previous chapter. The CAE will then take aspects of the mission and work out how audit can best fit into the corporate effort to make sure corporate goals are achieved.

Corporate SIC

The next item on the model is the statement on internal control (SIC) that the CEO and PFO are required to furnish as part of the annual and quarterly disclosure arrangements. This link between risk and control has been noted by the IIA:

> Any organization faces a number of uncertainties and risks which can both negatively or positively affect the organization. Risk can be managed in a number of different ways, including acceptance, avoidance, transfer, or control. Internal controls are a common method for reducing the potential negative impact of risk and uncertainty.[2]

Audit planning can be based around working backward from the need for each entity to make formal disclosures and then calculate the audit's role in this matter. The tremendous responsibilities that lay with the CEO and the board are brought out in IIA guidance on Sarbanes-Oxley:

> Section 302 requires management to evaluate and report on the effectiveness of disclosure controls and procedures with respect to the quarterly and annual reports. The principal executive and financial officers must certify that:
>
> They have reviewed the report, believe that the report does not contain untrue statements or omit material facts, and the financial statements and other financial information are fairly presented. They:
>
> 1. Are responsible for establishing and maintaining disclosure controls and procedures;
> 2. Have designed such disclosure controls and procedures to ensure that they are aware of material information;
> 3. Have evaluated the effectiveness of the company's disclosure controls and procedures; and
> 4. Have presented in the report their conclusions about the effectiveness of the disclosure controls and procedures.
>
> They have disclosed to the auditors and audit committee:
>
> 1. All significant deficiencies in the design or operation of internal controls which could adversely affect the issuer's ability to record,

process, summarize, and report financial data and have identified for the issuer's auditors any material weaknesses in internal controls; and

2. Any fraud, whether or not material, that involves management or other employees who have a significant role in the company's internal controls. They have indicated whether there have been significant changes in internal controls over financial reporting or in other factors that could significantly affect internal controls subsequent to the date of their evaluation, including any corrective actions with regard to significant deficiencies and material weaknesses.[3]

The pressures resulting from the above must be taken into consideration by the auditor when formulating audit plans. Hence, this is built into the top level of our model.

Corporate Risk Register (RR)

We arrive now at the corporate risk register (RR). The need to fulfill the corporate mission and the need to comply with disclosure requirements means there has to be a mechanism in place to capture and account for anything that interferes with these two aspirations; that is, there needs to be a risk profile, a risk map, and more importantly, some form of risk register in place. The risk register fulfils the following roles:

- A formal record of risks that have been identified by the management that also records the actions and strategies in place to ensure internal controls make sense and restrict risks to the appropriate level of risk appetite.
- A device that can be used to structure the risk management process by setting out what information is required to ensure that the management is able to apply the standards set out in the risk policy.
- A way of accelerating risks from local teams, from local management, and up to the head office through linked registers that ensure high impact/high probability risks may be reported upward throughout the organization.
- A means of supporting the process for reporting on internal controls that underpins the CEO's responsibilities for published disclosures.

Meanwhile, the influence of the risk register, and overall risk strategy, is recognized in audit standards:

> The organization's risk strategy should be reflected in the activity's plan. A coordinated approach should be applied to leverage synergies between the organization's risk management and internal audit processes.[4]

Moreover, the audit universe should reflect the way the organization's business lines are planned, structured, and administered:

> The audit universe can include components from the organization's strategic plan. By incorporating components of the organization's strategic plan, the audit universe will consider and reflect the overall business objectives. Strategic plans also likely reflect the organization's attitude toward risk and the degree of difficulty to achieving planned objectives. The audit universe will normally be influenced by the results of the risk management process. The organization's strategic plan should have been created considering the environment in which the organization operates. These same environmental factors would likely impact the audit universe and assessment of relative risk.[5]

Audit Mission

Having studied the corporate mission and extensively dealt with the corporate risk register, we are now in a position to develop a mission to guide audit's contribution. Audit is meant to help an organization improve its governance, risk management, and internal controls—and the mission needs to be developed with this in mind. In terms of disclosure requirements, the IIA's Sarbanes-Oxley guidance makes it clear that audit can make a huge contribution as a certifier in the disclosure process:

> The internal audit activity may be asked to complete some type of certification or to issue an opinion on financial controls as part of management's Sections 302 and 404 processes. The CAE should ensure that any certification or opinion is supported by adequate, appropriate audit evidence as required by the Standards to support the certification and/or opinion.[6]

It should be made clear that, although we have been referring to Sarbanes-Oxley and the resulting NYSE rules, many, if not all, types of organizations from private companies, government agencies, local authorities, charities, universities, and so on, each have their own similar disclosure requirements. These issues must feature in the audit-planning process and must become pivotal in the way risks are identified and assessed. Risk management has also been developing at some pace, as the old version of specialized risk assessments is giving way to the wider concept of risks that run across the entire business. A parallel development relates to the way audit perceives risk. In the past, the auditor's view of risk was related to the chance of error, fraud, and noncompliance, but this has moved on to all events that impact the business's ability to perform and meet the aspirations of the regulators. Paul Sobel has underlined how risk assessments at the ERM and audit level differ in the following ways:

- ERM focuses on identifying all business risks that could affect the company's achievement of its strategic objectives; audit focuses on identifying all process-level risks that could affect the achievement of individual process objectives.
- ERM risk assessments should be updated on the basis of significant changes in the business, or at some reasonable interval (e.g., one year); audit risk assessments typically are only updated at the time of the next audit.
- ERM risks are assessed relative to the company and its business model as a whole; audit risks are assessed based on process-level management's tolerance to risk relative to its specific objectives.
- Senior management typically has a general but realistic perception about how effectively enterprise risks are managed; process-level management typically has a more specific but occasionally overly optimistic perspective about how effectively process-level risks are managed.
- Enterprise risks may be external to the organization and, thus, somewhat difficult to manage; audit risks are typically manageable within the process, but many arise outside the process and are therefore challenging for the process owner to manage.[7]

Setting an audit mission within the context of the pressures on the business executives is all very well so long as the respective responsibilities of management and the auditor do not become blurred:

> This delicate but essential balance between management's responsibility regarding internal control monitoring and disclosure and the internal audit mission and its efforts has been successfully experienced for many years in industries and countries worldwide where similar regulations have been in place for some time. Sarbanes-Oxley promotes risk management and governance processes within an organization over which, according to the Standards, internal audit should be in a position to provide assurance and consulting without impairing objectivity and inde-

pendence. Management is responsible for developing the processes needed to ensure the company is in compliance with Sarbanes-Oxley. Internal audit's role should ideally be one of support through consulting and assurance. Internal auditors have been confronted with a range of questions and issues related to their role and involvement in Sections 302 and 404 initiatives. These questions include both short-term issues during the implementation phase of reporting processes, as well as longer-term questions on the role and responsibilities of internal audit in this process.[8]

CORPORATE RISK REGISTER MODEL: PHASE TWO

Our model is continued in Figure 3.2.

Each new aspect of the model is described in the following paragraphs.

Survival

The use of the corporate risk register to drive the audit-planning process brings the auditor firmly onto the board agenda. The increased profile has

Figure 3.2 Corporate Risk Register Model: Phase Two

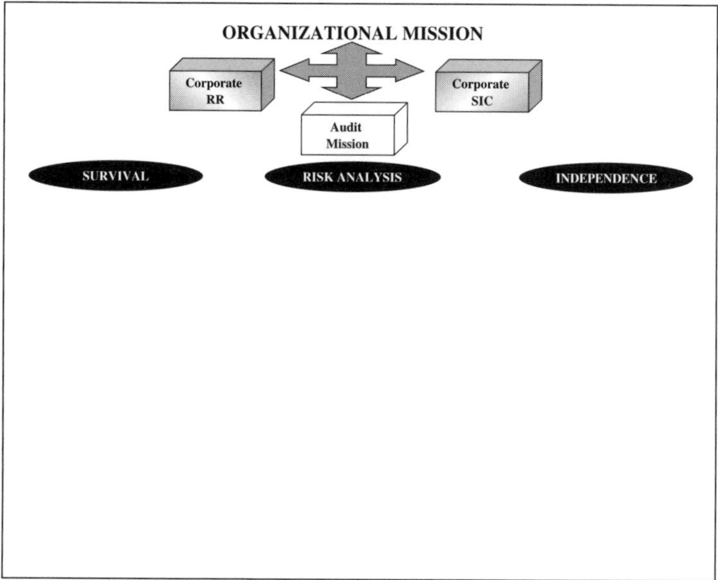

earned the CAE a boost in status, and quite possibly earnings, but there is a downside. Becoming locked into the controls disclosure regime may be what the CEO wants, but it may turn into a frenzied struggle to survive. The need for audit to get ERM going where this is not the case has been commented on in the past:

> Internal auditing's involvement in macro assessment will vary, depending on executive management's level of activity in this area. If management already has a process in place for assessing high-level risk as part of an overall enterprise risk management (ERM) system, then internal auditing should take its cues from that assessment. In many organizations, however, such a process is lacking and the internal audit activity may need to facilitate the process.[9]

Some audit teams have replaced their planning process with a disclosures compliance project where they help set up the arrangements for reporting on internal control over financial reporting. That is not to say, this is wrong. It is just that this situation has to be managed with care to ensure that audit does not assume survival mode as a norm. A strong CAE may be better off explaining how control disclosures is about changing the culture of organizations to promote transparency, ethical behavior, and good risk management. These ideals cannot simply be relegated to the audit office as they relate to the way the entire organization works. An appropriate warning has been issued by the IIA:

> If CAEs are to provide audit committees and senior management with an independent evaluation of risks and controls and contribution to risk management, control, and governance as outlined in the Standards, then the internal audit activity must maintain and effectively utilize those resources necessary to execute work in addition to that which is required for purposes of assisting management in the fulfillment of its responsibilities with respect to the financial reporting and disclosure processes.[10]

Independence

The other side of the survival factor relates to audit independence, which is defined as:

> The freedom from conditions that threaten objectivity or the appearance of objectivity. Such threats to objectivity must be managed at the individual auditor, engagement, functional and organizational levels.[11]

Instead of throwing out all audit plans, and focusing on controls disclosure/ERM preparedness, auditing may consider the need to assume a little distance from the frenzied activity and be able to report on progress. The first point is to ensure audit is not constrained by a narrow interpretation of risk that forms the measures within the remit of the regulators. Audit must always take an organization-wide view of the business and where ERM fits in. The internal auditor has little to gain from assuming an external audit's role and double-checking all verification work on the financial accounts. The core audit role should be retained, if it is not to be lost forever:

> While this guidance only addresses the role of the internal audit activity with regard to Sections 302 and 404 of Sarbanes-Oxley, the CAE should ensure that the internal audit activity's assessment of organizational risk extends beyond financial reporting and disclosure processes.[12]

There can be problems where the auditors take on too much responsibility for corporate governance.

CASE STUDY

Blurring ERM Responsibilities

A large federal government organization responded to the risk management challenge by establishing mandates to get ERM in place. These mandates were developed by the management board and given to the finance officer to implement. The CFO passed the project down to the CAE, who developed staff awareness programs, risk workshops, risk reporting systems, and surveys of control responsiveness across the organization. The reports from the CAE on progress on this project were sent up to the audit committee and board and eventually the board took less and less interest in the matter assuming that the CAE had everything under control. The board and senior management failed to assume any responsibility for ERM and felt it was simply an audit issue that did not relate to the business in question. The CAE eventually resigned, as the lack of interest and energy meant that, outside of the finance team, there was little real development of ERM capacity in the organization.

Risk Analysis

In the past, audit risk assessment came at the top of the audit-planning model. Nowadays, it comes a long way down to ensure that the risks that are being assessed make sense across the organization and not just in the private world of the CAE and audit team. We can set the tone for audit risk assessment by recalling examples from several audit teams:

CASE STUDY

Risk and Governance Issues

In one not-for-profit organization, the audit team developed risk-based audit plans using the corporate risk register as the basis for these plans. The audit strategy was formulated by applying the following process:

- The corporate risk register used by the board was analyzed and applied in identifying key audit priorities.
- Audit issues regarding compliance, information system projects, the control environment, IT security and data integrity, ethical maturity, and fraud policies were superimposed over the risk register to develop a further layer for the audit plans.
- Several aspects of the business that represented a material investment were also programmed into the plans.
- Issues that came from the regulators relating to oversight and public interest issues were also considered.

The above factors were discussed by the CAE, audit committee chair, and a senior operations director to derive an audit plan for the year based on achieving better business results, enhanced governance arrangements, and a well-controlled organization.

Some audit departments use a more structured approach to risk assessing the audit universe:

CASE STUDY

Ranking the Audit Universe

In one retail chain, the audit team attempted to rank the audit universe by going through the following process:

- Develop a clear audit mission based on adding value to the organization through assurance and consulting work.
- The CAE and audit managers define the audit universe.
- A working party consisting of the CFO, director of IT, and several business managers review the audit universe for consistency and structure.

The audit plan was then formulated as shown in Figure 3.3.

Ranking the Audit Universe *(continued)*

Figure 3.3 Audit Planning Allocation

HOURS	%
Direct hours: new audits	A
Follow-up audit hours	B
Indirect audit hours	C
Total audit hours	100%

CORPORATE RISK REGISTER MODEL: PHASE THREE

Our model continues in Figure 3.4.

Each new aspect of the model is described in the following paragraphs.

Figure 3.4 Corporate Risk Register Model: Phase Three

Risk Register

There is one train of thought that deems that the corporate risk register may be seen as representing the audit plan. These two concepts are seen as identical in terms of the auditor's need to drive the audit process into and inside the risk criteria that most impacts the organization.

CASE STUDY

Using the Risk Register

A newly formed audit department was asked to base their audit plan entirely around the corporate and business unit's risk registers. The CAE compiled a database of risk register reports and the relative high/low risk impacts and likelihood. The audit plan was directed toward verifying the reliability of these reports and whether all high-risk areas were being properly isolated and treated.

There is another train of thought, one that is supported here, that argues the need to assess the corporate risk register before determining how it can be used for audit planning. This later view is noted on our model and suggests that the corporate risk register needs to be assessed on four levels:

1. Standards
2. Categories
3. Documentation
4. Compliance

The idea is to work out whether the way the risk register is designed and applied within the organization makes sense and then determine whether this represents an adequate criterion of control:

> Adequate criteria are needed to evaluate controls. Internal auditors should ascertain the extent to which management has established adequate criteria to determine whether objectives and goals have been accomplished. If adequate, internal auditors should use such criteria in their evaluation. If inadequate, internal auditors should work with management to develop appropriate evaluation criteria.[13]

Risk registers are a product of ERM, which support the design, implementation, and reporting of internal controls. ERM therefore promotes compliance with Sarbanes-Oxley and other disclosure regulations:

> Sarbanes-Oxley promotes risk management and governance processes within an organization over which, according to the Standards, internal audit should be in a position to provide assurance and consulting without impairing objectivity and independence. Management is responsible for developing the processes needed to ensure the company is in compliance with Sarbanes-Oxley. The internal auditing activity's role should ideally be one of support through consulting and assurance.[14]

Standards

The first item to be considered when assessing the suitability of the corporate risk register is the way standards and guidance is set regarding the use of risk registers throughout the organization. An initial assessment of the reliability of these standards may include a consideration of the following five issues:

1. Whether there are documented standards on the use of risk registers in the organization that reflect current best practice.
2. Whether the board has endorsed a risk policy that sets out corporate aspirations regarding the development and implementation of ERM.
3. Whether people at all levels around the organization understand the need to document their risk management efforts.
4. Whether managers are concerned that ERM standards are being applied in a correct and consistent manager.
5. Whether the need to apply set standards on ERM activity is built into staff competencies that are used for recruitment, performance appraisal, and staff development programs.

Categories

The second item to be considered when assessing the suitability of the corporate risk register is the way risk categories are set and employed via risk registers throughout the organization. An initial assessment of the reliability of the way categories are established may include a consideration of the following five issues:

1. Whether there are documented standards on the type of categories that may be used to capture different types of risk to ensure consistency and reliability.
2. Whether the risk categories are sufficiently flexible to cater to all types of risk, including those that may not at first sight be obvious to many managers.

3. Whether the use of categories is being used by all parts of the organization.
4. Whether risk categories fit well with the definition of risk appetite that is promoted by the CEO and the board.
5. Whether the use of categories adds value to the way ERM is being applied.

Documents

The next item to be considered is the suitability of documentation relating to the use of risk registers throughout the organization. An initial assessment of the reliability of documentation may include a consideration of the following five issues:

1. Whether there is a concerted effort to update, improve, and further develop the way registers/databases/profiles/maps or methods are used to document the risks that impact the business.
2. Whether there is clear guidance on the use of risk registers to record the results of risk assessments and risk management strategies across the organization.
3. Whether the documentation relating to risk register is reliable and defensible.
4. Whether documentation is secured as confidential and does not lead to a potential competitive disadvantage to the organization in question.
5. Whether the documentation reflects the realities of risk and the way risk is being managed or is it simply the result of a form filling exercise to satisfy the regulators.

Compliance

The final item to be considered when assessing the suitability of the corporate risk register is the adequacy of adherence to the set standards and guidance regarding the use of risk registers throughout the organization. Compliance has been defined by the IIA as:

> Conformity and adherence to policies, plans, procedures, laws, regulations, contracts, or other requirements.[15]

An initial assessment of compliance with standards may include a consideration of the following five issues:

1. Whether the board has developed a system for assessing the extent to which risk registers have been prepared so as to meet their expectations.
2. Whether noncompliance among senior staff is seen as an important issue that may result in retraining or reprimands where appropriate.
3. Whether the documentation relating to risk register may be examined at a later date to track decisions made by management and work teams and the results of such decisions on the operation of internal control.
4. Whether there is ongoing training available for new staff and as part of performance management schemes that set out the need to comply with set ERM standards.
5. Whether risk registers are seen as worthwhile in promoting better business results and achieving a better understanding of respective priorities across the business.

CORPORATE RISK REGISTER MODEL: PHASE FOUR

Our model continues in Figure 3.5.

Figure 3.5 Corporate Risk Register Model: Phase Four

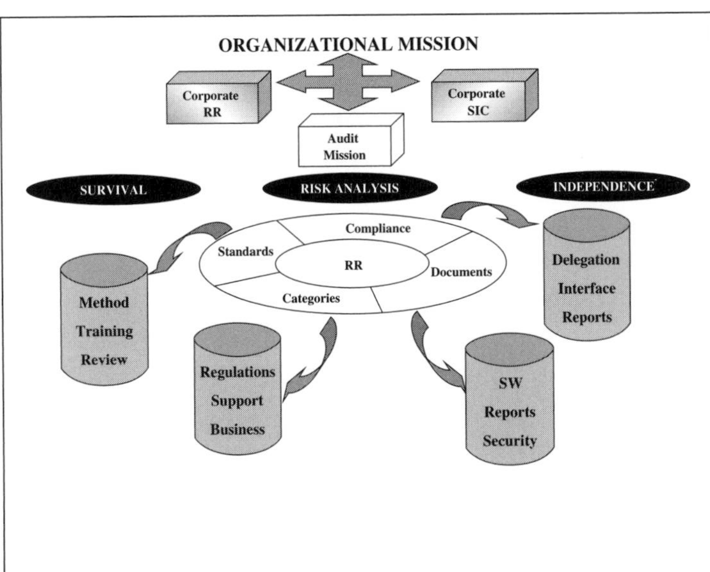

Each new aspect of the model is described in the following paragraphs.

Standards—Delegation, Interface, and Reports

Turning to a more detailed assessment of the way standards are employed for risk registers, the auditor will need to make a careful consideration of three key factors:

1. **Delegation.** Standards need to be designed at the top and sent down through the organization in a way that fits the structure and authorities in place.
2. **Interfaces.** The risk registers need to be set up in a way that provides a road map of the organization relating each department, section, team, and project. In this way, risks, such as IT security concerns, may be linked between the registers where they cross over different parts of the business.
3. **Reports.** The registers should be designed to allow suitable reports that can be generated about high-profile risks that get reported up through the business. They should also be suited for an overview of internal control that forms the basis of the CEO's formal certifications.

Categories—Regulations, Support, and Business

Turning to a more detailed assessment of the way standards are employed for risk registers, the auditor will need to make a careful consideration of three key factors:

1. **Regulations.** Risk categories should incorporate matters that relate to the regulators and legal obligations facing the organization.
2. **Support.** They should also cover support services such as finance, IT, business planning, marketing, and so on.
3. **Business.** The main part of the register's risk categories should be relevant to the actual core business of the organization and not just to financial accounting systems.

Documentation—Software Reports and Security

Turning to a more detailed assessment of the way standards are employed for risk registers, the auditor will need to make a careful consideration of three key factors:

1. **Software.** The registers should be supported by sound software systems that enhance the value of the underlying information.
2. **Reports.** The documentation should enable robust reports that move the business forward.
3. **Security.** The data and information contained in the registers should be properly protected against unauthorized access.

Compliance—Methods, Training, and Review

Turning to a more detailed assessment of the way standards are employed for risk registers, the auditor will need to make a careful consideration of three key factors:

1. **Methods.** Registers should be developed through a sound methodology that has been agreed with the board.
2. **Training.** All staff should have a basic if not good understanding of the process for recording risks to their part of the business.
3. **Review.** The entire risk recording system should be subject to regular review and improvement.

CORPORATE RISK REGISTER MODEL: FINAL

Our complete model is presented in Figure 3.6.

Each new aspect of the final model is described in the following paragraphs.

Horizon Scanning

We have noted that the auditor may use all or part of the corporate risk register in formulating audit plans depending on the reliability and maturity of ERM within the organization. A separate point to note is the need to perform horizon scanning to ensure each register is up to date and vibrant and that audit plans also retain this feature:

> Changes in management direction, objectives, emphasis, and focus should be reflected in updates to the audit universe and related audit plan. It is advisable to assess the audit universe on at least an annual basis to reflect the most current strategies and direction of the organization. In some situations, audit plans may need to be updated frequently (e.g.,

Figure 3.6 The Complete Model

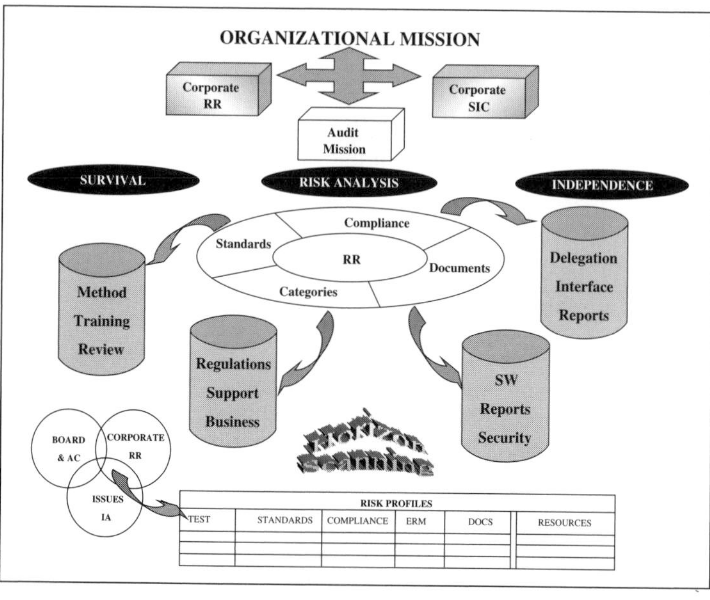

quarterly) in response to changes in the organization's environment of management activities.[16]

Audit plans need to be aligned to important and changing risks that impact the organization as a key aspect of audit planning and a simple case study will help illustrate this idea.

CASE STUDY

Keeping Plans Vibrant

An audit department for a large university found that its audit planning process was inflexible and old fashioned. The main performance target set by the audit committee related to the completion of the annual audit plan, and this single factor more or less drove the audit mission. Hence, most of the quality assurance review process established by audit management involved checking progress on the audit against the budgeted hours that were set at the planning stage. The CAE was convinced that a local consulting firm was seeking to take over the audit by promising to deliver a higher number of planned

Keeping Plans Vibrant *(continued)*

audits than the existing in-house team. Audit staff were given bonuses if they could complete the planned audits in as short a time as possible. Unfortunately, even when the audit plan was delivered, the CAE and the audit team were still seen as a waste of space by most of the executives and were not invited to any meetings of note. During a heart to heart talk with the chief finance officer, it was made clear to the CAE that the audit team appeared to be stuck in the past and were working on audits that had been planned up to a year ago, when many corporate issues had moved on. In response, the CAE prepared a paper aimed at redesigning the audit-planning process to adopt risk-based planning. To capture changing risks, the CAE assigned various topical developments that impacted the university to the three audit managers and five senior auditors. Each audit staff member was given an aspect of university business to track and monitor, holding regular meetings with the unit head or budget holder who had most responsibility for the area in question. The annual audit plan was updated each quarter using intelligence gathered through this new process and reapproved by the audit committee, again on a quarterly basis. In this way, the audit plan was always vibrant and up to date and reflected the current concerns of key players in the organization. The categories of audit work performed were:

- Corporate governance
- Risk management
- Partnerships and joint ventures
- Key financial systems
- Fraud and regularity
- Establishment visits
- Computer audit
- Follow-ups

Newer plans were then based on an organic developmental process that reflected the emerging risks facing the organization in the following way:

- *April–June.* Review the draft plans that have already been prepared and flex them to take on board new issues that have occurred recently and lessons learnt on the governance front.
- *July–Sept.* Develop an audit strategy based around the goals set for improving ERM and publicize them.
- *Oct–Dec.* Develop an issues analysis in which problems with the corporate risk assessments are documented and prepare a theme paper on current issues and stakeholder expectations.
- *Jan–March.* Consult and discuss emerging issues and themes through meetings with senior management and prepare next year's draft audit plans.

Keeping Plans Vibrant *(continued)*

Strategic plans appeared from the above process and revolved around set goals for the audit resources that were aligned to audits to ensure these goals were achieved broken down as in Figure 3.7.

Figure 3.7 Sample Structure for Alignment of Goals to Audit Resources

Goals	Audit Staff	Comment	Quarter for Coverage
1.			
2.			
3.			
4.			

Risk Profile

To capture much of what has been discussed so far in this chapter, the auditor may wish to develop a risk profiling mechanism in which the assessment of ERM and the risk registers can be documented. The elements of this risk profiling are set out in our model and include:

- *Test.* The auditor should test a sample of the risk registers in use to ensure that the information found in the registers matches the realities of risk assessment and risk management for the area in question.
- *Standards.* The auditor should consider the standards that are established to cater to ERM and assess whether this is sufficiently robust to ensure a sound and effective risk management process.
- *Compliance.* The auditor will be concerned with the extent to which there is compliance with the standards that cover the use of ERM in the organization.
- *ERM.* The auditor should consider the extent to which an integrated and holistic risk management process that covers the traditional risk assessment activities such as finance, IT, security, insurance and contingency planning and also addresses nontraditional areas that relate to core business lines is in place.
- *Documentation.* The auditor should examine the adequacy of documentation relating to risk management and the reviews of internal control that this necessarily entails.
- *Resources.* The auditor should consider the type of resources that are applied in getting good risk management in place and ensuring that risk registers are reliable.

CASE STUDY

Visit-Based Planning

In a large retail company, which had a major acquisition program, the audit-planning approach was based on visiting retail outlets using the following criteria:

- Newly acquired
- Results of self-assessment survey
- Performance issues
- Other factors

Several overseas sites had differing interpretations of risk and differing approaches. One problem is that some branches viewed low risk as attractive in keeping attention away from their area, while others took the opposite view in that high risk meant better bonuses as they dealt with important corporate issues. Each country was affected by its culture and way of dealing with risk. Meanwhile, the local in-house internal auditors would have their own approach to planning their work and the head office audit team would have to assess the reliability of local arrangements. The main problems revolved around the use of self-assessment surveys where the reliability of the returns from various countries had to be assessed before they could be input to the head office risk logs.

Some audit teams use the board's perspective to help them develop their audit plans:

CASE STUDY

The Board's Risk Assessment

An audit department used the board's risk assessment to underpin their audit plans, based on three levels of risk for impact and three levels for likelihood:

Impact of Risk:

Level	Importance	Impact of Losses and Liabilities	Operational Complexity	Impact on Reputation
3	Severe	Major loss	Disruption	Media outcry
2	Moderate	Some loss	Delays	Negative reports
1	Minor	Minimal loss	Inconvenience	Unfavorable

Likelihood of Risk:

3	HIGH—event expected to occur
2	MEDIUM—event may occur
1	LOW—event unlikely to occur

Each part of the organization was assessed for impact and likelihood using these two scales, and high scoring systems then featured in the audit plans.

Corporate Risk Register

We are now in a position to decide the extent to which audit can use the corporate risk register to drive the audit plan. A short case study follows:

CASE STUDY

Fine-Tuning the Risks

An audit team located within an international oil company had a policy of visiting each of its 120 sites once a year. During the visits, the audit team would check the standard of documentation for each main operation and examine a sample of transactions to verify that they complied with the set procedures. After a short project that involved helping the head office business management compile a corporate risk register, it became clear that some 15 sites in three of the main regions accounted for over 85% of the key risks. Each of these 15 sites comprised a miniature town with office buildings, accommodation, shops, family areas, and recreational facilities built within the local company owned compound. Using the drivers from the corporate risk register, the CAE compiled an annual audit plan that focused on the 15 high-risk sites that would be visited each year and relegated the remaining sites for a visit once every 5 years.

Issues—Internal Audit

The risk register is one of the three factors that feed into audit's risk profile, and the next item relates to issues that are of special concern to audit. These may include some or all of the following key questions:

- *Compliance.* How many internal controls fail because of noncompliance with set operational standards?
- *Fraud.* What parts of the organization are susceptible to material levels of internal and external fraud?
- *Information Systems.* What information systems and new development projects are critical to the success of the business?
- *Ethics.* What aspects of the business depend on high standards of ethical behavior to ensure fair play?
- *Contingencies.* What aspects of the business need to be protected by well-defined and well-tested contingency plans?
- *Follow-ups.* What parts of the organization would be exposed to unnecessary risk if previously agreed audit recommendations fail to be implemented?

- *Error.* What parts of the organization have a track record of error and poor functioning, which means the ability to deliver the intended results is impaired?

Audit may want to include issues like the above in the planning process even where they do not appear on high-profile risk registers.

Board and Audit Committee

The board must be fitted into the planning process as dictated by IIA standards:

> The chief audit executive should communicate the internal audit activity's plans and resource requirements, including significant interim changes, to senior management and the board for review and approval. The chief audit executive should also communicate the impact of resource limitations.[17]

As such, the third item that may be fed into the audit risk profile is high-level concerns that sit with the board and/or audit committee. These concerns will vary from organization to organization, but may, for example, include the following questions:

- *Regulators.* Are there any fines or penalties (or worse) that may hit board members through a failure to act or through actions that are deemed inappropriate?
- *Competitors.* Are we doing enough to stay ahead of the competition?
- *Legal claims.* Are we potentially exposed to any material legal claims through something that we are or are not currently doing?
- *Personal liability.* Is there any mud that will stick to board members through anything that we are doing or failing to do?
- *Performance.* Is our overall performance good enough to ensure a healthy future?
- *Takeovers.* Are we susceptible to takeover due to any weaknesses that result from a failure in strategy or through other reasons?
- *International trends.* Are we doing enough to keep up with international developments that may impact our business?
- *Workforce problems.* Are our people behaving in a way that promotes success and a sustainable future?
- *Reputational.* Are we seen as the best in the business by the people who matter most?

The idea is to add these and other relevant issues to the corporate risk register, along with audit issues to form a better risk profiling process to support the annual plan. The purist would argue that world-class risk registers should really include audit issues and boardroom issues if such issues are derived from a well-developed ERM process. In fact, some see ERM as being a tool that allows one to capture all important issues in one place and not as a tool that captures just operational and technical matters. In this scenario, the main corporate risk register could become the basis for the annual audit plan.

CASE STUDY

Risk Criteria

One private sector audit shop based its audit-planning strategy around several key concepts:

1. Items taken from the corporate risk register that by definition were based on areas deemed high strategic risk to the organization.
2. Audit issues that were important but that tended to get left off the risk register—such as change programs, ethics management, and performance management.
3. Requests from senior management for audit input on various high-profile projects, some of which arose from an earlier audit report.
4. Concerns expressed by the audit committee in terms of the way various governance-related initiatives were being implemented across the business.
5. Movement of key audit staff on loan to various parts of the business and seconded to various short projects.
6. Issues that were emerging from audit work that was being carried out during the year.
7. Changing priorities owing to rapid developments that impacted the business, normally resulting from external changes in the marketplace and/or market regulators.

The CAE would put the above "in the pot" and discuss the results with the audit committee (or audit committee chair) and juggle audit resources each quarter until a pragmatic solution emerged. The generic concept of corporate risk was merged with value add concerns that hit the bottom line to allow competing projects to be assessed and some dropped while others were added in. The audit committee was quite used to discussing the relative merits and demerits of respective audits and assignments. This process worked because the audit committee was astute, and had a good working relationship with the CAE, who in turn had the authority to stand firm in the face of conflicting demands on the audit resource.

SUMMARY

Risk registers may be used in the audit-planning process to ensure that audit plans reflect the commercial reality of business life facing the organization. Unfortunately, the CAE cannot simply take the corporate risk register without paying close attention to the adequacy of this facility and whether there are other issues that need to be part of the planning framework. One way to realize the benefits of using aspects of the corporate risk register is to go through the following five steps:

Step 1. Have a good handle on the corporate risk register used by the board and top management and make sure this is aligned to the internal controls disclosure reporting system.

Step 2. Balance the need to help improve ERM with the need to retain some degree of objectivity in providing an independent assurance on the overall state of ERM.

Step 3. Develop a benchmark against which to assess the reliability of the organization's ERM and whether the process reaches across the entire organization.

Step 4. Compare the ERM process against the benchmark looking at standards, risk categories, documentation, and the extent to which there is compliance with the adopted ERM arrangements—and that the resulting risk registers reflect current risks in a meaningful way.

Step 5. Test a selection of entries on the corporate risk register to determine whether the role of the register in risk-based audit planning and whether other issues outside the remit of the register need to be factored into audit plans.

Note that Appendix A contains a checklist that can be used to assess the overall quality of risk-based audit planning.

NOTES

1. Institute of Internal Auditors, Practice Advisory 2020-1.
2. Institute of Internal Auditors, Practice Advisory 2010-2.
3. Internal Auditing's Role in Sections 302 and 404 of the U.S. Sarbanes-Oxley Act of 2002, May 26, 2004, IIA.
4. Institute of Internal Auditors, Practice Advisory 2010-2.
5. Institute of Internal Auditors, Practice Advisory 2010-2.

6. Internal Auditing's Role in Sections 302 and 404 of the U.S. Sarbanes-Oxley Act of 2002, May 26, 2004, IIA.
7. Auditors Risk Management Guide, Integrating Risk Management and ERM, Paul J Sobel, CCH Incorporated (Chicago) 2004, page 2.14.
8. Internal Auditing's Role in Sections 302 and 404 of the U.S. Sarbanes-Oxley Act of 2002, May 26, 2004, IIA.
9. Anderson, Urton and Chapman, Christy (2002), "The IIA Handbook Series" in *Implementing The Professional Practices Framework*, IIA, p. 94.
10. Internal Auditing's Role in Sections 302 and 404 of the U.S. Sarbanes-Oxley Act of 2002, May 26, 2004, IIA.
11. Institute of Internal Auditors, Glossary of Terms.
12. Internal Auditing's Role in Sections 302 and 404 of the U.S. Sarbanes-Oxley Act of 2002, May 26, 2004, IIA.
13. Institute of Internal Auditors, Standard 2120.A4.
14. Internal Auditing's Role in Sections 302 and 404 of the U.S. Sarbanes-Oxley Act of 2002, May 26, 2004, IIA.
15. Institute of Internal Auditors, Glossary of Terms.
16. Institute of Internal Auditors, Practice Advisory 2010-2.
17. Institute of Internal Auditors, Standard 2020.

4

THE ANNUAL AUDIT PLAN

> The chief audit executive should establish risk-based plans to determine the design of the internal audit priorities of the internal audit activity, consistent with the organization's goals.
>
> —IIA Standard 2010

INTRODUCTION

We arrive now at the all-important annual audit plan. This plan should be designed to ensure discharge of the internal audit's responsibilities, which include:

- Improving and assuring governance, risk management, and internal controls.
- Promoting self-assessment of internal control.
- Coordinating audit activities with the external auditor.
- Promoting good information systems, compliance with procedures, value for money, and safeguarding assets and interests.
- Forming a view of the corporate attestations on internal control.

Audit planning conjures up several key questions as described by Paul Sobel:

> When conducting the annual audit-planning process, the auditor must answer the following questions:
>
> 1. What represents success for the company?
> 2. What are the barriers to achieving that success?
> 3. How does the company manage those barriers?
> 4. How do we know the barriers are managed to the desired level?[1]

In quoted companies, the auditor will want to consider Section 404 attestations and will want the audit plan to cover items such as the need to ensure that:

- Significant controls are documented, assessed, and tested.
- A clear methodology is applied to internal control reviews and reporting.
- External audit has a clear role in testing the internal control framework.
- A form of steering committee or resource is established to govern Section 404 reporting.
- The overall risk management framework is sound and material risks are being addressed in line with stakeholder expectations.

Internal audit should be able to provide assurances on the reliability of published disclosures, the state of entity risk management processes, the reliability of key controls, the overall state of internal controls over financial reporting, and the reliability of self-assessment reviews. If the audit plans start with this objective in mind, there is a much better chance that they will deliver the goods.

ANNUAL AUDIT-PLANNING MODEL: PHASE ONE

Our first model is presented in Figure 4.1.

Each aspect of the model is described in the following paragraphs.

The Annual Audit Plan

We design our model by placing the annual audit plan at the top. All the elements that follow will become components of the plan that audit should design and get approved each year—that is, to focus the work of the audit resource for the coming year.

> There are a variety of approaches that can be used to conduct a business risk assessment. However, each risk assessment approach generally has the same broad phases:
>
> Phase 1: Create risk universe
>
> Phase 2: Understand risk characteristics

Figure 4.1 Annual Audit-Planning Model: Phase One

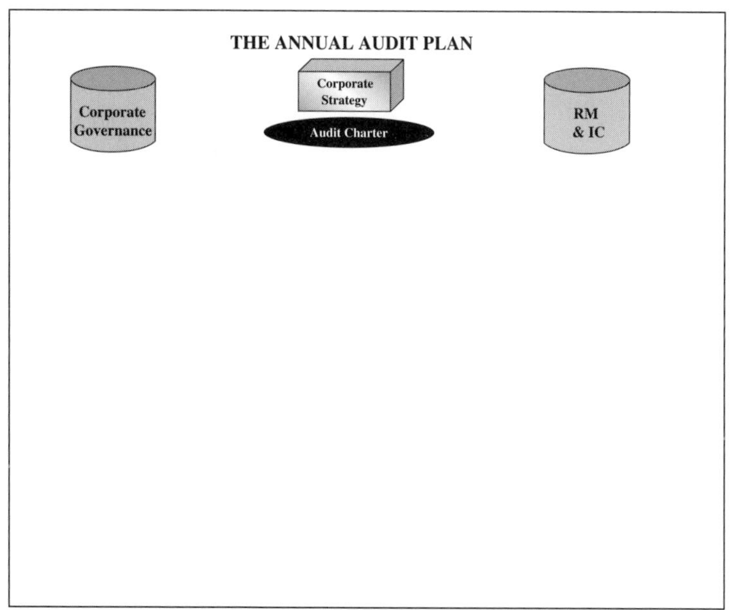

Phase 3: Assess and prioritize risks
Phase 4: Determine next steps[2]

Corporate Governance

Governance appears next on the model as it is one of the main influencing factors. Moeller has described audit's role in disclosure reporting as:

> Internal audit and/or the section 404 compliance team needs to review all organization processes and select the ones that are financially significant...[3]

Sarbanes-Oxley has had much impact on audit teams and some audit teams have grown because of the need to build the implications into audit plans as well as perform other planned audit work.

Risk Management and Internal Control

The concepts of risk management and internal control regime stand on the other side of the top level of our model. These two items sit alongside governance and interdependent concepts, much as the two wings of a plane keep it airborne. COSO ERM sets the pace:

> Internal auditors should consider the breadth of their focus on enterprise risk management.[4]

CASE STUDY

Staff Surveys

A large audit department within a commercial company starts its planning process by carrying out a review of the risk management and control environment. The results of this survey are used to focus the audit plans toward parts of the business where there are known or suspected problems. The results also indicate where there is scope for audit to provide consulting work to help deliver a better understanding of risk management and internal control. Some of the statements that appear in the annual survey include the following, where the response is disagree/agree and various ranges in between:

- Our work goals are clear.
- We identify risks to the achievement of our work goals.
- We understand which risks are important.
- We seek to mitigate risk by controls.
- Mitigation is aligned to risk appetite.
- We stick to set procedures.
- Problems are notified to senior management.

As a result of the survey, the auditors are able to provide a more focused role in assuring the ERM process. The team also scheduled ongoing testing for the more significant financial reporting systems, while ensuring there is detailed documentation to support the audit opinion. The CAE looked to provide positive assurances rather than saying nothing untoward was found. A further development was to examine the way the business units were assessing and testing their own controls and whether this self-assessment was reliable. Finally, the plans incorporated a review of the some of the work performed by the external audit and whether this was designed to deal with material weaknesses. In this company, many of the audit staff were lent out to a Sarbanes-Oxley project that lasted over six months, blowing a hole in the current audit plan. The risk profile used by internal audit was eventually extended to feature the risk of not complying with Sarbanes-Oxley requirements.

Corporate Strategy

The next factor that feeds into the annual audit-planning process relates to the corporate strategy set by the organization, and this is ignored by the auditors at their peril—the following case study illustrates the importance of corporate strategy:

CASE STUDY

Aligning Plans with Strategy

A small audit team based in a management training company took their annual audit plan from the corporate strategy. Each year the business planning division produced a corporate plan and more detailed plans for each of the business lines. The plans were designed to deliver the set targets for the ensuing year and were risk assessed in terms of responding to the various risks that impacted the set objectives and underlying performance targets. The items from the corporate strategy were then entered into the audit-planning mechanism and they set the agenda for the audit plan. In this way, the measures that would be implemented by the business were broken down into four quarters and audit would either be programmed into the ensuing projects or would undertake assurance reviews aimed at assessing the state of controls that were being relied on in the target areas in question. As and when the corporate strategy was revised each quarter to accommodate new developments, the audit plans were altered to include these changes.

Audit Charter

The issues we have so far discussed should influence the audit charter. The audit charter in turn sets the agenda for the audit service and gives shape and form to the annual audit plan. The audit charter has already been discussed in Chapter One, and it is important in audit planning because it sets the tone for the role of the auditors.

ANNUAL AUDIT-PLANNING MODEL: PHASE TWO

Our model is further enhanced in Figure 4.2.

Each new aspect of the model is described in the following paragraphs.

Audit Committee

The audit committee appears next on our model as this forum has a role to play in the design and implementation of the annual audit plan. The audit committee has a great deal of new areas of responsibility in the governance arena:

> Although Sections 302 and 404 of the Sarbanes-Oxley Act of 2002 do not assign specific responsibilities to audit committees, Sections 301

Figure 4.2 Annual Audit-Planning Model: Phase Two

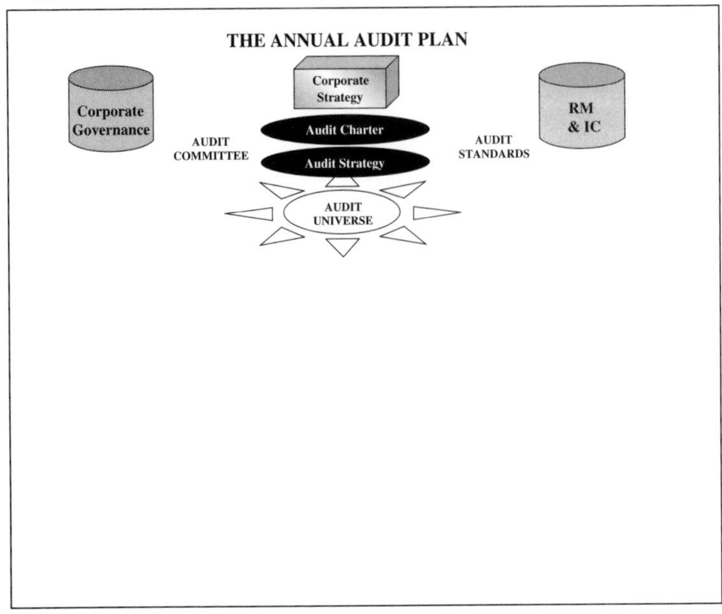

and 407 establish broad standards for and disclosures regarding audit committees. Section 301 establishes certain general standards with which audit committee members are required to comply. These standards are:

Except for board of director fees, audit committee members may not accept consulting, advisory, or other compensatory fees from the issuer and its subsidiaries.

Audit committee members must also not be an affiliated person of the issuer and its subsidiaries.

Audit committees must be directly responsible for the appointment, compensation, retention, and oversight of all registered public accounting firms that prepare or issue audit reports or perform other audit, review, or attest services for the issuer.

Audit committees must establish procedures for receiving, retaining, and addressing complaints received by the issuer related to accounting, internal controls, and auditing.

Audit committees must have the authority to engage independent counsel, as they deem necessary. Issuers must provide the audit committee with appropriate funding to enable it to fulfill its responsibilities.[5]

As such, the audit committee tends to turn to the auditors for help, advice, and support in this task.

The CAE should ensure that the audit committee is kept up to date on the role and activities of internal audit in the company's efforts to comply with Section 404. Instances where independence or objectivity will be impaired by the role that internal audit assumes should be discussed with the audit committee prior to assuming this role. In addition, the implications, as well as any impact on both current and future audit plans because of devoting resources to assisting in Section 404 compliance efforts, should be discussed with the audit committee.[6]

Audit Standards

Having taken on board the expectations of the audit committee, the other influence over audit strategy is the demands of auditing standards. Standards are defined as:

> A professional pronouncement promulgated by the Internal Auditing Standards Board that delineates the requirements for performing a broad range of internal audit activities, and for evaluating internal audit performance.[7]

Complying with audit standards means that certain aspects of the audit-planning process must be geared toward best practice in assigning audit resources and not just fulfilling what the audit committee and board might desire. For example, the annual audit plan should incorporate brought forward items following up from the previous year's audits:

> The chief audit executive should establish a follow-up process to monitor and ensure that management actions have been effectively implemented or that senior management has accepted the risk of not taking action.[8]

Another example is that IIA practice advisories, although not mandatory, represent good practice and should be considered in the course of managing and delivering the audit product. One set of guidance provides an outline of the risk-based planning approach:

> Audit work schedules should be based on, among other factors, an assessment of risk priority and exposure. Prioritizing is needed to make decisions for applying relative resources based on the significance of risk and exposure. A variety of risk models exist to assist the chief audit executive in prioritizing potential audit subject areas. Most risk models utilize risk factors to establish the priority of engagements such as:

financial impact;
asset liquidity;
management competence;
quality of internal controls;
degree of change or stability;
time of last audit engagement;
complexity;
employee, and government relations, etc.

> In conducting audit engagements, methods and techniques for testing and validating exposures should be reflective of the risk materiality and likelihood of occurrence.[9]

There are many sources of guidance that fall outside formal audit standards, and authoritative texts can be useful in setting the scene for good audit planning. Christy Chapman has developed this idea of using high–low risk impacts and probability for audit planning:

> A precise, detailed quantification of risk can also be detrimental, since such processes can complicate the assessment effort and slow down progress. More often, organizations are quantifying risk based simply on their impact on the achievement of company objectives and the likelihood that they will occur. Identified risks are assigned one of four ratings: high impact-high likelihood, high impact-low likelihood, low impact-high likelihood, and low impact-low likelihood.[10]

The bottom line is that all audit standards, guidance, and recognized texts should be reviewed to assess whether the auditors are providing a sound basis for planning their work. Any divergence between adopted practice and audit standards should be reconsidered and justified as part of the annual review process that should determine how audit plans are put together.

Audit Universe

The final part of this stage of the annual audit-planning model relates to the audit universe, that is, the map that represents all aspects of the organization that fall within the remit of the audit service, broken down into defined units or items. IIA guidance suggests a link between the audit universe and the organizational strategy to keep the resulting plans grounded and realistic:

> The audit universe can include components from the organization's strategic plan. By incorporating components of the organization's strate-

> gic plan, the audit universe will consider and reflect the overall business objectives. Strategic plans also likely reflect the organization's attitude toward risk and the degree of difficulty to achieving planned objectives. The audit universe will normally be influenced by the results of the risk management process. The organization's strategic plan should have been created considering the environment in which the organization operates. These same environmental factors would likely impact the audit universe and assessment of relative risk.[11]

A short case study will help consolidate the points that we have so far noted:

CASE STUDY

Defining the Audit Universe

After the merger of two large companies providing project management to the realty sector, the formation of a new audit department was approved. This new audit team started off with two audit staff with a budget to recruit additional two staffers the following year. The first three months were spent developing an audit resource and isolating an audit universe. The universe was devised using the following principles:

1. All main financial systems that fed into the final accounts were identified and noted.
2. All local area offices that were spread across a number of states were listed.
3. All head office functions were included in the list.
4. All major projects were also noted.
5. Finally, a log of corporate issues was compiled, including matters such as succession planning reviews, pension concerns, the ethical impact program, the antifraud program, and other items that appeared on the boardroom agenda.

The audit universe was defined as comprising the above categories of areas that would be risk assessed to determine the planned audit coverage. Each different aspect was risk assessed using a relevant perspective on risk profiling, until the important parts of the audit universe featured in the annual audit plan, in line with a formal policy on consulting and assurance work.

ANNUAL AUDIT-PLANNING MODEL: PHASE THREE

Our model continues in Figure 4.3.

Figure 4.3 Annual Audit-Planning Model: Phase Three

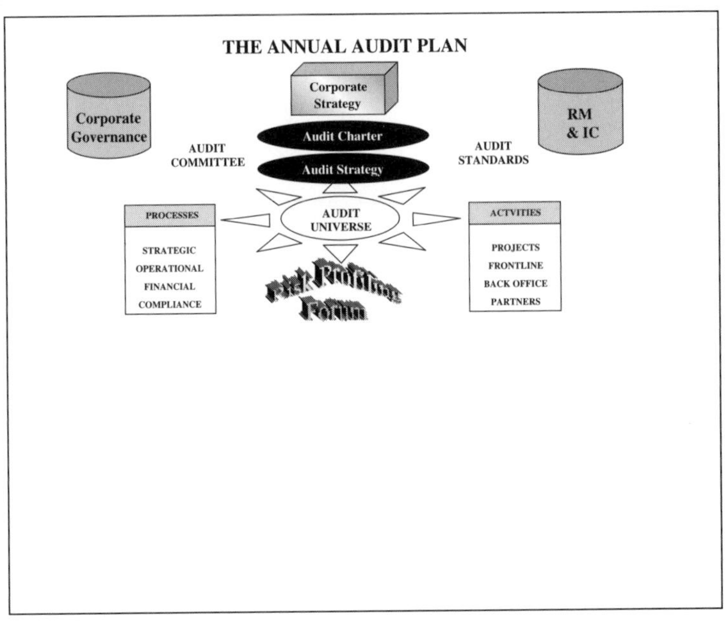

Each new aspect of the model is described in the following paragraphs.

Risk-Profiling Forum

Our model suggests that there is a formal forum that considers the inputs to the annual audit-planning process, which we have called the risk-profiling forum.

Case Study

Scoring Risks

In one manufacturing company, the risk factors that were used to drive the annual audit plan consisted of:

Risk Factor	Risk Scored by
1. Cash	Auditor scores
2 . Materiality	Auditor scores
3. Importance	Management scores
4. Date last audited	Auditor scores

Scoring Risks *(continued)*

The above matters are then discussed in a risk-profiling forum comprising audit management and senior business managers. The workshop also considers factors such as:

- Changes in processes
- Changes in staff
- Fraud and errors
- Instances of noncompliance
- New regulations
- Sensitive information
- IT systems
- Growth in large financial systems

The forum attempts to define an audit unit, profiles risks, and prepares an outline risk score that is taken away by the CAE for later consideration by the CAE and the audit management team. An annual audit plan is derived from this information and sent up to the audit committee for discussion before it is sent out to senior management for comments. The audit committee will consider issues such as:

- Soft risks such as ethical culture
- CSA reviews and their reliability
- New risks that the organization will face over the ensuing year
- Management requests for audit cover
- Allegations, fraud, wastes, abuse
- The audit budget and types of services provided by the audit team

If the risk-profiling forum can be used to represent the views of stakeholders, then the auditors can move closer to adding value to the organization:

> The type of work or services that constitute value-added practice, then, is largely situation specific. What adds the most value for one organization, or even one area within an organization, might be a waste of resources somewhere else. Hence, the influence of individual circumstances gives rise to the question, "How can auditors identify the practices that will add the most value given their own specific situation? The obvious answer is; Ask your stakeholders."... Today, the best audit departments are minimizing or eliminating cyclical audits. Those that still use computerized risk models employ this tool simply as a starting point for discussions with executive managers. Ultimately, the goal of the department is to

> align its audit plan with the organization's strategic plan, helping management accomplish its objectives without costly or time-consuming surprises along the way... To allow for this real-time risk assessment, annual audit plans are becoming more flexible, with a higher percentage of time remaining unallocated... Some leading audit departments are increasing audit plan flexibility by assigning a percentage or audit time to major functional areas, like finance or information technology, without committing to any specific projects within these areas;... At every step of the way, the auditors ask themselves questions such as, "Given all the risks in the organization, is this the best use of my time?"[12]

One further consideration is the work carried out by other review agencies, and it is important that parts of the organization are not over-audited, with duplication, confusion, and embarrassment all around:

> In determining the proposed audit plan, the CAE should consider relevant work that will be performed by others. To minimize duplication and inefficiencies, the work planned or recently completed by management in its assessments of the risk management process, controls, and quality improvement processes as well as the work planned by the external auditors should be considered in determining the expected coverage of the audit plan for the coming year.[13]

Process

The audit universe and the way risks are profiled to ensure a high-impact annual audit plan have so far featured in our model. The two ancillary issues relate to the way audit categorizes an organization as a set of processes or as a set of activities. The first perspective, where the audit universe is related to various processes, covers the following classification:

- *Strategic.* These will include all those matters that arise from the boardroom corporate strategy and that lie with "head office thinking".
- *Operational.* These matters come from the core business functions and front line operations that deliver the products and services in question.
- *Financial.* These tend to consist of systems that support the published accounts and the internal financial management and budgeting process.
- *Compliance.* These are arrangements that are designed to ensure there is good compliance with set policies, procedures, standards and operational routines.

This is useful where the organization itself classified risk along similar lines and audit can align itself with the corporate viewpoint on risk management. Risk based audit planning becomes, then an extension of ERM. A short example will illustrate this point:

CASE STUDY

Risk and Audit Frequency

A government audit agency developed a risk assessment based on several high-risk concepts:

- Quality of controls
- Flow of funds
- Qualitative aspects of management
- Public disclosure implications
- Top management risks
- Complexity of operations.

The above define the audit priorities that were then entered into the first draft of the auditing plans covering strategic issues. A further planning element was visit-based audits covering the numerous local offices scattered throughout the country, based on:

- Materiality
- Inherent complexity
- Recent changes
- Previous audit cover

This last assessment determined the visit cycle, which was scheduled as follows:

Assessment	Frequency
Fundamental risk	Annual
Very high risk	Annual
High risk	Every 2 years
Medium risk	Every 4 years
Low risk	Every 6 years

One advantage in this type of classification is that it reinforces the scope of audit work, which is again noted in IIA standards:

The internal audit activity should evaluate risk exposures relating to the organization's governance, operations, and information systems regarding the

Reliability and integrity of financial and operational information.

Effectiveness and efficiency of operations.

Safeguarding of assets.

Compliance with laws, regulations, and contracts.[14]

Activities

The other consideration that is noted on our annual audit-planning model is the way an organization may be broken down into a series of activities:

- *Projects.* Here, the organization is broken down into a series of projects, programs, change strategies, and new developments.
- *Frontline.* This classification sees the organization as a series of services or products that will appear in the audit plans.
- *Back office.* Support and back-office functions can be seen as a separate classification of the organization.
- *Partners.* Increasingly, the biggest risks arise where an organization works with partners and associates to get things done.

CASE STUDY

Using Objectives

A financial services organization used objectives-based risk assessments to drive its audit plans:

	Systems Objective	Risk Score Impact %	Recent Changes	Update Position	Revised Risk Scores
1. Information Systems					
2. Operational Processes					
3. Support Services					
4. Projects and Ventures					

ANNUAL AUDIT-PLANNING MODEL: PHASE FOUR

Our model continues in Figure 4.4.

Each new aspect of the model is described in the following paragraphs.

Core, Strategic, and Themed

We now arrive at three new lines to our model of the annual audit-planning process, that is, core, strategic, and themed matters that should fall somewhere within the annual audit plan.

Core:

There are some audit services that fall firmly within the remit of audit's role and should be considered in any annual audit plan. Some of the core audit services have already been discussed and may include:

- *Compliance.* A concern for the adequacy and effectiveness of the corporate arrangements to ensure there is good compliance with procedures across the organization.

Figure 4.4 Annual Audit-Planning Model: Phase Four

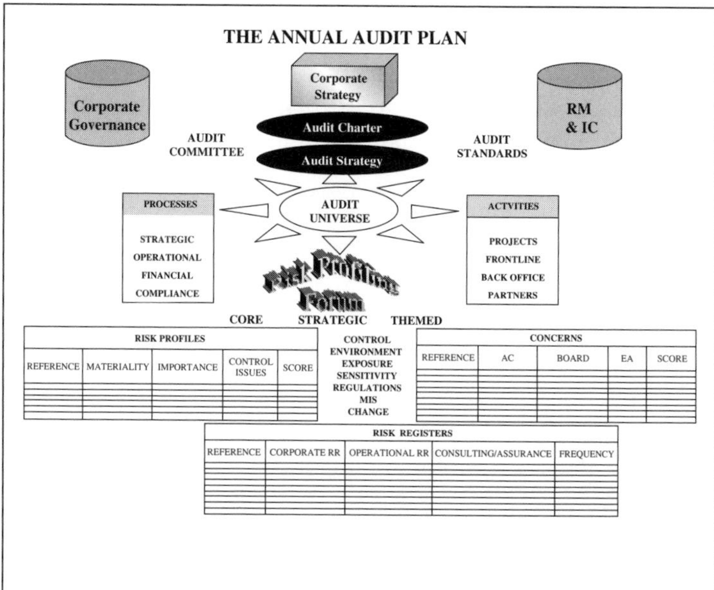

- *Fraud.* A concern that there are sound fraud prevention and detection measures in place to guard against loss from abuse, misappropriation, and fraud in general.
- *Consultancy.* The need to respond to requests from management for consulting services provided by the internal audit department.
- *Interrogations.* The ability to run interrogation programs against significant information systems to detect error, abuse, and poor controls.
- *Project support.* The need to respond to requests for audit input in projects and programs where appropriate.
- *Training and facilitating.* The provision of risk and control training and facilitation of risk workshops.
- *Financial systems.* A focus on reviewing the integrity of financial systems, particularly those that have a material bearing on the accuracy of the final accounts.
- *Site visits.* The provision of an outreach audit program that enables the audit staff to visit remote sites as part of the review of risk management and internal control.
- *VFM.* The need to ensure there are suitable arrangements in place throughout the organization to promote economy, efficiency, and effectiveness in the use of resources.

IS auditing is another important aspect of audit work that may well feature in most year's annual audit plans. Some audit departments create a separate IT audit plan to feed into the main annual audit plan. The characteristics of a robust IT audit plan are summarized below:

- Consultation and communication
- Cooperation
- Alignment with business objectives
- Alignment with the wider context of assurance across the organization
- Use of recognized methodologies
- Flexibility and allowing for contingencies
- Independence reinforced and signed off by the audit committee
- Clearly explained logic that is transparent
- Sustainability to adapt to the structure of the business over time.[15]

Strategic:

The second planning concept relates to getting strategic issues into the annual audit plan. The idea is quite simple. All those issues that are of strategic importance to an organization will have some bearing on the way audit plans are put together because of the fact that audit needs to target high-risk areas if it is to be of any real value. Many of these strategic issues will appear in the corporate risk register, which was discussed in the previous chapter. A short case study will help illustrate this point.

CASE STUDY

Structuring Audit Teams

The CAE in an audit team of ten staffers defined the audit universe as consisting of:

- Corporate objectives
- Corporate processes
- Business systems
- Projects

The risks associated with the above had been captured in the corporate risk register and was thus used as a basis for the annual audit plan. The audit universe was assigned to audit teams A, B, and C current in line with the strategic risk assessment as shown in Figure 4.5.

Figure 4.5 Sample Assignments of Audit Teams

	Strategy	**Operational**	**Financial**	**Frontline**	**Support**
	Project 1	Division 1	System 1	Business 1	Service 1
	Project 2	Division 2	System 2	Business 2	Service 2
	Project 3	Division 3	System 3	Business 3	Service 3
Audit Team:	A	B	B	C	C

Themed:

The final basic consideration is the idea of themed annual audit plans. Audit plans are put together on the basis of the audit universe of key parts of the organization that are risk assessed and which score highly as a result of high impact and high probability risks. Meanwhile, there are certain core audit services such as compliance visits to newly acquired sites or due diligence reviews in sensitive areas. Over and above these items, the CAE may write in certain "themes" that need to be covered each year, which include matters that the CAE needs to kick-start within the organization, because to leave them out would leave the organization exposed. Some of the themes that have appeared in audit departments in the past include:

- *IS exposures.* Sound information systems are crucial to sound internal control and this fact is not always appreciated by top management and the board. If there is no director of IS who sits on the main board, the strategic importance of existing, new, and proposed information systems may be missed. In fact there is a whole movement that suggests IT governance is a fundamental part of the overall corporate governance arrangements.
- *Security and contingency.* Like IS, security over the corporate resource and its information systems is another issue that may be seen as high risk by the auditors, but perhaps this may not be the view of the corporate management team.
- *Project management.* Many new developments in an organization depend on good project management practices and this is another area that audit may focus on because of its wide implications across the business.
- *Fraud and abuse.* Fast moving organizations that are chasing tight targets may not have the time or the inclination to worry about employee frauds or external frauds. Some managers feel that frauds and irregularities can be written off against the bottom line and do not fully understand their fiduciary duty to protect the organization.
- *Compliance.* As we have mentioned earlier, compliance and the need to ensure it happens in all parts of the organization is always a concern to the auditors—even where it may not be seen as such by the board.
- *VFM.* The need to review the way resources are employed to turn over the business is built into the terms of reference for internal audit and therefore should appear as a possible theme for the annual plan.
- *MIS and reporting models.* Audit should review the way an organization reports back to its stakeholders, particularly where there are legal, accounting, and regulatory requirements in place that rely on the accuracy of these reports.
- *Partnering and associates.* Many audit teams are thinking outside the box, by considering the external partners who work with the organization, for the organization, and alongside the organization. The main problem is that accountabilities may get lost where the relationship evolves over the years and it is not clear who is respon-

sible for what. Many risk workshops miss the partnering aspects of the business because the manager in charge of the arrangement believes that responsibility has been contracted out to a third party—which is not really the case.

- *Internal control environment.* Many organizations are unable to get around the concept of the control environment and feel that control is about specific routines recommended by the auditors—normally concerning basic accounting systems. The auditors are now concentrating on the control environment as a way of measuring progress in making internal control work and work well.
- *Communications.* Governance, risk management, and internal control are mainly about doing the right things and letting people know about it. In this sense, communications is an important part of the overall governance equation and may well become one of the themes for the annual audit plan.
- *Strategic development.* Risk management is about getting strategy to work well in the face of known and unknown influences on the business. The way strategy is developed should take on board risks in achieving objectives and the way strategy is implemented should likewise be properly controlled, this being another possible theme for the audit review process.
- *Contracting.* Procurement systems and large contracts can make or break an organization if they are not properly controlled, and this item may become a regular feature of the annual audit plan.

Besides the above items, the overall governance arrangements in an organization may well appear as annual themes, where the audit team reviews aspects of governance such as:

- Audit committee
- Effectiveness of the board
- External audit contract
- Nonexecutive directors
- Compensation committee
- ERM arrangements
- Control disclosure reporting
- Ethics and whistle blowing
- Accounting policies
- Fraud risk management

The final point to note is that many theme topics should be board-room top table issues and as such should be assigned to high-risk categories. In well-run organizations, these issues should feature in the corporate risk register. In this scenario, the risk register may become closely aligned to the audit universe and drive the risk-based planning profile system. The hope is that all audit work can be linked back to the wider picture presented by the corporate risk register and add-on issues that are also of some concern to the future success of an organization.

CASE STUDY

Bottom-Line Risks

A financial services company decided that its main risk lay in unreliable systems processing as it dealt with many thousands of on-line customers each year. The audit plan involved reviewing many of these core business systems to ensure each one was audited each year. In conjunction with these planned audits, the audit team would run a concurrent audit testing schedule using their database interrogation package. The testing examined a sample of transactions and isolated many cases of possible error, abuse, or breach of procedure. The outputs from this system were then placed in the audit plan that was revised each quarter. The idea was to track each reported problem and seek to isolate a systems failure or areas where the system needed to be improved. Wherever possible, an attempt was made to link transaction issues with the wider systems reviews that were being conducted by the auditors.

Control Environment and So On...

We have already mentioned the control environment as a possible theme for the annual audit plan and it also appears on the model along with subjects such as:

- *Exposures.* Risks to business operations.
- *Sensitivities.* Issues that cause concern to the board.
- *Regulations.* Requirements that derive from the regulatory framework for the organization in question.
- Management information systems (MIS).
- Change management, programs, and projects.

These items are important because audit may be set an overall goal of improving the control environment within the organization. This overriding goal may be fed into everything that audit does and may be seen as the culmination of the items in the annual audit plan. It is possible to build the above aspects of the control environment into the annual plan as specific attempts to raise the way the workforce appreciates, designs, implements, and reviews their internal controls.

Risk Profiles

It is possible to take much of the material that has so far been featured on our model, and translate the content into three interrelated schedules. The first is the risk-profiling schedule that may contain the following items:

- *Reference.* Each audit should have a unique reference number.
- *Materiality.* The size of the audit area, wherever possible to assess, should also be indicated.
- *Importance.* The degree to which the area in question relates to the key objectives of the organization should be documented.
- *Control issues.* Any issues that suggest good, poor, or changing controls may appear in this part of the document.
- *Score.* The score from the above factors should be recorded.

The risk profile will contain the basic risk-assessed profile of the audit universe and will score each audit unit appropriately. This "hard" risk-scoring device is used by many audit shops as a simple way of assessing the entire organization and results in basic audit plans.

CASE STUDY

IT-Based Plans

A CAE in a dot.com company developed the concept of covering the entire organization but focusing only on those high-risk areas in information systems that need audit attention. The risk assessment scoring systems took this on board. Risk-based IT planning was seen as important in identifying those systems data and facilities that should feature in audit plans, focusing on those information systems crucial to organizational success. The following assessment criteria are applied to each information system:

- IT infrastructure and operating environment.
- Size of the unit where applicable.
- Impact on critical business processes.

IT-Based Plans *(continued)*

- Security rating—information, equipment, and premises.
- Previous audit results.
- Importance of control compliance.
- Recent changes including changes in personnel, systems, and objectives.

The risk assessment followed a set methodology including the documentation, input from management, timing levels decided on, and change control and new systems coming on line. The audit plans were seen as part of the overall audit process that is detailed in the following steps:

- *Define the Audit Universe.* These were seen as areas that can be audited, defined by function or activity, by section or division, or by project or change program.
- *The Audit Plan.* The plan establishes the priorities of the internal audit activity, in line with the organization's goals and objectives and progress that has been made in establishing an effective risk management process. Requests for audits would also be considered and placed in the plan where appropriate.
- *Engagement Plan.* This is the plan for the actual audit in question, focusing on objectives, risks, and key controls, and an audit's terms of reference.
- *Audit Field Work.* This is about obtaining evidence to support the audit conclusions through a systematic approach to reviewing risks and controls.
- *Audit Reporting.* This is based on a set template that was used after the exit meeting had discussed the main findings in the audit. The draft report was then sent out for comments before a final version is prepared and published.
- *Follow-up and Monitoring.* The agreed recommendations are tracked to ensure that they are implemented.

In this way, the planned work gets translated into action to improve controls.

Concerns

It is possible to take much of the material that has so far been featured on our model, and translate the content into three interrelated schedules. The second issue that may be incorporated into the planning schedules is the concerns of key stakeholders. The "Concerns" schedule may contain the following items:

- *Reference.*
- *Audit committee.* Any matters that the audit committee wishes to see in the plan would be included here. Bearing in mind that at least one audit-committee member must be a financial expert, there should be important issues that come from this forum.
- *Board.* Again, issues that the board wish to see reviewed would be recorded in this part of the document.
- *External audit.* The external auditor should be allowed to input into the internal auditor's annual audit plan and hence this column is provided. The external auditor's concept of materiality is different from that of the internal auditor as it is based on the maximum extent by which financial statements can be misstated and still not affect decisions made by most users of these statements.
- *Score.* The final score from the above issues should appear here.

The risk profile will contain the various specific requests or concerns that are held by important groups within and outside the organization. These sensitivities may be scored and fed into the annual audit-planning process so as to help the organization perform. This is achieved by the appropriate behavior of the auditors, as suggested by two contrasting auditing standards:

> Internal auditors should ascertain the extent to which operating and program goals and objectives have been established and conform to those of the organization.[16]
>
> Internal auditors and the internal audit activity should take an active role in support of the organization's ethical culture. They possess a high level of trust and integrity within the organization and the skills to be effective advocates of ethical conduct as leaders. They have the competence and capacity to appeal to the enterprise managers, and other employees to comply with the legal, ethical, and societal responsibilities of the organization.[17]

Risk Registers

It is possible to take much of the material that has so far been featured in our models and translate the content into three interrelated schedules. The final input that may be incorporated into the audit-planning schedule concerns the outputs from the various risk registers across the organization, and these registers may contain the following items:

- *Reference.*
- *Corporate risks.* These risks should be measured for impact and likelihood and the results entered here.
- *Operational risks.* These risks should be measured for impact and likelihood and the results entered here.
- *Consulting/Assurance.* Assurance work will be prioritized when the risk registers are based on a sound risk management process, while consulting work is needed when the organization is at an early stage in developing risk management and ERM.
- *Frequency.* The document should indicate which parts of the organization need to be visited in terms of reviewing the state of the risk registers.
- *Score.* The final score from the above issues should appear here.

The risk profile will contain the basic risk-assessed profile of the audit universe and score each audit unit appropriately. This "hard" risk-scoring device is used by many audit shops as a simple way of assessing the entire organization and results in basic audit plans.

ANNUAL AUDIT-PLANNING MODEL: FINAL

Our complete model is presented in Figure 4.6.

Each new aspect of the final model is described in the following paragraphs.

Service Stratum

One complication that needs to be addressed in the annual audit-planning process is the way the audit role is broken down into defined services strata. This subdivision works on two levels—one approach is to assess the service strata and feed the audit plans into the predefined aspects of audit work. The other approach is to plan the audit universe, using the three schedules above (risk profiles, concerns, and risk registers), and then derive the type of audit services that would deliver the best results. The audit service strata used in our model are:

- *Assurances.* This is the basic service providing a formal opinion on the adequacy and effectiveness of governance, risk management, and internal control.

Figure 4.6 The Complete Model

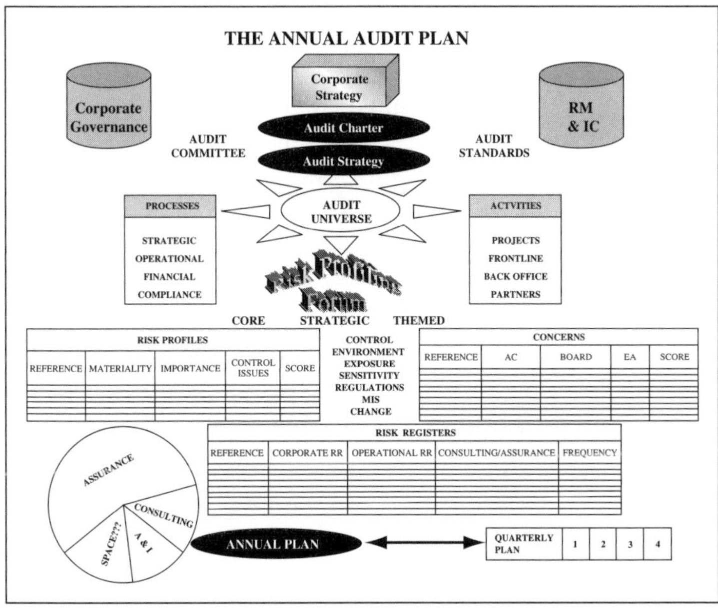

- *Consulting.* This is the additional service provided by the auditors to help improve the adequacy and effectiveness of governance, risk management, and internal control.
- *Advice and information (A&I).* This is the possible facility to provide ad hoc advice and assistance on issues and concerns relating to governance, risk management, and internal control.
- *Space.* It is a good idea to add in an extra space to provide for additional services that may be demanded from the auditors and that fall in line with the overall focus on issues that relate directly or indirectly to governance, risk management, and internal control.

There are obvious links between the different types of audit work that are recognized in audit standards:

> Internal auditors should incorporate knowledge of controls gained from consulting engagements into the process of identifying and evaluating significant risk exposures of the organization.[18]
>
> If significant consulting opportunities arise during an assurance engagement, a specific written understanding as to the objectives, scope,

respective responsibilities and other expectations should be reached and the results of the consulting engagement communicated in accordance with consulting standards.[19]

Annual Audit Plan

We are now in a position to formulate the annual audit plan. The best way to illustrate the options is to relay several relevant case studies starting with traditional risk assessments.

CASE STUDY

Traditional Risk Assessment

A large government agency audit department developed a fairly straightforward audit-planning process. The annual plan was based on risk assessing the audit universe by assigning a score for each of the audit units on the basis of:

- Materiality
- Control concerns
- Risk register rating
- The last audited date
- Special factors

The scores were further weighted to reflect the relative significance of each risk factor according to the table in Figure 4.7.

The annual audit plan consisted of the high-risk audit units, which were then placed into one of four quarters and the audits broken down into different types of audit services:

A. Assurances:
 A1. Planned
 A2. Carried forward
 A3. Follow up
B. Investigations
C. Consulting:
 C1. SDLC
 C2. Projects
 C3. Control awareness
 C4. Advice and information
D. Audit Management:
 D1. Planning
 D2. QA
 D3. AC support

Traditional Risk Assessment *(continued)*

Figure 4.7 Sample Audit Unit Risk Breakdown

Audit Unit	Factor 1, 2, 3, 4, 5	Weight 1, 2, 3, 3, 2, 1	Score	Comment

The net required hours are broken down in Figure 4.8.

Figure 4.8 Net Required Hours

QTR 1	QTR 2	QTR 3	QTR 4	Total
840	740	1040	940	3560

The required hours were then resourced by audit staff using the following schedule:

	QTR 1	QTR 2	QTR 3	QTR 4	Total
Hours	1040	1040	1040	1040	4160
Contract hours	200	200	300	100	800
	1240	1240	1340	1140	4960
Less					
Non controllable Hours	400	500	300	200	1400
Net available Hours	840	740	1040	940	3560

There are many different ways that an audit universe can be risk scored as shown in the next case study:

CASE STUDY

Risk Assessing the Universe

In one division, the approach outlined in Figure 4.9 was adopted to risk score the audit universe.

The audits that scored high using the scoring table in Figure 4.9 were designated to categories and assigned to quarters, as shown in Figure 4.10.

Risk Assessing the Universe *(continued)*

Figure 4.9 Sample Audit Approach and Factors

Audit	Title	Expenditure	Revenue	Staff	Last Audited	Requests	Score

Factor	Score 1	Score 2	Score 3	Comment
Expenditure (£)	a-b	c-d	e-f	
Revenue (£)	a-b	c-d	e-f	
Staff numbers	a-b	c-d	e-f	
Last audited (year)	1	2	3	
Requests	0	1–5	Over 5	

Figure 4.10 Sample Audit Categories and Quarter Designations

Planned Audits	**QTR 1**	**QTR 1**	**QTR 1**	**QTR 1**	**Total Days**
Corporate system	x	x	x	x	x
Financial systems	x	x	x	x	x
IS	x	x	x	x	x
Follow up	x	x	x	x	x
VFM	x	x	x	x	x
TOTAL					**AD**
Audits Hours:					
Planning	x				
Audit committee	x				
Audit management	x				
Audit admin	x				
Total available audit days	**AD**				

A further case study shows how one audit shop was able to demonstrate progress on planned work through regular reports to their audit committee.

CASE STUDY

Reporting Progress

In one audit division, audit planning was designed to allow the audit committee to ensure that audit resources were being used properly. It was also designed to monitor progress on audits and target high-risk areas across the organization. Risk assessment for each part of the organization was based on:

- Impact on the organization
- Systems development and change
- Regularity compliance issues
- Known problems
- Audit history

At each audit-committee meeting, the CAE presented the progress report, as in Figure 4.11, to help monitor progress in completing the audit plan.

Figure 4.11 Audit Progress Report

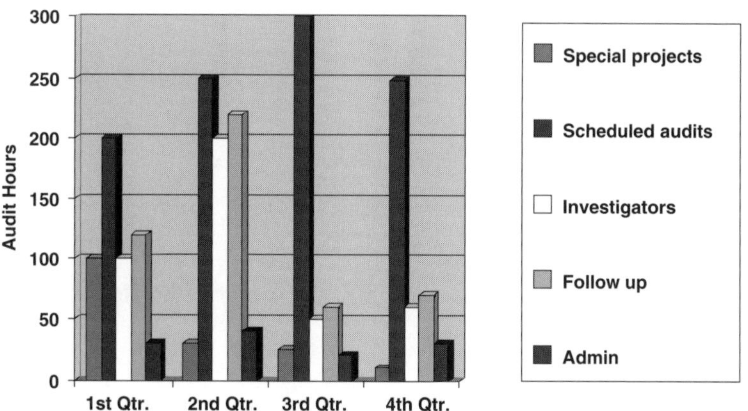

The CAE also reported a percentage breakdown of audit time used in the period:

Scheduled audits	x
Special projects	x
Investigations	x
Follow up	x
Admin	x
	100%

Reporting Progress *(continued)*

This time was then applied to the type of audit completed:

Operational	x
IS	x
Financial	x
Other	x
	100%

Audit staff budget were also compared to actual over the following categories:

- Special projects
- Investigations
- Follow up
- Audit admin

The audit hours required to support the audit plan was built up in the following manner:

Assurance services		x	
Consulting services		x	
Follow up audits		x	
Contingency		x	
			x
Audit planning	x		
Audit committee support	x		
Quality assurance	x		
Admin	x		
Vacation	x		
Sick	x		
Development	x		
			x
	Total Audit hours		**x**

The final case study looks at the way plans can be flexed to take on board a change in circumstances.

CASE STUDY

Agreeing with Changes in Plans

In a newly formed audit shop, changes to the audit plan are approved by the CEO and there are regular meetings with the chair of the audit committee to discuss progress and planned changes due to new developments, special requests for audit supports, frauds, and other issues. The changes would have to be approved by the audit committee and urgent projects are notified to the CEO and chair of the audit committee as soon as practicable (they were then

Agreeing with Changes in Plans *(continued)*

discussed at the next audit committee meeting). Planned audits are curtailed where they are seen as representing low levels of risk in the context of changing circumstances. The target is that 70% of planned work should to be completed allowing much scope to respond to changes and opportunities to add value to the business. The main issue is the relationship between the audit and the audit committee and the level of mutual trust therein. For example there has been a move away from ongoing compliance testing to much more focus on strategic issues facing the organization. In terms of working out whether there are sufficient audit resources to cover the work required, the focus is on planned work and responding to urgent issues. Plans are good if they meet the expectations of:

- Management, including requests for help.
- Important projects to tackle high-risk areas in the governance agenda.
- External auditors.
- Top management and the need to report on risk management and internal controls.
- Audit committee that wants the audit to identify significant business risks and opportunities to add value.

Quarterly Audit Plan

The final part of the annual audit-planning model is the quarterly audit plan. This is an important stage in the planning process since it is possible to fine-tune the annual plan and provide detailed staff work schedules for the ensuing three months. Quarterly plans work best where they are seen as the primary planning period to get to grips with real-time issues that are facing the organization, using real-time resources that are available for this task. Some argue that quarterly plans are much more realistic than the annual audit plans, which have been the basis for the audit service for many years.

CASE STUDY

Contingencies

In one audit division, the CAE would run with a 25% level of contingency built into their audit plans for unforeseen work and responding to clients' concerns. The audit committee accepts the need to change the plan in most quarters and the focus is on auditing high-risk areas. The audit committee monitors progress on the plan on a quarterly basis.

Quarterly tracking of audit work is a good way to help ensure that plans are achieved.

CASE STUDY

Quarterly Tracking

The audit committee of one large organization was mainly concerned with the quarterly audit plans and which audits were completed and which were noted as dropped, changed or put off. These issues were discussed with the committee on the basis of the concept of relative risk to the business and advances in Sarbanes-Oxley preparations. The quarterly audit report included the table shown in Figure 4.12.

Figure 4.12 Quarterly Audit Report—Progress

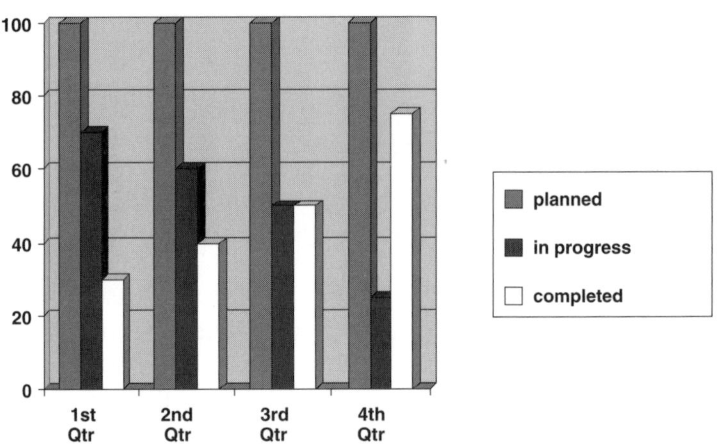

The report also contained a progress table:

REFERENCE	AUDIT	CODE A–E	NOT STARTED	IN PROGRESS	COMPLETED

Quarterly Tracking *(continued)*

CODE:

A Assurance
B Follow up
C Consulting
D Investigations
E Issues studies

The changes in the annual audit planning over the years can be said to move through the following stages:

- *Chaotic*. Audit lurched from engagement to engagement on the basis of the whims of the more long standing auditors.
- *Traditional.* Auditors tried to visit every site, office, and department over a set time frame looking for error, abuse, and fraud.
- *Systematic.* Many audit shops develop a rigid risk assessment model and then formulate audit plans and try to complete various audits on the basis of those that had come out on top of the risk assessments.
- *Business sense.* In its most developed state, auditing may well engage in a sensible dialogue with its key stakeholders and work out how to use the corporate risk profiles to provide a good blend of assurance and consulting work to enhance the success of the organization in the face of rapidly changing risks.

Some auditors simply use a set of principles to underpin the way they formulate their audit plans.

CASE STUDY

Setting Out the Planning Concepts

A newly appointed CAE developed a strategy whereby audit plans were based on the following policies:

- Risk assessment model developed on the basis of tackling high-risk areas as defined by the board.
- Stakeholders consulted to get their views on the risk model and changes made to reflect the business realities facing the organization.

Setting Out the Planning Concepts *(continued)*

- Audit plans seek to reflect best practice in risk-based planning using the concepts of inherent risk, control risk, residual risk, and a scoring index.
- The corporate risk profile was used as the starting place for the audit-planning profiles.
- Key issues included regular themes such as IT security, procurement and contracts, Sarbanes-Oxley, project management, and recent and planned changes.
- Formal risk assessment was then used to add to the profile covering factors such as impact on business, process change, compliance issues, known problems, and audit history.
- Audit areas are identified and timing agreed so that audit resources could be assigned to engagements, projects, and tasks.
- CAE authorizes the start of the engagement and the scope is reviewed before the detailed field work stage covering discussion on matters such as manager's proposals, corporate systems interfaces, any specific requests, support systems, past audit cover, new developments, emerging issues, budgets, personnel, operational processes, products, IT support, KPI, stakeholders' concerns, marketing issues, resources competence, and the type of risk language in use.
- Engagement terms of reference focus on the above.
- Audit report talks about inherent risk, control risk, residual risk, and the state of risk management in the area in question.

SUMMARY

The annual audit plan has a key role in auditing, and it should be prepared after much care and attention. One way to realize the benefits from risk-based annual audit plans is to go through the following five steps:

Step 1. Ensure that the annual audit plan is derived from an audit charter that makes clear the role of internal audit and how it has to interface well with the rest of the organization as well as maintain professional standards of work.

Step 2. Define an audit universe that represents the organization and provides a suitable framework for developing a considered audit coverage of all parts of the organization.

Step 3. Acquire a conceptual view of the organization based on the processes and activities at all levels and in all parts of the organization, including associates, partners, local offices, and international concerns.

Step 4. Make clear what services audit provides in conjunction with the views of key stakeholders, including a good balance between assurance and consulting work.

Step 5. Construct a suitable methodology for ensuring that audit is able to target high-risk aspects of the organization, which may involve assessing the corporate risk register, concerns of stakeholders, and the need to provide assurance and assistance in ERM development and internal control reporting.

Note that Appendix A contains a checklist that can be used to assess the overall quality of risk-based audit planning.

NOTES

1. Auditors Risk Management Guide, Integrating Risk Management and ERM, Paul J Sobel, CCH Incorporated (Chicago) 2004, page 4.04.
2. Auditors Risk Management Guide, Integrating Risk Management and ERM, Paul J Sobel, CCH Incorporated (Chicago) 2004, page 5.05.
3. Moeller, Robert and Witt, Herbert (1999), *Brink's Modern Internal Auditing*, 5th edition, New York: John Wiley and Sons, page 116.
4. Committee of Sponsoring Organizations, Enterprise Risk Management, September 2004, page 9.
5. Internal Auditing's Role In Sections 302 and 404 of the U.S. Sarbanes-Oxley Act of 2002, May 26, 2004, IIA.
6. Internal Auditing's Role In Sections 302 and 404 of the U.S. Sarbanes-Oxley Act of 2002, May 26, 2004, IIA.
7. Institute of Internal Auditors, Glossary of Terms.
8. Institute of Internal Auditors, Standard 2500.A1.
9. Institute of Internal Auditors, Practice Advisory 2010-2.
10. Anderson, Urton and Chapman, Christy (2002), "The IIA Handbook Series" in *Implementing The Professional Practices Framework*, IIA, page 98.
11. Institute of Internal Auditors, Practice Advisory 2010-2.
12. Internal Auditor, February 2003, how do internal audit add value pages 33–37 James Roth.
13. Institute of Internal Auditors, Practice Advisory 2120.A1-1.
14. Institute of Internal Auditors, Standard 2110.A2.
15. Internal Audit and Business Risk Journal, February 2005, pages 22–26 Arthur Piper—reporting on; Charting the course, the evolution and future of IA Survey by Ernst and Young, Characteristics of a robust IT audit plan (summarized).
16. Institute of Internal Auditors, Standard 2120.A2.
17. Institute of Internal Auditors, Practice Advisory 2130-1.
18. Institute of Internal Auditors, Standards 2120.C2.
19. Institute of Internal Auditors, Standards 2220.A2.

5

ENGAGEMENT PLANNING

> Internal auditors should develop and record a plan for each engagement, including the scope, objectives, timing and resource allocations.
>
> —IIA Standard 2200

INTRODUCTION

We arrive now at detailed engagement planning, where long-term plans get translated into actual audits. An audit engagement is described as:

> A specific internal audit assignment, task, or review activity, such as an internal audit, Control Self-Assessment review, fraud examination, or consultancy. An engagement may include multiple tasks or activities designed to accomplish a specific set of related objectives.[1]

Each engagement should be planned and a work program that can be used to guide the auditor through the work needed to complete the engagement should be prepared. An engagement work program is described as:

> A document that lists the procedures to be followed during an engagement, designed to achieve the engagement plan.[2]

IIA standards help set the scene for this all-important aspect of risk-based audit planning:

> In planning the engagement, internal auditors should consider:
>
> The objectives of the activity being reviewed and the means by which the activity controls its performance.
>
> The significant risks to the activity, its objectives, resources, and operations and the means by which the potential impact of risk is kept to an acceptable level.

The adequacy and effectiveness of the activity's risk management and control systems compared to a relevant control framework or model.

The opportunities for making significant improvements to the activity's risk management and control systems.[3]

The model used in this chapter is designed to ensure that the above happens.

ENGAGEMENT PLANNING MODEL: PHASE ONE

Our first model appears in Figure 5.1.

Each aspect of the model is described in the following paragraphs.

ERM

We start our model with the overriding concept of ERM, that is, the organization's need to ensure there is an adequate risk management process that runs across the entire entity. This point cannot be over emphasized.

Figure 5.1 Engagement Planning Model: Phase One

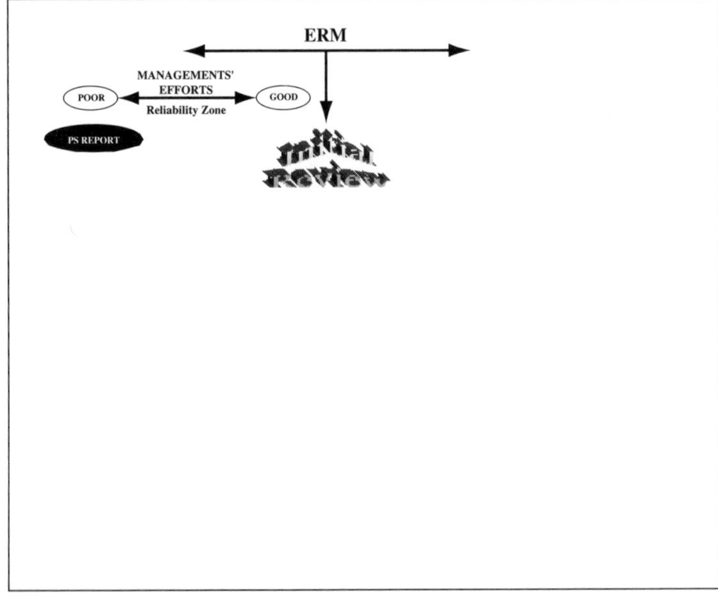

Good Governance, performance, behavior, and success can be earned by all organizations that understand the way risks that get in the way of these aspirations can be tackled. This is not to say success can be guaranteed. It is just that risks can be addressed in the best way possible, and the chance of ongoing success can be enhanced. The audit engagement is about helping the part of the business being audited get to grips with the way risks are controlled through helping, prompting, warning, cajoling, and by all other legitimate means. Christy Chapman has observed the way risk assessment can be used in engagement planning:

> Risk assessment during a specific audit engagement is designed to identify and evaluate exposures at the operations or micro level of the organization. In addition to understanding the business products, services, markets, and other strategic issues, effective engagement level assessments require the audit team to consider the business process risks, the quality of the local management team and the various ways individuals might behave given differing situations.[4]

CASE STUDY

Engagement Risk Assessment

The engagement planning stage used by a newly established audit team involved developing a detailed profile of the business unit in question. The profile included the following risk factors:

Risk Factor:	Source of Information:
Transaction volume	Information systems
Materiality	System and financial accounts
Previous audit results	Audit files and briefings with audit manager
Regulations	Research codes and local laws
Emerging issues	Interviews with the management

The profile was used to determine how much time should be spent on the audit and where the terms of reference should be focused.

Initial Review

It is tempting to strip the next audit from the annual audit plan and send out the assigned auditors to start the audit with a predetermined terms of reference. The team may be told to go and sniff out errors, problems, and anything that is untoward. While this approach worked well in the past, as auditors assumed a greater degree of professionalism, the old ways no longer represent a valid use of the audit resource. Before we can start the audit, there needs to be an initial assessment of the area under review to determine the scope, direction, and approach for the coming audit. Good audit work is not just about achieving set plans, but it is about achieving good results by focusing the plans in a way that optimizes the input from the auditors. IIA standards help clarify this matter:

> Internal auditors should conduct a preliminary assessment of the risks relevant to the activity under review. Engagement objectives should reflect the results of this assessment.[5]

The initial survey is about gathering information to set the direction for the audit and audit guidance makes it clear that this survey has the following objectives:

- Understand the activity under review.
- Identify significant areas warranting special emphasis.
- Obtain information for use in performing the engagement.
- Determine whether further auditing is necessary.[6]

The initial assessment that is aimed at arriving at good engagement plans may well involve the following steps:

Step 1. Assess the known facts about the audit area from the annual audit plan.

Step 2. Review the previous audit report and any outstanding matters, including agreed recommendations and any subsequent follow-ups that have been carried out.

Step 3. Talk to auditors who have had contact with the area under review for any information that is not obvious from the previous audit file.

Step 4. Consider developments within the organization that impact on the area in question, including recent restructuring or change programs and any relevant performance reports.

Step 5. Interview the line manager and get an idea of the current state of risk management and the reliability of existing controls against the background of the type of challenges and pressures that are happening and planned.

Step 6. Prepare a risk profile based on the managers' own risk assessment and any other concerns that have been identified from the above-mentioned tasks.

Management's Efforts

An important aspect of the initial review in our engagement planning model is the progress that has been made by the management in the area in question. The audit approach will be based on the needs determined from an initial assessment of the adequacy of the risk management arrangements that are being operated by local management, hopefully in conjunction with the corporate risk management policy for the organization. Before we can isolate the terms of reference for the engagement, the auditor must find out what needs to be done in terms of establishing a sound system of internal control in the context of the risks that face the area under review. This approach is endorsed by IIA standards:

> The internal auditor should consider management's assessment of risk:
>
> The reliability of management's assessment of risk.
>
> Management's monitoring and reporting of risk issues.
>
> Management reports of events that have exceeded the agreed limits for risk toleration.
>
> Whether there are risks identified by management elsewhere in the organization in related activities or supporting systems that may be relevant to the activity under review.
>
> Management's own assessment of controls related to risks.[7]

A short case study details the way management's efforts are assessed and built into engagement plans:

CASE STUDY

Developing the Terms of Reference

One audit team developed a template for assessing the state of key issues that would need to be taken into account when developing the engagement terms of reference (Figure 5.2).

Developing the Terms of Reference *(continued)*

Figure 5.2 Sample Terms of Reference

ERM Element	Factor	Audit Test
Applied risk policy	Extent of risk awareness	Check managers' understanding
Clear objectives and performance targets	Comply with corporate standards	Staff surveys and review target-setting arrangements
Formal reporting lines	Authorization levels and responsibilities	Check responsibilities in line with authority
Risk identification and management	Formal ERM process	Examine current risk strategy and registers
Reliable disclosure reports on internal control	Formal reports and certifications	Check sample of control reports
Ongoing improvement to controls	Control review embedded into business	Examine extent to which controls updated in line with changing risks
Suitable tools in place	Range of corporate tools and help applied	Examine near misses, contingency plans, software tools, and KPIs
Training programs	Staff competence encouraged	Review staff training and development on ERM and controls
Evidence based ERM	All risk management documented	Check the way decisions can be traced back to risk assessments
Graded quality system	ERM maturity range in place	Check progress on ERM against set corporate benchmarks

Reliability Zone

After having assessed the managements' efforts, it is possible to form a view on the reliability of the current risk management arrangements along the lines of say "poor" or "good"—or any degree between these two extremes. Remember this is an initial assessment at this stage and apparently poor arrangements may be in an early stage of development, while apparently good arrangements may not work well in practice. This assessment of reliability is in consonance with IIA guidance that suggests:

> In planning the engagement, internal auditors should consider:
>
> The objectives of the activity being reviewed and the means by which the activity controls its performance and achievement of those objectives.
>
> The significant risks to the activity, its objectives, resources, and operations and the means by which the potential impact and/or likelihood of risk is kept to an acceptable level.
>
> The adequacy and effectiveness of the activity's risk management and control systems compared to a relevant control framework or model.
>
> The opportunities for making significant improvements to the activity's risk management and control systems.[8]

Reliability can be assessed by considering the following aspects of risk management:

- Is good ERM happening?
- Is it in line with corporate standards?
- Is it more than just a paper exercise?
- Do staffs believe ERM helps them to do their jobs?
- Can the outputs from the ERM process be relied upon by the senior management?

One aspect of reliability that should be considered is the extent to which the corporate internal control model has been applied in the area in question. This big picture thinking has been remarked on by Christy Chapman.

> Using the organization's broad-based internal control framework to plan an engagement helps internal auditors ensure their work is not too

narrowly focused on the policies and procedures of the reviewed area but instead reflects the "big picture" concerns of the organization as a whole.[9]

CASE STUDY

Dealing with Remote Sites

One audit team relied on visits to the many remote sites to discharge the audit role and an annual plan was developed to identify those offices that attracted the most risk. A self-assessment questionnaire that sought information on the types of issues that were impacting the objectives at the site in question was sent out a month before the planned visit. This questionnaire had queries about plans to mitigate the high-risk factors facing local management and when the feedback was analyzed it formed the basis for developing an audit's terms of reference for the engagement. The opening interview with the business manager and subsequent initial appraisals were directed at assessing the way the management was identifying and dealing with local risk and ensuring compliance with head office procedures.

PS Report

The final part of this stage of the model is the Preliminary Survey (PS) report based on what we have called the initial survey, which is the report prepared by the lead auditor after completing the initial review stage of engagement planning. IIA guidance suggests that a great deal of activity should occur before the detailed engagement field work can be started:

> The chief audit executive is responsible for determining how, when, and to whom engagement results will be communicated. This determination should be documented and communicated to management, to the extent deemed practical, during the planning phase of the engagement. Subsequent changes, which affect the timing or reporting of engagement results, should also be communicated to management, if appropriate.[10]

This is important since management research suggests that good planning is necessary whenever a project or venture is being started. And it is the failure to plan properly that leads to poor results in all walks of business, including the audit process. The use of preliminary survey reports is detailed in the following case study:

CASE STUDY

Risk Workshops

The auditor's risk assessment at engagement level was based around steps taken by the business management to understand their risks, and each audit assurance engagement went through the following stages:

- A risk workshop was conducted with the business management team for the area in question.
- The in-house review processes such as exception reporting and budget monitoring were also examined.
- Heat maps were prepared with the business manager, which isolated priority areas of high residual risk and aspects of the operation that were dependent on key controls.
- The risk management strategy for high risk, control reviews, and compliance arrangements formed the basis for the engagement plan that was agreed upon with the management team.

ENGAGEMENT PLANNING MODEL: PHASE TWO

Our model is further enhanced in Figure 5.3 by building in steps instigated by auditors to ensure that the terms of reference for the engagement are well focused.

Each new aspect of the model is described in the following paragraphs.

Audit's Efforts

Audit's efforts should be viewed in conjunction with the management's efforts that we discussed earlier. During the initial review, and before we can set a clear terms of reference for the engagement, a review would have been carried out of management's efforts to establish an effective risk the management process. If the reliability scale suggests that there is a sound process in place, then audit can set about reviewing this process and providing formal assurances on ensuring it meets the standards set by the organization. If however the process is poor, then audit may well feel that a consulting engagement will be a better way of using their resources. Whatever the adopted approach, auditing will need to bring something to the party and make clear their contribution. In deciding how

Figure 5.3 Engagement Planning Model: Phase Two

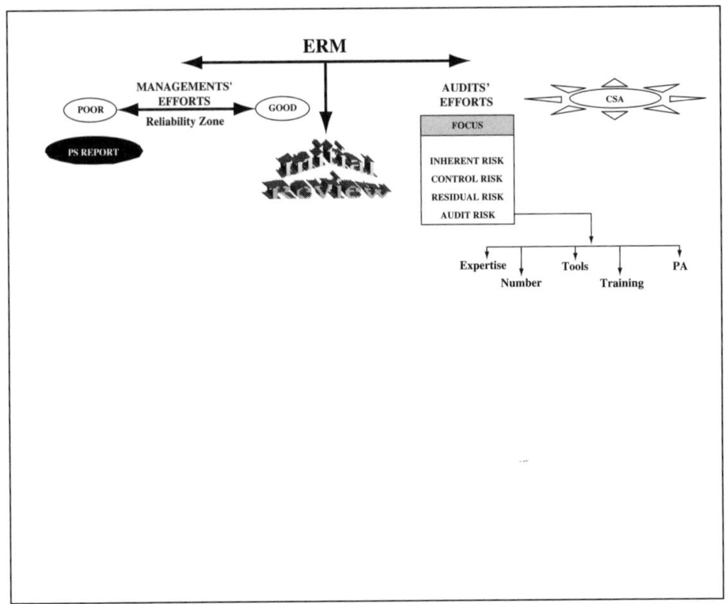

best to approach the task of risk-based audit planning, the auditors may wish to consider certain types of risks:

Inherent risk:

Audit will wish to judge the extent of risk inherent in the area under review. The fact that the audit has featured in the annual audit plan, and has been selected for inclusion in a particular quarter, means the operation must have some degree of material risk attached to it. Regard may be had to IIA guidance in reviewing background information such as those noted below:

- Objectives and goals.
- Policies, plans, procedures, laws, regulations, and contracts that could have a significant impact on operations and reports.
- Organizational information, for example, number and names of employees, key employees, job descriptions, and details about recent changes in the organization, including major system changes.

- Budget information, operating results, and financial data of the activity to be reviewed.
- Prior engagement working papers.
- Results of other engagements, including the work of external auditors, completed or in process.
- Correspondence files to determine potential significant engagement issues.
- Authoritative and technical literature appropriate to the activity.[11]

The engagement planning stage will involve the auditor revisiting this consideration and working out how big the risk currently stands by having reference to certain factors:

- The corporate risk appetite.
- New and emerging developments and projects.
- The level of innovation that was expected from the business area in terms of internal stakeholders' views.
- The criticality of the business objectives in the overall success of the organization, taking onboard the needs of both external and internal customers.
- The scope for error, fraud, and abuse and the impact of such matters on the reputation and functioning of the business.

Control risk:

The auditor will also be concerned with the risk that controls, although they appear to be in place, do not work well or may be ignored, or flouted. This control risk could make the difference between a successful part of the business and a major cause of concern. Control has been defined as:

> Any action taken by management, the board, and other parties *to manage risk* and increase the likelihood that established objectives and goals will be achieved. Management plans, organizes, and directs the performance of sufficient actions to provide reasonable assurance that objectives and goals will be achieved.[12]

When controls fail, risks that the controls are meant to guard against may materialize and underline the business, as it happened in the following case study:

CASE STUDY

Audit Interventions

A dynamic new audit team set clear goals for improving controls, processes, performance, governance, and helping the business exploit opportunities to streamline the business lines. Each engagement was based on the scope to hit these key targets and concentrated on risks that got in the way of such progress. Meanwhile, the extent to which known problems and threats were being tackled was also built into the audit work. The auditors did their own risk assessments on the basis that they needed to ensure improvements in governance, risk management, and more reliable controls as a result of the intervention of the audit team.

The risk that controls could fail should be uppermost in the auditor's mind when planning the engagement. We have already referred to one useful framework for assessing the scope of controls that are of concern to the auditors rests with IIA standards, as reproduced here:

> Based on the results of the risk assessment, the internal audit activity should evaluate the adequacy and effectiveness of controls encompassing the organization's governance, operations, and information systems. This should include:
>
> Reliability and integrity of financial and operational information.
>
> Effectiveness and efficiency of operations.
>
> Safeguarding of assets.
>
> Compliance with laws, regulations, and contracts.[13]

Poor or failed controls means the above may not be achieved, and audit engagement planning should address this possibility within the planned terms of reference for assurance work, bearing in mind that:

> Internal auditors are expected to identify and evaluate significant risk exposures in the normal course of their duties. [14]

Residual risk:

The other risk that the auditor should build into engagement plans relates to the risk from a lack of controls, that is, where inherent risk has not been contained below the threshold set by the corporate risk appetite. Residual risk is defined as:

> The risk remaining after management takes action to reduce the impact and likelihood of an adverse event, including control activities in responding to a risk.[15]

Operations that hold high levels of inherent risk and that have poor internal controls will tend to have high levels of residual risk. Risk-based engagement planning will need to focus on this equation to be of any real use.

Audit risk:

There is one last risk that is often overlooked by the auditor. This is audit risk. Many auditors have moved far ahead in the ERM field and insist that it is the management and only the management that is responsible for ensuring ERM works and makes sense. Audit simply helps them to discharge this responsibility wherever possible and reports the results of the management's efforts in this respect. But all parts of a business bear some responsibility and it is wrong for auditing to hide behind their cloak of independence and argue that they are not really accountable except for checking up on progress and reporting the results. There are many risks that reside fairly and squarely with the CAE and the audit staff and these include the failure to achieve the following:

> The internal auditor should prepare a summary of results from the reviews of management's assessment of risk, the background information, and findings from any survey work carried out. The summary should identify:
>
> Significant engagement issues and reasons for pursuing them in more depth. Pertinent information acquired from all sources.
>
> Engagement objectives, engagement procedures, and special approaches, such as computer-assisted audit techniques.
>
> Potential critical control points, control deficiencies, and/or excess controls.
>
> Preliminary estimates of time and resource requirements.
>
> Revised dates for reporting phases and completing the engagement.
>
> When applicable, reasons for not continuing the engagement.[16]

A further concern is that auditing gets tied in too closely with improving the area under review and is not able to stand back and consider whether they have been able to deliver an objective assessment of the state of internal controls:

> Objectivity requires internal auditors to perform engagements in such a manner that they have an honest belief in their work product and that no significant quality compromises are made. Internal auditors are not to be placed in situations in which they feel unable to make objective professional judgments.[17]

There is tremendous pressure on the audit team to deliver a wide range of products that enhance the organization governance framework. The auditors are being asked to appraise risk management standards and specific key controls and are also in demand as consultants in helping to promote good performance, value for money, quality systems, good compliance, and antifraud measures across the entire business. Much hinges on the way engagements are planned and the way they target real issues and concerns:

> The internal auditor is responsible for planning and conducting the engagement assignment, subject to supervisory review and approval. The engagement program should:
>
> Document the internal auditor's procedures for collecting, analyzing, interpreting, and documenting information during the engagement.
>
> State the objectives of the engagement.
>
> Set forth the scope and degree of testing required to achieve the engagement objectives in each phase of the engagement.
>
> Identify technical aspects, activity objectives, risks, processes, and transactions that should be examined.
>
> State the nature and extent of testing required.
>
> Be prepared prior to the commencement of engagement work and modified, as appropriate, during the course of the engagement.[18]

Another risk that faces the auditor is derived from the need to work to professional standards and perform with reasonable skill and care.

> Internal auditors should possess the knowledge, skills, and other competencies needed to perform their individual responsibilities. The internal audit activity collectively should possess or obtain the knowledge, skills, and other competencies needed to perform its responsibilities.[19]

The final point to note is the need to ensure that scarce audit resources are applied in a suitable manner:

> Internal auditors should determine appropriate resources to achieve engagement objectives. Staffing should be based on an evaluation of the nature and complexity of each engagement, time constraints, and available resources.[20]

The engagement plan is designed to address all the above-mentioned risks and lead to a well-constructed and valuable audit. Anything less is unacceptable even if the audit's role in organizations is not always defined by the regulators:

> Sarbanes-Oxley specifies the various roles of management, the audit committee, and the external auditors; however, the Act does not specifically address the role of internal auditors.[21]

Where the right skills are not available to perform the audit, effort must be made to address the shortfall:

> The chief audit executive should obtain competent advice and assistance if the internal audit staff lacks the knowledge, skills, or other competencies needed to perform all or part of the engagement.[22]

CSA

We have included Control Self-Assessment (CSA) as a useful tool for focusing the audit. CSA may be used by the management as a tool for assessing risk at a local level as a contribution to ERM throughout the organization. CSA may be used by the auditor to help the management understand and deal with risks to their business. It may also be used to work alongside management in isolating risks in an area that is due to be audited so that the audit may focus on these risks and kick-start the CSA process that management may wish to adopt in the future. It is clear that CSA can be a very powerful technique that fits nicely into the governance, risk management, and internal control agenda. IIA guidance makes clear the benefits from a well-constructed CSA program:

> A methodology encompassing self-assessment surveys and facilitated workshops called CSA is a useful and efficient approach for managers and internal auditors to collaborate in assessing and evaluating control procedures. In its purest form, CSA integrates business objectives and risks with control processes. Control self-assessment is also referred to as Control/risk self-assessment or CRSA. Although CSA practitioners

use a number of differing techniques and formats, most implemented programs share some key features and goals. An organization that uses self-assessment will have a formal, documented process that allows management and work teams, who are directly involved in a business unit, function, or process to participate in a structured manner for the purpose of:

Identifying risks and exposures;

Assessing the control processes that mitigate or manage those risks;

Developing action plans to reduce risks to acceptable levels; and

Determining the likelihood of achieving the business objectives.[23]

The auditor may use this facilitated approach in engagement planning to get to a useful terms of reference for the audit:

> Internal audit activity acquires more information about the control processes within the organization and can leverage that additional information in allocating their scarce resources so as to spend a greater effort in investigating and performing tests of business units or functions that have significant control weaknesses or high residual risks.[24]

This approach may be demonstrated in a case study:

CASE STUDY

The Initial Review

In an audit shop, the initial review for each major audit involves a detailed assessment of risk areas and issues that should form the terms of reference for the planned audit. The risk assessment involves the following stages:

- Review of the corporate risk register and risks that relate to the area in question.
- Review of matters brought forward from the previous audit including any follow-up of past recommendations.
- Discussions with the line management regarding any risk assessments that have been conducted within the business over the last six months.
- A facilitated meeting with the management team to establish the business objectives, the risks that impact on the objectives, an assessment of these risks, and a consideration on the state of the existing risk management strategy.

> **The Initial Review** *(continued)*
>
> A draft terms of reference is built from the above four sources and this is fed back to the line manager for discussion and formulation into a final terms of reference. The engagement plan will then comment on each of the four elements of risk:
>
> 1. Corporate risk register
> 2. Previous audit
> 3. Discussions with the line management risk assessments
> 4. Facilitated management team workshop

There is full recognition of the role that internal audit may play in stimulating effective control self-assessments within an organization, so long as audit does not assume responsibility for what is a management tool:

> The internal audit activity is often the source for expertise regarding control self-assessment (CSA) and for skilled facilitators. CSA may be used as an effective and efficient means for management to document and/or assess controls. If an internal auditor provides information, training, and/or facilitates a CSA, objectivity is not likely to be impaired. However, if during the CSA the internal auditor owns the assessment or is the main source of the documentation, then objectivity is impaired.[25]

ENGAGEMENT PLANNING MODEL: PHASE THREE

Our model continues in Figure 5.4.

Each new aspect of the model is described in the following paragraphs.

Compliance

The concept of compliance comes back into the frame in our model as we need to determine the audit approach where an initial assessment of the risk management process suggests that there is a reasonably good set of arrangements in place. The auditor will need to determine a reliability zone in terms of compliance, and this matter is dealt with next.

Figure 5.4 Engagement Planning Model: Phase Three

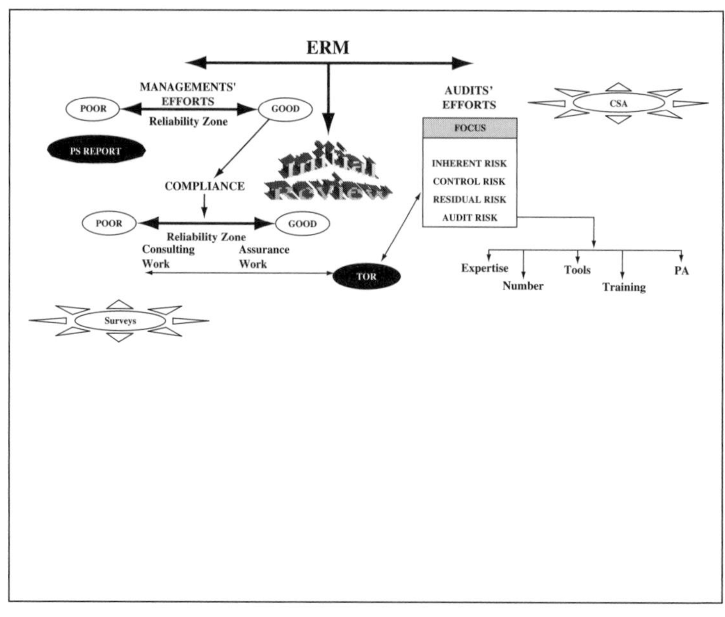

Reliability Zone

The level of compliance with corporate standards on internal control and the organization's risk management policy may be judged to be either poor, good, or a level between these two ranges. Good risk management arrangements will tend to be:

- Reliable
- Integrated into the business
- Seen as worthwhile
- Resourced
- Constantly updated

Poor arrangements will exhibit the following features:

- Annual exercises
- Filed for the auditors
- Out of date

- Not properly understood
- Focused around financial compliance issues only

Consulting—Assurance Work

Having made an initial assessment of the state of risk management in terms of the extent to which it fits corporate standards, the type of audit can be planned. The audit approach may be based on a consulting style or an assurance style. Some annual audit plans set out the type of audit beforehand and ensure that the audit team follows the format that was prescribed previously. While this makes for an easily managed engagement, for the risk-based approach to audit planning, it may not always be appropriate. Risks change from year to year, quarter to quarter, and even over shorter time frames. And it is best to design the audit approach that adds most value to the organization on the basis of the latest position for the operation in question. There is firm guidance on the audit's role in the context of Sarbanes-Oxley and, for that matter, other relevant disclosure provisions for, say, public sector organizations:

> Internal auditors acting in a consulting role may be asked to assist the organization in identifying, evaluating, and implementing risk and control assessment methodologies as well as recommending controls to address related risks. However, decisions to adopt or implement recommendations made as a result of an internal audit advisory service should be made by management. An internal auditor may be asked to participate in the design and implementation of a new process for management to assess their internal controls over financial reporting. If the internal auditor's activities are limited to evaluating the new processes and defining a reference guide on recommended controls addressing related risks, the internal auditor's objectivity is not likely impaired. Additionally, if the internal auditor is a member of the project team which selects the assessment methodology and tools, and/or defines the documentation standards management is going to use, objectivity is not likely considered impaired. On the other hand, if the internal auditor implements new processes to remediate control gaps, the internal auditor's objectivity may be considered impaired.[26]

The equation suggested in our model is that where there are poor risk management arrangements the auditor may well assume a consulting style to help management set up a suitable infrastructure. Audit's consulting role may involve assisting with formal projects that are set up to help establish sound internal control disclosure practices and an effective risk management process. A less onerous version may be to facilitate CSA workshops, or help the management set up a program of CSA events to stimulate risk management at local level. The other side of the equation means that, where the risk management arrangements are firmly in place, audit may adopt a more traditional assurance role and simply audit these arrangements to ensure they are both robust and reliable. A case study follows:

CASE STUDY

Using Templates

An audit team used the template shown in Figure 5.5 to assign risk categories in audit work.

Figure 5.5 Sample Risk Categories Template

Audit Area	Inherent Risk	Control Risk	Emerging Issues	Type of Audit
XXX	XXX	XXX	XXX	A
XXX	XXX	XXX	XXX	B
XXX	XXX	XXX	XXX	C

A: advice and information
B: issues paper
C: formal audit report

Surveys

One useful technique that appears in our planning model is the use of surveys. Some audit teams send out self-assessment surveys to local offices and overseas sites asking the management to score their risks through a variety of set factors, or the survey will provide a diagnostic tool to score the control environment again through a selection of set questions designed to probe the way staff design, implement, and review their controls, using an assessment of operational risk in this task. The results of the survey not only enable the audit team to assign a score to the unit in terms of the potential exposure to high levels of risk but once the results are fed into the engagement planning cycle they help the auditor direct the terms of reference toward apparent weaknesses or high risk aspects of the business area under review. IIA guidance provides support for the use of survey during the planning stage of an audit:

> A survey permits an informed approach to planning and carrying out engagement work, and is an effective tool for applying the internal auditing activity's resources where they can be used most effectively. The focus of a survey will vary depending upon the nature of the engagement. The scope of work and the time requirements of a survey will vary. Contributing factors include the internal auditor's training and experience, knowledge of the activity being examined, the type of engagement being performed, and whether the survey is part of a recurring or follow-up assignment. Time requirements will also be influenced by the size and complexity of the activity being examined, and by the geographical dispersion of the activity.[27]

This type of approach is used by the audit team, which is discussed in the following case study.

CASE STUDY

Planning Questions

In one not-for-profit organization, an initial survey was used to judge where to focus the subsequent audit (Figure 5.6).

Figure 5.6 Sample Survey Terms of Reference (TOR)

Planning Question	Survey: Managers' Response	Auditor's Initial Examination of Response	Impact on Engagement Terms of Reference
1. Managers aware of risks that face them?			
2. Managers have robust systems for identifying new risks?			
3. Risks have been adequately assessed?			
4. Risk management is accurate, robust, and reliable?			
5. Others			

Everything that has been discussed in our model so far, when taken together, will enable the auditor to agree with the line manager on a terms of reference for the area under review. The risk-based approach to audit planning is quite dynamic in that it does not start with a set terms of reference. It requires that some preplanning work be carried out before the potentially high-risk areas can be isolated and placed into the terms of reference for the audit, to ensure the work makes sense on a wider front. Good terms of reference will:

- Focus on real risks.
- Take on board management steps to implement ERM.
- Distinguish assurance from consulting work.
- Be agreed with the business manager and work team.
- Reflect the best use of audit resources.

One final point to note in setting a terms of reference is that the scope of the engagement should not be limited without any good reason as this will impair audit independence:

> A scope limitation is a restriction placed upon the internal audit activity that precludes the audit activity from accomplishing its objectives and plans. Among other things, a scope limitation may restrict the:
>
> Scope defined in the charter.
>
> Internal audit activity's access to records, personnel, and physical properties relevant to the performance of engagements.
>
> Approved engagement work schedule.
>
> Performance of necessary engagement procedures.
>
> Approved staffing plan and financial budget.[28]

Where the audit is a consulting engagement, the action that should be taken when independence is impaired is spelt out in audit standards:

> If internal auditors have potential impairments to independence or objectivity relating to proposed consulting services, disclosure should be made to the engagement client prior to accepting the engagement.[29]

Once the terms of reference have been agreed upon, they will have to be communicated to all relevant parties:

> When planning an engagement for parties outside the organization, internal auditors should establish a written understanding with them about objectives, scope, respective responsibilities and other expectations, including restrictions on distribution of the results of the engagement and access to engagement records.[30]

This basic requirement also applies to consulting work:

> Internal auditors should establish an understanding with consulting engagement clients about objectives, scope, respective responsibilities, and other client expectations. For significant engagements, this understanding should be documented.[31]

The audit plan needs to be sufficiently comprehensive to help determine the shape and form of the audit and the practical aspects of getting the job done:

> Other requirements of the engagement, such as the engagement period covered and estimated completion dates, should be determined. The final engagement communication format should be considered, since proper planning at this stage facilitates preparing the final engagement communication.[32]

ENGAGEMENT PLANNING MODEL: PHASE FOUR

Our model continues in Figure 5.7.

Each new aspect of the model is described in the following paragraphs.

Figure 5.7 Engagement Planning Model: Phase Four

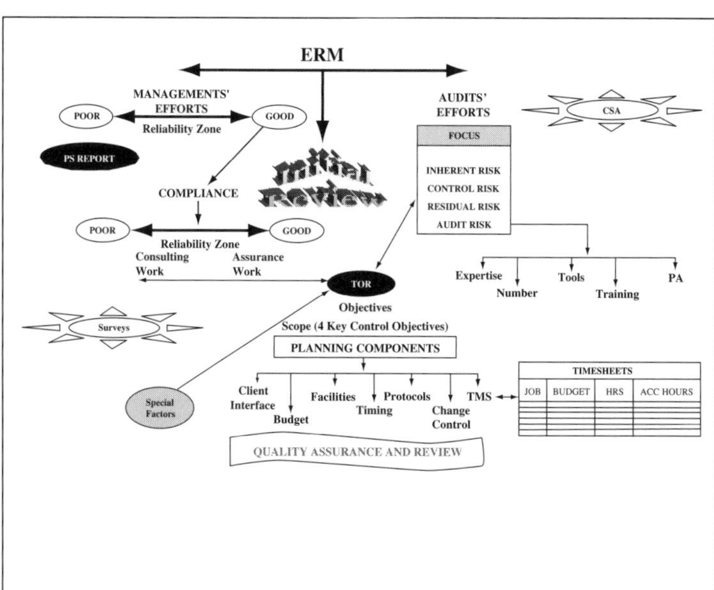

Objectives and Scope

The engagement planning exercise is based on defining clear objectives for an audit, and IIA standards require that:

> Objectives should be established for each engagement.[33]

Examples of the objectives that may be defined for an audit engagement are set out below:

- To review the adequacy and effectiveness of the risk management process relating to the operation of system ABC.
- To review the arrangements to ensure compliance with corporate procedures relating to ABC in department XYZ.
- To review the extent to which the significant risks to business systems ABC are being addressed so that they fall in line with the corporate risk strategy.
- To help management establish the control framework agreed to by the board to ensure that an effective ERM process is implemented and operated as part of the business systems in department XYZ.
- To assess the state of fraud prevention and detection in section YYY.

It is crucial that the objectives set are precise and lead to a well-defined and successful audit. This is particularly important where there is a large team of auditors assigned to the work, as a lack of clarity may imply that each team member is working in the dark, or even worse having a different interpretation of the outputs that are expected from the audit. An engagement objective has been defined as:

> Broad statements developed by internal auditors that define intended engagement accomplishments.[34]

Objectives define what is going to be achieved by the audit and scope dictates the issues that fall within the remit of the audit:

> The established scope should be sufficient to satisfy the objectives of the engagement.[35]

Having decided what falls within the remit of the audit, by default it is clear that certain aspects of the operation under review will not feature in the work that will be carried out by the auditor. This may be because parts of the business have a lower risk rating, or perhaps these areas were reviewed by a previous audit or by a different review team. Or it may be the case that the audit is driven by specific concerns that impact the current strategic position. The other benefit in setting the scope of the audit is that it helps define the type of issues that will be considered by the auditor, and IIA standards have provided a useful framework for making this decision, using the well-known Scope of Key Control Objectives that has been mentioned several times in this book:

> Based on the results of the risk assessment, the internal audit activity should evaluate the adequacy and effectiveness of controls encompassing the organization governance, operations, and information systems. This should include:
>
> Reliability and integrity of financial and operational information.
>
> Effectiveness and efficiency of operations.
>
> Safeguarding of assets.
>
> Compliance with laws, regulations, and contracts.[36]

The third feature of Scope is that it indicates how the audit will be tackled in terms of the use of evidence and information as suggested below:

> The scope of the engagement should include consideration of relevant systems, records, personnel, and physical properties, including those under the control of third parties.[37]

As regards IIA guidance, there is a great deal of useful information regarding engagement objectives that should be noted by the auditor, including the following:

> Engagement objectives and procedures should address the risks associated with the activity under review. The term risk is the uncertainty of an event occurring that could have an impact on the achievement of objectives. Risk is measured in terms of consequences and likelihood. The purpose of the risk assessment during the planning phase of the engagement is to identify significant areas of activity that should be examined as potential engagement objectives.[38]

Special Factors

We have placed "special factors" within the risk-based engagement planning model to allow the audit space to breathe. If planning models are too concise and promote a rigid scoring system that turns the audit into a rather mechanical process, then this may lead to good results, but probably not excellent results. Allowing room for special factors gives the auditor discretion to work not on instinct, but to respond to intangible issues that may creep into the minds of the auditor and the management alike. These special items will vary from place to place, but may relate to what some people call, "soft controls"—such as the way people relate to each other at work and whether there is an aggressive culture of "succeed at all costs" or a laid back culture of "do anything you like" that in fact affects the way control routines are perceived and applied.

CASE STUDY

Isolating Concerns

An audit engagement to review the way clients who needed business loans were being assessed by the customer services division of a large financial services company found that the process for checking affordability was being applied in a slapdash manner by most staff. The audit changed its approach and focused on the staff bonus scheme that was placing the services team under tremendous pressure to sign off new loans even where some detailed checking of data could not be fully completed. The risks presented by the poorly conceived bonus scheme were found to increase the risk of defaults and breaching of regulator's provisions, and the audit terms of reference was further flexed to form a consulting project to help improve matters in this part of the organization.

There are several areas in which audit can contribute for making clear improvements to the existing arrangements, and these could form part of what we have called special factors for planning the engagement. For example:

> Internal audit can and should play an important role in business continuity planning (BCP) development as well as its testing processes. It may offer resources to observe and comment on the results of the BCP tests, suggest testing scenarios, or offer consultative advice on the progress of the BCP development.[39]

Planning Components

The items noted under the planning components box in our model are explained below:

- *Client interface.* The task of setting the terms of reference for the audit at hand provides a great opportunity to get to know client managers and understand their risk profiles and how these profiles are developed and managed. It is also a chance for auditing to demonstrate how they can help the management team in their efforts to make ERM a reality.
- *Budget.* A budget needs to be set for the audit on the basis of the audit staff assigned to the job, traveling and hotel expenses, and any other expenses that need to be built into the engagement plan. Like all good budgets, the figures need to be monitored and discrepancies resolved.
- *Facilities.* Each audit plan should include a bid for any facilities that may be required to support the work, including input from, say, external experts, help from IS audit or contract audit staff, and any additional data interrogation facilities that may need to be applied.
- *Timing.* The way the audit is planned needs to take on board timing issues relating to travel, staff absences, review work by the audit managers, important reporting dates for, say, audit-committee updates, and timing issues facing the area under review.
- *Protocols.* Everyone in an organization will be busy and it is easy to forget protocols when developing the audit plan. A client needs to be given sufficient notice of the audit to ensure it goes smoothly, and dates, meetings, and fieldwork need to be programmed in a way that is fair to all sides.
- *Change control.* Audit standards call for the setting of work programs for each audit engagement:

  > Work programs should establish the procedures for identifying, analyzing, evaluating, and recording information during the engagement. The work program should be approved prior to the commencement of work, and any adjustments approved promptly.[40]

  When changes are made to these programs, they need to go through a formal agreement process involving the audit manager to ensure the work retains direction and is an efficient use of audit resources.
- *Time sheets.* Finally, each auditor who works on an engagement should record the time spent on the job against the code that represents the job in hand, and this is discussed below in more detail.

Time Sheets

The way the auditor accounts for time is one of the basic planning components listed above. The reason for giving this more emphasis is because time is very important for the auditor and it is time (along with quality) that needs to be tightly controlled to ensure that the audit staff are focused and able to deliver. Each audit engagement should be given a time budget that is based on the work that needs to be completed and the number and type of auditors that are assigned to the tasks. Meanwhile, each auditor should be required to account for his/her time and record chargeable hours to live jobs. The time sheet will record:

- The audit engagement in question.
- The hours charged by the auditor.
- The relevant dates.
- The type of work performed.
- Whether the hours were preapproved by the lead auditor, audit manager, or CAE.

The engagement plan should record the time needed to complete various parts of the audit and this budget should be signed off by the audit manager in question. One version of a time sheet is shown in Figure 5.8.

Quality Assurance

Quality is included in the planning model because it should be built into all models that relate to audit work. In fact, quality is relevant to engagement planning on two different levels:

1. Planning should be carried out to quality standards.
2. Plans in themselves set standards that can be used to address the quality of the ensuing audit engagement.

Quality has always been recognized by the audit profession, and IIA standards cover this topic in some detail:

> The chief audit executive should develop and maintain a quality assurance and improvement program that covers all aspects of the internal audit activity and continuously monitors its effectiveness. This program includes periodic internal and external quality assessments and ongoing

Figure 5.8 Sample Timesheet

EMPLOYEE Week Commencing;							DATE			
JOB	**CODE**	**HOURS**	**MON**	**TUES**	**WED**	**THUR**	**FRI**	**SAT**	**SUN**	**TOTAL**
OTHER										
ADMIN										
TRAINING										
VACATION										
SICK										
OTHER										
TOTALS										
AUDITOR SIGNS **(OR SIMPLY INPUTS DATA TO SYSTEM)**							**AUDIT MANAGER SIGNS** **(MANAGER REVIEWS DATA)**			

internal monitoring. Each part of the program should be designed to help the internal auditing activity add value and improve the organization's operations and to provide assurance that the internal audit activity is in conformity with the Standards and the Code of Ethics.[41]

In the past, the quality concept was based mainly on assessing whether that work had been performed to acceptable standards and this involved a great deal of double checking. Nowadays, quality is more about having five basic structures in place:

1. A clear set of standards that are applied to the job.
2. Staff who are adequately trained, recourced, and motivated to perform to these standards.
3. A culture in place that promotes compliance with quality standards and procedures.
4. Supervision by management that the above is firmly in place.
5. Suitable documentation that demonstrates that the above is in place.

For auditors, these five elements should be fully employed:

1. **Standards.** There are comprehensive standards and guidance issued by the IIA and these should be accompanied by a suitable audit manual that expands on the matters covered in the standards. For example, not all consulting engagements will be taken on by the auditors without a careful consideration of how they help the organization move forward:

 > In performing consulting engagements, internal auditors should ensure that the scope of the engagement is sufficient to address the agreed-upon objectives. If internal auditors develop reservations about the scope during the engagement, these reservations should be discussed with the client to determine whether to continue with the engagement. [42]

2. **Staffing.** Audit staff should be trained as certified internal auditors and should be given the required level of funding and support to perform their work properly:

 > In determining the resources necessary to perform the engagement, evaluation of the following is important:
 >
 > The number and experience level of the internal auditing staff required should be based on an evaluation of the nature and complexity of the engagement assignment, time constraints, and available resources.
 >
 > Knowledge, skills, and other competencies of the internal audit staff should be considered in selecting internal auditors for the engagement.
 >
 > Training needs of internal auditors should be considered, since each engagement assignment serves as a basis for meeting developmental needs of the internal auditing activity.
 >
 > Consideration of the use of external resources in instances where additional knowledge, skills, and other competencies are needed.[43]

3. **Culture.** This is more difficult. The CAE should ensure there is a positive culture in place and that compliance with procedure is not seen as just following a set of mundane tasks.

4. **Supervision.** Audit standards require that an adequate level of supervision is in place, and there is normally a lead auditor appointed to take charge of planning and performing the audit. In addition, the audit manager will tend to be involved in the engage-

ment planning stage and then assume a review role as well as provide advice whenever this is requested by the lead auditor. IIA standards take a lead in this matter:

> Engagements should be properly supervised to ensure objectives are achieved, quality is assured, and staff is developed.[44]

5. **Documentation.** There are clear standards covering working paper files and documentation in general, and these principles are ingrained in most professional audit staff. IIA standards address the need for engagement work programs in both assurance work and consulting work:

> Internal auditors should develop work programs that achieve the engagement objectives. These work programs should be recorded.[45]
>
> Work programs should establish the procedures for identifying, analyzing, evaluating, and recording information during the engagement. The work program should be approved prior to its implementation, and any adjustments approved promptly.[46]
>
> Work programs for consulting engagements may vary in form and content depending upon the nature of the engagement.[47]

The audit manager needs to ensure that whatever was planned for the auditor has actually been achieved. This means that review mechanisms should be built into engagement plans so that there is provision for carrying out regular reviews of work carried out by the audit team as the work progresses:

> All engagement working papers should be reviewed to ensure that they properly support the engagement communications and that all necessary audit procedures have been performed. Evidence of supervisory review should consist of the reviewer initialing and dating each working paper after it is reviewed. Other techniques that provide evidence of supervisory review include completing an engagement working paper review checklist, preparing a memorandum specifying the nature, extent, and results of the review, and/or evaluation and acceptance within electronic working paper software.[48]

Good-quality internal audit means that the results can be used by others:

> If an internal audit activity maintains its independence and objectivity, the external auditor could use their work to the greatest extent an audi-

tor could use the work of others; therefore, reducing the extent of testing, which may otherwise be performed by the external auditor. In this situation, the organization's external auditor fees may be reduced.[49]

ENGAGEMENT PLANNING MODEL: FINAL

Our complete model is presented in Figure 5.9.

Each new aspect of the final model is described in the following paragraphs.

Work Schedules

Engagement plans should result in work schedules or what audit standards have referred to as audit programs. In our model, we would want the lead auditor to prepare a schedule on the basis of the stages of an assurance audit process, covering:

Figure 5.9 The Complete Model

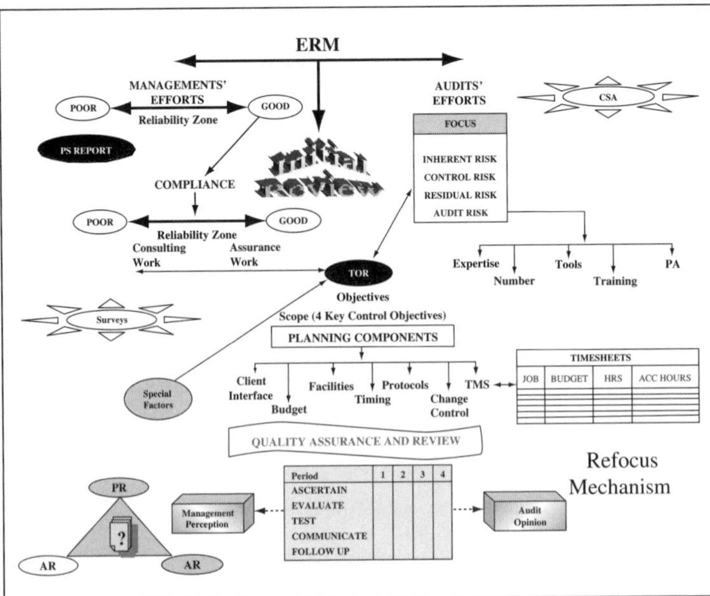

- *Ascertain.* The engagement plan should isolate which system or which aspects of a system are being reviewed. This decision will determine the start and end place of the system that is being "captured" by the auditor. Engagement work schedules should, at a minimum, include the following items:
  - What activities are to be performed;
  - When they will be performed; and
  - The estimated time required, taking into account the scope of the engagement work planned.
  - The nature and extent of related work performed by others.[50]

  There are also various issues to be considered in establishing engagement work schedule priorities, which should include:
  - The dates and results of the last engagement;
  - Updated assessments of risks and effectiveness of risk management and control processes;
  - Requests by the board and the senior management;
  - Current issues relating to organizational governance;
  - Controls;
  - Major programs, systems, and/or changes in enterprise's business and operations,
  - Opportunities to achieve operating benefits; and
  - Changes to and capabilities of the audit staff.
  - The work schedules should be sufficiently flexible to cover unanticipated demands on the internal audit activity.[51]
- *Evaluate.* The engagement plan should indicate how the system will be evaluated. This evaluation will ideally be carried out using a risk-based approach where:
  - Objectives are ascertained.
  - Risks that impact these objectives are identified.
  - The risks in question are assessed for impact on objectives and the likelihood that the risks will materialize.
  - The controls that guard against the high-impact/likelihood risks are evaluated for effectiveness.
  - The results are communicated.

  A decision will have to be made as to whether this evaluation process is carried out by the auditor alone, or in conjunction with management. Staff surveys have already been discussed and the use of surveys has been endorsed in auditing standards:

> A survey permits an informed approach to planning and carrying out engagement work, and is an effective tool for applying the internal auditing activity's resources where they can be used most effectively. The focus of a survey will vary depending upon the nature of the engagement. The scope of work and the time requirements of a survey will vary. Contributing factors include the internal auditor's training and experience, knowledge of the activity being examined, the type of engagement being performed, and whether the survey is part of a recurring or follow-up assignment. Time requirements will also be influenced by the size and complexity of the activity being examined, and by the geographical dispersion of the activity.[52]

- *Test.* The engagement plan may give some direction on the testing stage of the audit, including the use of computerized interrogations using live or downloaded data. The guidance on testing should not be too extensive as this decision should ideally be based on the results of the evaluation of controls. Standards for testing should be set on the basis of best practice guidance issued by auditing standard sets:

> Information should be sufficient, competent, relevant, and useful to provide a sound basis for engagement observations and recommendations. Sufficient information is factual, adequate, and convincing so that a prudent, informed person would reach the same conclusions as the auditor. Competent information is reliable and the best attainable through the use of appropriate engagement techniques. Relevant information supports engagement observations and recommendations and is consistent with the objectives for the engagement. Useful information helps the organization meet its goals.[53]

- *Communicate.* The engagement plan should state how audit findings will be communicated and who will receive the draft and final reports that result from the engagement. It is important that communication channels are defined at an early stage and not made up as the audit progresses. Professional guidance recognizes the need to keep the management appraised about progress on the audit:

> All those in management who need to know about the engagement should be informed. Meetings should be held with management responsible for the activity being examined. A summary of matters discussed at meetings and any conclusions reached should be prepared, distributed to individuals, as appro-

priate, and retained in the engagement working papers. Topics of discussion may include:

Planned engagement objectives and scope of work.

The timing of engagement work.

Internal auditors assigned to the engagement.

The process of communicating throughout the engagement, including the methods, time frames, and individuals who will be responsible.

Business conditions and operations of the activity being reviewed, including recent changes in management or major systems.

Concerns or any requests of management.

Matters of particular interest or concern to the internal auditor.

Description of the internal auditing activity's reporting procedures and follow-up process. [54]

The work required to fulfill the matters noted above should be recorded in an engagement planning record or schedule that covers period one onwards, be it days or weeks—depending on the length of the audit. Note that for some larger projects the audit may last several months. The audit manager should be involved in the compilation of work schedules at the planning stage as these schedules can act as a key control over the audit.

Management Perceptions versus Audit Opinion

There are two boxes on either side of the work schedule item in our engagement planning model. The first relates to management's perception of their risk management and internal control arrangements. The other relates to the audit opinion that results from the audit work that is being planned. The engagement plan should seek to determine whether the audit opinion on the adequacy of internal controls equates to management's own view of their systems. One important aspect of this equation is the certification of controls disclosures by the auditor, because this involves considering whether management assertions are as reliable as the management believes they are:

> The internal audit activity may be asked to complete some type of certification or to issue an opinion on financial controls as part of management's Sections 302 and 404 processes. The CAE should ensure that any

> certification or opinion is supported by adequate, appropriate audit evidence as required by the Standards to support the certification and/or opinion. Additionally, under the requirements of Section 404, the external auditor will perform tests of management's assertion that key financial controls have been identified, designed appropriately, and management has a sufficient basis to know that the key controls are functioning.[55]

The audit opinion is not just a matter of perception or impression. It is the result of detailed analysis and assessment that arrives at a considered and defensible viewpoint. The engagement plan needs to be constructed to have a reasonable chance of obtaining the necessary evidence, and IIA standards make clear the need to obtain credible information.

> Engagement observations and recommendations emerge by a process of comparing what should be with what is. Whether or not there is a difference, the internal auditor has a foundation on which to build the report. When conditions meet the criteria, acknowledgment in the engagement communications of satisfactory performance may be appropriate. Observations and recommendations should be based on the following attributes:
>
> *Criteria.* The standards, measures, or expectations used in making an evaluation and/or verification (what should exist).
>
> *Condition.* The factual evidence that the internal auditor found in the course of the examination (what does exist).
>
> *Cause.* The reason for the difference between the expected and actual conditions (why the difference exists).
>
> *Effect.* The risk or exposure the organization and/or others encounter because the condition is not consistent with the criteria (the impact of the difference).[56]

The audit will aim to secure information about the effectiveness of risk management arrangements. Although risk management can be a matter of perception, there is fortunately an opt-out where the management and audit views differ and there is no agreement to compromise on either side:

> When the chief audit executive believes that senior management has accepted a level of residual risk that is unacceptable to the organization, the chief audit executive should discuss the matter with senior management. If the decision regarding residual risk is not resolved, the chief audit executive and senior management should report the matter to the board for resolution.[57]

Refocus mechanism:

We have added a refocus mechanism into the engagement planning model so as to allow for the peculiarities of risk management. By definition, risks change over time and this change can happen very quickly in volatile environments. Some changes result from new influences that appear on the horizon while other changes are a response to new information that was previously hidden or not properly appreciated. Errors and problems found by the auditor will influence the direction of the audit and may encourage the auditor to probe potential contentious areas. The possibility of such occurrences should be considered at the planning stage:

> The internal auditor should consider the probability of significant errors, irregularities, noncompliance, and other exposures when developing the engagement objectives.[58]

Any changes made will need to be approved before they are adopted:

> In obtaining approval of the engagement work plan, such plans should be approved in writing by the chief audit executive or designee prior to the commencement of engagement work, where practicable. Initially, approval may be obtained orally, if factors preclude obtaining written approval prior to commencing engagement work. Adjustments to engagement work plans should be approved in a timely manner.[59]

PR, AR, and AR:

The final part of the model presents an interesting dilemma for the auditor based on three different interpretations of risk:

1. **PR (perceived risk).** This is the perceived risk that we have mentioned earlier—that is, the level of risk that the management believes remains after their controls have been established and administered. It is the level of risk that the management is currently living with. The problem with risk management systems is that they depend on a careful evaluation of objectives as a start to the process, and it is these objectives that may become too narrowly focused in operational performance and not the wider governance issues:

   > The internal audit activity should evaluate the design, implementation, and effectiveness of the organization's ethics-related objectives, programs and activities.[60]

2. **AR (actual risk).** The actual risk is the risk that is present after controls, as verified by the auditors testing routines. The level of risk

may in fact be the same as management's own perception if there is a robust risk management process in place:

> Management reporting and communication should convey risk management conclusions and recommendations to reduce exposures. For management to fully understand the degree of exposure, it is critical that audit reporting identify the criticality and consequence of the risk exposure to achieving objectives.[61]

3. **AR (acceptable risk).** The final risk concept is the level of risk that fits with the risk appetite set by the organization in line with the type of business environment and the demands of key stakeholders.

The engagement plan should have as a basic aim the need to identify these three types of risks and assess whether there is sufficient alignment to enable a positive report to be sent out to the management, the board, and the audit committee. If engagement plans are constructed with this simple aim in mind, there is much more chance that the plan and, therefore, the resulting audit will have value to the organization and help it move forward and make progress in the ERM stakes, although ultimate responsibilities should always be borne in mind:

> Ultimately, it is the role of executive management and the audit committee to determine the role of internal audit in the risk management process. Management's view on internal audit role is likely to be determined by factors such as the culture of the organization, ability of the internal auditing staff, and local conditions and customs of the country.[62]

SUMMARY

Audit engagement planning is essentially about making the audit itself sharp and well focused. One way to realize the benefits from good engagement planning is to go through the following five steps:

Step 1. The engagement's terms of reference should be set only after an initial survey (often called a preliminary) has been undertaken in the area in question.

Step 2. One aspect of the initial survey is a consideration of the management's efforts to establish effective risk management and sound internal controls in their areas of responsibility.

Step 3. Having carried out the initial survey, the auditors should focus their efforts on working out, for the areas under review, the inherent risks, control risk, residual risk, and risk in the successful completion of the audit engagement itself.

Step 4. CSA should be considered in all assurance engagements in terms of what risk management efforts have been achieved by management and what risk management efforts can be promoted by the auditor to help determine the focus of the audit engagement. For consulting engagements, the initial survey should enable the auditor to determine the scope and form of the engagement, including aspects of the areas under review that will need to be examined in more detail.

Step 5. Each engagement should apply the full range of quality assurance mechanisms including supervision, review, audit budget, time sheeting, audit documentation, and a clear methodology for performing the audit and preparing a high-impact audit reports.

Note that Appendix A contains a checklist that can be used to assess the overall quality of risk-based audit planning.

NOTES

1. Institute of Internal Auditors, Glossary of Terms.
2. Institute of Internal Auditors, Glossary of Terms.
3. Institute of Internal Auditors, Standard 2201.
4. Anderson, Urton and Chapman, Christy (2002), "The IIA Handbook Series" in *Implementing The Professional Practices Framework*, IIA, page 96.
5. Institute of Internal Auditors, Standard 2210.A1.
6. Institute of Internal Auditors, Practice Advisory 2210.A1-1.
7. Institute of Internal Auditors, Practice Advisory 2210.A1-1.
8. Institute of Internal Auditors, Practice Advisory 2200–1.
9. Anderson, Urton and Chapman, Christy (2002), "The IIA Handbook Series" in *Implementing The Professional Practices Framework*, IIA, Page 161.
10. Institute of Internal Auditors, Practice Advisory 2200–1.
11. Institute of Internal Auditors, Practice Advisory 2210.A1-1.
12. Institute of Internal Auditors, Glossary of Terms.
13. Institute of Internal Auditors, Standard 2120.A1.
14. Institute of Internal Auditors, Practice Advisory 2100–3.
15. Institute of Internal Auditors, Glossary of Terms.
16. Institute of Internal Auditors, Practice Advisory 2210.A1-1.
17. Institute of Internal Auditors, Practice Advisory 1120–1.
18. Institute of Internal Auditors, Practice Advisory 2200–1.
19. Institute of Internal Auditors, Standard 1210.
20. Institute of Internal Auditors, Standard 2230.
21. Internal Auditing's Role in Sections 302 and 404 of The U.S. Sarbanes-Oxley Act of 2002, May 26, 2004, IIA.

22. Institute of Internal Auditors, Standard 1210.A1.
23. Institute of Internal Auditors, Practice Advisory 2120.A1-2.
24. Institute of Internal Auditors, Practice Advisory 2120.A1-2.
25. Internal Auditing's Role in Sections 302 and 404 of The U.S. Sarbanes-Oxley Act of 2002, May 26, 2004, IIA.
26. Internal Auditing's Role in Sections 302 and 404 of The U.S. Sarbanes-Oxley Act of 2002, May 26, 2004, IIA.
27. Institute of Internal Auditors, Practice Advisory 2210.A1-1.
28. Institute of Internal Auditors, Practice Advisory 1130–1.
29. Institute of Internal Auditors, Standard 1130.C2.
30. Institute of Internal Auditors, Standard 2201.A1.
31. Institute of Internal Auditors, Standards 2201.C1.
32. Institute of Internal Auditors, Practice Advisory 2200–1.
33. Institute of Internal Auditors, Standards 2210.
34. Institute of Internal Auditors, Glossary of Terms.
35. Institute of Internal Auditors, Standard 2220.
36. Institute of Internal Auditors, Standard 2120.A1.
37. Institute of Internal Auditors, Standard 2220.A1.
38. Institute of Internal Auditors, Practice Advisory 2210–1.
39. Moeller, Robert and Witt, Herbert (1999), *Brink's Modern Internal Auditing*, 5th edition, New York: John Wiley and Sons, page 209.
40. Institute of Internal Auditors, Standard 2240.A1.
41. Institute of Internal Auditors, Standard 1300.
42. Institute of Internal Auditors, Standard 2220.C1.
43. Institute of Internal Auditors, Practice Advisory 2230–1.
44. Institute of Internal Auditors, Standard 2340.
45. Institute of Internal Auditors, standard 2240.
46. Institute of Internal Auditors, standard 2240.A1.
47. Institute of Internal Auditors, standard 2240.C1.
48. Institute of Internal Auditors, Practice Advisory 2340–1.
49. Internal Auditing's Role in Sections 302 and 404 of The U.S. Sarbanes-Oxley Act of 2002, May 26, 2004, IIA.
50. Institute of Internal Auditors, Practice Advisory 2010–1.
51. Institute of Internal Auditors, Practice Advisory 2010–1.
52. Institute of Internal Auditors, Practice Advisory 2210.A1-1.
53. Institute of Internal Auditors, Practice Advisory 2310–1.
54. Institute of Internal Auditors, Practice Advisory 2200–1.
55. Internal Auditing's Role in Sections 302 and 404 of The U.S. Sarbanes-Oxley Act of 2002, May 26, 2004, IIA.
56. Institute of Internal Auditors, Practice Advisory 2410–1.
57. Institute of Internal Auditors, Standard 2600.
58. Institute of Internal Auditors, Standards 2210.A2.
59. Institute of Internal Auditors, Practice Advisory 2240.A1-1.
60. Institute of Internal Auditors, Standard 2130.A1.
61. Institute of Internal Auditors, Practice Advisory 2010–2.
62. Institute of Internal Auditors, Practice Advisory 2100–3.

6

PROJECT MANAGEMENT

Internal auditors should enhance their knowledge, skills, and other competencies through continuing professional development.

—IIA Standard 1230

INTRODUCTION

This chapter sets out some of the basics regarding project management as a complement to risk-based audit planning. Many auditors get involved in long-winded projects during their career but have no particular training at planning larger projects over and above the basic audit engagement planning that relates to smaller pieces of work. Sarbanes-Oxley, ERM, control frameworks, ethics initiatives, performance management schemes, value for money initiatives, CSA programs, contingency planning, and a whole assortment of emerging topics can be led by internal audit under the consulting role. In fact, there is a call for auditors to lead on Sarbanes-Oxley preparations:

> Internal auditors frequently are skilled at managing large or complicated projects, ensuring key deliverables are produced on time. The internal auditor may be asked to take on the role of lead project manager for all or part of the efforts related to complying with Section 404. A project manager may generally be responsible for monitoring progress of a project, arranging for appropriate communication of project results during the project, and monitoring adherence to the established timetable. If the internal auditor's role is restricted to these administrative tasks, objectivity would not likely be impaired. However, if the project manager's role extends to being the primary decision maker as to acceptability of work product, approving successful completion of stages of the project, authorizing redirection of resources within the project team, or other similar management activities, the internal auditor's objectivity is impaired.[1]

Internal auditors have started to take center stage as they reign supreme in their review and analysis skills, along with their ability to stand outside the day-to-day politics that can blur even the most determined professional's opinion. This development has good as well as less attractive implications. One plus point is that bigger and wider projects are being thrown at the audit team as the best people to review and advise on ways to go forward, particularly on the consulting front. The problem is that many auditors may not be equipped to take on significant engagements that last for some time, since they are used to performing their work in a matter of days, or perhaps weeks at the most. What is needed is good project management skills to ensure that planned work that involves substantial resources and which may last for many months is designed and scheduled in a way that promotes the successful accomplishment of audit goals.

PROJECT MANAGEMENT PLANNING MODEL: PHASE ONE

Our first model appears in Figure 6.1.

Each aspect of the model is described in the following paragraphs.

Figure 6.1 The Project Management Planning Model: Phase One

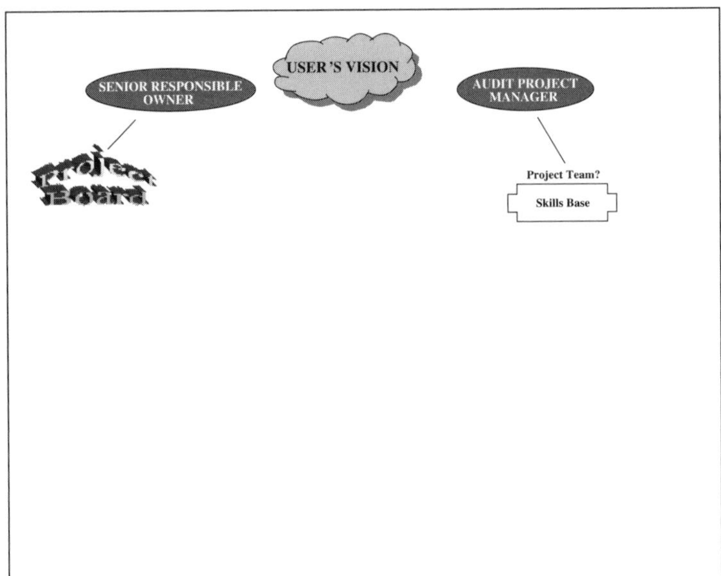

User's Vision

Many projects start with a vision that guides the shape, form, and content of the detailed work that is subsequently performed. A consulting project for developing a world-class appreciation of agreed control models across all business groups may be based on a vision that staff take responsibility for their work in a robust and motivated way. This vision may show the organization as the best in the business for making sharp and sensible decisions at the customer contact level. It is best that the vision comes from the user as they are the most responsible for the products that result from the project.

Case Study

The Project Goal

In a large state agency, the auditors were asked to embark on a major project to identify and record all assets that were held across the many dozens of local offices. This was planned to take three months, with one auditor acting as project manager, along with two admin staff from a local office. The work was based on a vision held by the Director of Resources to develop an on-line asset register that could be updated and applied to secure federal government grants. The project team prepared a color document that illustrated the on-line register and this represented the final goal toward which they moved forward over the three months.

Senior Responsible Owner

Having a vision and having this vision derived from the front-line business is a start. But there is more to a solid project than blue-sky thinking and putting ideas into action. Most projects need to be driven by a person who is committed to ensuring that it happens, even when all is not plain sailing. This is where the Senior Responsible Owner (SRO) swings into action. That is someone who is powerful enough to break down barriers to project development and at times simply ensure that whatever needs to happen, happens. Many projects get lost when the steering group, or team members, or project board, become suits that talk a lot but do not deliver. Consensus management can become agreed fudges that fail to move anything forward as this entails more risk. An SRO is a person who has a major stake in making sure that the project is a success and as such stands out from boards, committees, and loosely associated groups of people.

CASE STUDY

The Project SRO

In one commercial organization, the board voted the director of Planning as the SRO for an important project to establish ERM throughout the organization and this person was able to make decisions regarding the project and the size of the preimplementation pilot study. All major changes were passed through the SRO who kept a close eye on project changes, facility acquisitions, rationalization programs, and other matters that fell in line with the project mandate. The SRO also studied the risk log and, in particular, red risks that were high impact, high likelihood. The ERM program was rolled out to strategic head office teams, the business units, and support processes based on Sarbanes-Oxley disclosure rules, and sound financial accounts. One spin-off requested by the SRO was the development of a control framework that was used in conjunction with the ERM process.

While there will be an SRO to help guide and direct the project, audit projects are slightly different from normal business projects. This is because the Chief Audit Executive (CAE) is responsible for managing the audit resource and making sure that professional standards and professional dignity are retained at all times. In this sense, the CAE becomes an additional level of SRO:

> All internal audit assignments, whether performed by or for the internal audit activity, remain the responsibility of the CAE. The CAE is responsible for all significant professional judgments made in the planning, examination, evaluation, report, and follow-up phases of the engagement. The CAE should adopt suitable means to ensure that this responsibility is met. Suitable means include policies and procedures designed to:
>
> Minimize the risk that professional judgments may be made by internal auditors or others performing work for the internal audit activity that are inconsistent with the professional judgment of the CAE such that a significant adverse effect on the engagement could result.
>
> Resolve differences in professional judgment between the CAE and internal audit staff members over significant issues relating to the engagement. Such means may include: (a) discussion of pertinent facts; (b) further inquiry and/or research; and (c) documentation and disposition of the differing viewpoints in the engagement working papers. In instances of a difference in pro-

> fessional judgment over an ethical issue, suitable means may include referral of the issue to those individuals in the organization having responsibility over ethical matters.[2]

Project Board

For larger projects, say on designing an internal controls reporting infrastructure across an entire group of companies, there should be a group of senior figures who should constitute a board to oversee the project and make decisions involving the use of corporate resources that need to be approved at a higher level. The project board is responsible for making decisions that are outside the authority levels of the project manager, that is, such decisions that fall outside of the set scope, spend levels, and tolerances agreed to, at the outset, for the project manager. The board members should include three types of representatives:

1. A senior supplier who ensures that resources are available throughout the duration of the project.
2. A project sponsor who approves decisions affecting the progress of the project.
3. A senior user who ensures that the solution meets the needs of end users and happens within the set time, and budget, and meets quality standards.

Meanwhile, the SRO will have a great impact on the project and will also want to attend project board meetings.

CASE STUDY

Project Procedures

When an audit project that is planned to last over 12 weeks (and involves at least two auditors) is set up by the CAE, the project management system swings into action, which entails the following procedures:

- The project is requested by a nominated sponsor through the CAE.
- The sponsor is normally a senior business manager or audit-committee member.
- The CAE presents a business case to the audit committee, including the project terms, source, justification, costs, duration, resources, and products.

Project Procedures *(continued)*

- The CAE appoints a project manager from the audit staff.
- The audit committee appoints a projects board who will hear monthly progress reports and will monitor progress.
- A budget monitoring system is applied, using an assigned budget code and agreed cost profile. The template includes costs classified in accordance with financial procedures from an agreed budget.
- A project plan is approved by the project board and discussed with the users.
- A project team is assigned the tasks under the remit of the project manager using audit staff, contract staff, and others where appropriate.
- The project manager is required to prepare and maintain a risk register.
- The project board assesses the status of the project and reviews the risk register and action plans before endorsing the work to continue. Each project board meeting contains a revised summary business case and risk register that supports continuation of the work.
- Changes have to be approved by the project board and budget increases go to the Principal Finance Officer for approval.
- The project manager will incorporate a change management strategy and implementation plan that will be presented to the project board when the project is more than 50% complete. This strategy will be agreed to by the users.
- All changes made will be supported by pilot exercises that are reported to the project board and the sponsor for consideration.

Audit Project Manager

The success of many a project has depended on the skills, dexterity, and determination of the project manager assigned to the task. This will be a senior auditor who will be in charge of the day-to-day running of the project. The audit project manager will take on the following tasks:

- Day-to-day management of the project.
- Maintenance of the risk log, issues log, and lessons learnt log, as matters arise.
- Highlighting reports that go to the project board, normally on a monthly basis.
- Stakeholder communication, including contact with the people who will be using the new systems.

- Using interpersonal skills to get everyone who will be affected by the project energized and positive.

CASE STUDY

Project Risks

A CAE assigned a corporate project to an audit manager who was asked to prepare a business case that was then sent to a newly established project board. The audit manager was asked to lead on developing a security template that could be used to assess the state of security in all buildings and a specialist security firm to work on the main operational matters using the corporate security policy for guidance. The audit manager was concerned about security risks to the organization but also kept an eye on the risks to the project in terms of failing to deliver the goods.

Project Team

Our model suggests that projects are engagements of strategic importance that consume large amounts of resources. By definition, this means that there is likely to be a team of auditors, or a mix of audit and nonaudit staff, assigned to the project. Like all teams, they will need to be carefully managed, mainly by setting clear roles and ensuring that members understand where they fit into the big picture, are competent in the assigned role, and behave in an acceptable manner:

> The Code of Ethics of The Institute of Internal Auditors (IIA) are Principles relevant to the profession and practice of internal auditing, and Rules of Conduct that describe behavior expected of internal auditors. The Code of Ethics applies to both parties and entities that provide internal audit services. The purpose of the Code of Ethics is to promote an ethical culture in the global profession of internal auditing.[3]

The project manager will also want the team to be energized and motivated to deliver the goods, and have real belief in what they are trying to achieve.

Skills Base

The next item that appears on our model is the skills required for the project manager and team. We have already noted the downside of auditing assuming a key role in governance, risk, and control issues. It is relatively easy to be given a major project to help establish governance arrangements in all or parts of a business, but it is less easy to make rapid progress on these matters. One major risk facing the CAE and audit team is the lack of appropriate skills to perform high-level work, available in the audit shop. It may be a good idea to send a select number of audit staff on project management training so that they learn a suitable methodology for performing this type of work. It is wrong to send a team of auditors out on a large project without ensuring they understand and are using a methodology that is either the approach adopted by the organization to manage projects or is a set of standards that will lead to the successful delivery of project results—or at least maximize the chances of such success. Moeller has a view on this issue:

> Internal auditors might benefit from using these Project Management Institute (PMI) risk management concepts as part of normal audit activities. Every internal audit faces a range of uncertainties ranging from having no information about some subject area to total certainty and complete information, and internal audits should be planned and managed with this concept in mind.[4]

PROJECT MANAGEMENT PLANNING MODEL: PHASE TWO

Our model continues in Figure 6.2.

Each new aspect of the model is described in the following paragraphs.

Stakeholders

So far we have covered infrastructure matters that promote good projects and now we turn to the actual process for getting a project off the ground and into action. Armed with the users' vision of what we are trying to achieve, we then need to consult widely with defined stakeholders to:

- Identify where they stand in terms of supporting the vision.
- Determine what they would like to see from the project.
- Promote buy-in from people who have a stake in what is being planned.

A vision that floats across an organization has little real value if those people who can influence the vision becoming a reality either do not know

Figure 6.2 The Project Management Planning Model: Phase Two

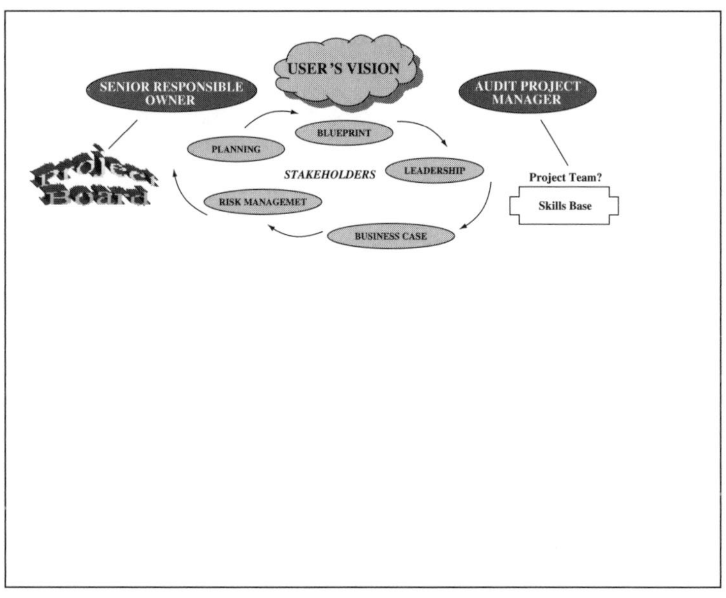

about the projects, or have had no input on defining the project's scope and direction.

Project design cycle:

The vision needs to be translated into defined products that, if achieved, will mean the accomplishment of project objectives. In our model, this involves the following aspects:

- *Blueprint.* A map should be developed by the project manager, in consultation with the SRO, showing what the new position will be like, once the project is completed—much like a "before and after position", where the defined benefits are clear from the map or blueprint itself.
- *Leadership.* At an early stage, the concept of leadership needs to be built into the project plan in recognition of the need to drive change and make progress. Most projects involve making changes, and many people feel uncomfortable where these changes bring forth new or unclear risks that they feel they may not be able to handle. Without leadership, many projects would flounder as people wonder

whether they need to bother to change, when the changes themselves may create much bother.

- *Business case.* An important part of the project approval and launching process involves the development of a business plan. This is normally a detailed document, set out using the corporate template, that addresses the basic concepts of "Why do it?"; "What is it about?"; "What will it cost in terms of time, money and disruption?" and "What benefits will be delivered?" The business plan will set a number of tests that the project will have to pass for it to be approved and moved on to the planning stage.
- *Risk management.* Project management turns the concept of risk management on its head and asks what risks are derived from launching this project that may interfere with the ability of the project to deliver its stated objectives. ERM is about getting the concept of risk into an organization in a way that touches on all aspects of work. Projects entail the movement of resources toward defined goals that are part of the overall strategic direction of an organization. If these project goals are not achieved, there is less chance that strategic goals will themselves be accomplished. As such, all major projects need to be risk assessed and the project manager should be asked to set up suitable measures to manage these risks. Many an auditor has come unstuck by preaching good risk management to the business lines but failing to use the agreed approach in their own work.
- *Planning.* The final stage of this part of the model relates to project planning, where the more detailed work has to be defined and planned. It is important to work through the earlier stages of the project design cycle and not jump straight into matters of practical planning, to ensure there are more chances of a well-planned project. Planning is about scheduling tasks and dates and working out who will do what and forms the basis for much of the next part of our model.

CASE STUDY

Sorting Out Problems

After auditing a fairly new inventory management system for a large national mail-order company, the auditor found that there were many problems with the current arrangements. Five different warehouses were involved in delivering

Sorting Out Problems *(continued)*

items to customers, depending on the type of goods. Customers were experiencing delays, poor information, incorrect deliveries, and the drivers could not tell how many packages related to each flat packed item. Order number, and delivery numbers did not tie up and, all in all, the weaknesses in the way the system worked was leading to the real risk of customer disloyalty and a poor reputation. The audit report was well received and the director of operations asked the lead auditor to undertake a development project to improve the system and get rid of the weaknesses. The project was supported by a clear business case and it was overseen by a board comprising the director of operations, and other senior figures. The audit project manager made a presentation to the main board of directors that emphasized that the entire company business revolved around the movement of goods and that faults in the system would undermine the entire enterprise. The audit project manager used an operations manager and an admin staff to resource the work and based most of the decisions on an ongoing and detailed risk assessment process built into the project, which highlighted aspects that could interfere with the goal of making the existing inventory system work properly. Most of these risks revolved around the timing of project tasks and interdependencies that meant certain tasks had to be completed before others could start. A Gant chart was used to illustrate the relationship between tasks, relationships, project products, and planning dates.

PROJECT MANAGEMENT PLANNING MODEL: PHASE THREE

Our model continues in Figure 6.3.

Each new aspect of the model is described in the following paragraphs.

Progress Reports

We have already mentioned the role of the project board and noted that it is an important component of the overall project management process. The project manager needs to report to the CAE on progress, using the normal auditing facilities that cover engagement planning and monitoring. In addition, the project manager needs to use a further monitoring process involving information provided to the project board at what should be the

Figure 6.3 The Project Management Planning Model: Phase Three

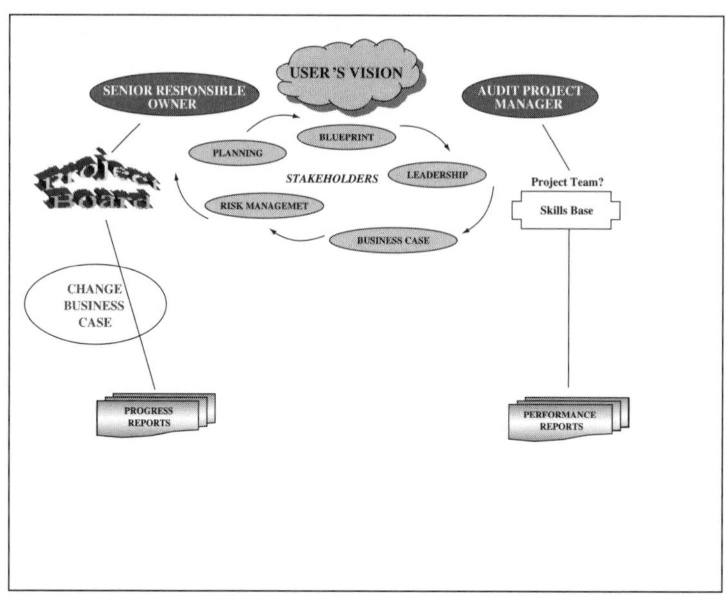

regular presentations to this forum. The project board will want information directly from the project manager concerning:

- Highlights of the month in terms of progress and issues that came up.
- The project status in terms of the budget and resources spent.
- Requests for additional funding and financial concerns.
- The status of the risk register and high risks that may have developed over the month, along with details of the major issues that have emerged.
- Anything that has a significant impact on the project.

Performance Reports

Projects cost time and money and for this reason, they need to be controlled at all stages. Each project promises to make an impact on the organization and all key external and internal stakeholders expect these promises to become a reality in line with the project objectives. One useful device is to set a number of performance targets that get reported out as a routine part of the project management methodology, including targets such as:

- Budget, with spending against plans.
- Scheduled tasks achieved against plans.
- Time spent by project team against plans.
- Quality targets set by the project board.

Change Business Case

A great deal of work is normally spent in developing a project plan; for larger projects, this may involve authorizations to spend on new resources, new facilities, and even entire new systems. Once this has been agreed upon, the project board can get back to the job and assess progress reports and presentations to check that everything is going as planned. Superimposed on this is the change dynamic that impacts many projects as factors influence the shape, form, timing and, at times, the set goals of a project, and a request for change has to be made to the project board. It may be that:

- The business case may have been unrealistic.
- Costs of facilities may have increased.
- Unforeseen factors may need to be addressed.
- The project may get extended to other parts of the business and require a change in the scope.

In this situation, it would be wrong to simply change a project in response to changing circumstances and not undergo a formal process for dealing with important changes or increased spends. The case study below relates to a short audit-driven project:

CASE STUDY

Setting the Tone

In a not for profits organization, the CAE was asked to set up a project to develop an ethics code for the workforce, a code that could be understood and used to support the antifraud policy. The CAE in turn assigned the task to a senior audit manager, who spent several weeks researching the topic and talking to similar organizations about their arrangements before designing the policy and implementation plan. The Director of Personnel chaired the project board and much of the work revolved around training seminars to deliver the key messages and expectations from employees. The first seminar was held with the board of directors who used this to set the tone for the rest of the training.

PROJECT MANAGEMENT PLANNING MODEL: PHASE FOUR

Our model continues in Figure 6.4.

Each new aspect of the model is described in the following paragraphs.

TOR and PID

The project needs to have a tight Terms of Reference (TOR) and a formal Project Initiation Document (PID) to ensure success. The TOR sets out exactly what is expected from the project and what aspect of the business will be affected. Most systems cross over and interface with other systems and processes to form an integrated whole that drives the business in question. One vexing issue that is starting to annoy many existing and would-be customers is the lack of good integration with business systems, where customers are passed from one department to another as they have to embark on a highly pressured search to find out which team deals with which part of their enquiry. Automated phone

Figure 6.4 The Project Management Planning Model: Phase Four

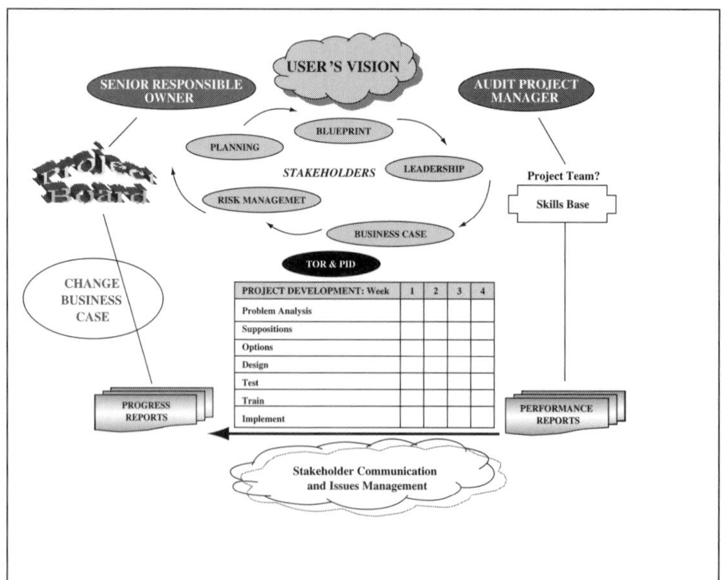

lines can sometimes exasperate this problem as the enquirer is asked to press 1, 2, or 3 as they desperately search for someone to help them sort out their problem. Projects that involve changes to these business systems need to make clear exactly which aspects they are addressing and how the change may impact other parts of the business. Otherwise, the net result could be poorly conceived processes that are difficult to administer. The PID is the project initiation document that appears after the outline business case. The PID starts the project proper and is presented to the project board with the outline business case to secure authority to start the project as it moves from a basic study to a full-blown project.

Project Development Plan

The next aspect of the project management model is the development plan. At this stage of project planning, it is suggested that the project manager draw up a detailed schedule, based on defined stages of the project and timed deadlines for each task under each stage. In our model, we have derived the following main components of the project development plan:

- *Problem analysis.* Projects are designed for a reason. Developing a new CSA program is about getting risk management into business operations through suitable devices. Control awareness programs are about establishing good control frameworks to promote a successful organization. Fraud prevention and detection projects are about making vulnerable parts of the business more secure from fraud, abuse, and negligence. There needs to be a careful consideration of the problems that the project is trying to resolve by analyzing these problems and why they exist.
- *Suppositions.* The next stage is to develop suppositions as to why we have these problems and the underlying causes; normally it is because of poor systems or weak procedures.
- *Options.* There has to be some consideration of ways forward, not as one line recommendations, but as comprehensive discussions on options and alternative solutions. These options may be further assessed by considering many factors such as the practicality, costs, changing contexts, possible resistance, impact on customers, and stakeholder views.

- *Design.* Next comes the design of new systems, procedures, or developmental programs that are geared to making what needs to happen, happen.
- *Test.* An important stage of a project is to test the solutions and check that they make sense and have a good chance of working out. Phased pilots may make a huge task much more manageable.
- *Implement.* The implementation stage moves from project planning to making actual changes, and must be planned over the set time frame.

Stakeholder Communication

At all stages in a project, it is a good idea to keep the stakeholder in touch with what is happening. Buzz groups, risk workshops, presentations, and one-to-one meetings may all be used to obtain views, develop ideas, and to keep all players up to date with the project as it is developing. The CAE should be a key stakeholder in all relevant activity, as this person needs to keep a hold on whether the audit is in line with professional standards, its charter, and the need to secure an acceptable level of independent assurance reporting. Auditing standards are quite clear on this front:

> Consulting engagements cannot be rendered in a manner that masks information that in the chief audit executive's (CAE) judgment should be presented to senior executives and board members. All consulting is to be understood in that context. An internal auditor is first and foremost an internal auditor. Thus, in the performance of all services the internal auditor is guided by The IIA s Code of Ethics and the Attribute and Performance Standards of the International Standards for the Professional Practice of Internal Auditing (Standards). Any unforeseen conflicts or activities should be resolved consistent with the Code of Ethics and Standards.[5]

Issues Management

It is rare for a project to sail through from start to finish with no problems along the way. It is a good idea to build in an issues management facility at the planning stage of a project so that the rules need not be made up in an ad hoc manner. The issues management policy is not about predicting which problems will arise during the project, but is more about developing a methodology for resolving any such problems if and when they arise. A good issues management system will tend to ensure that:

- Issues are documented and dealt with as and when they arise.
- An issue is a risk that has materialized and therefore should have been in the risk register along with a mitigation strategy to deal with the risk.
- A brand-new issue may appear and this again needs to be dealt with by a full analysis of the circumstances, in conjunction with guidance from the project board.

PROJECT MANAGEMENT PLANNING MODEL: FINAL

Our complete model is presented in Figure 6.5.

Each new aspect of the final model is described in the following paragraphs.

Figure 6.5 The Complete Model

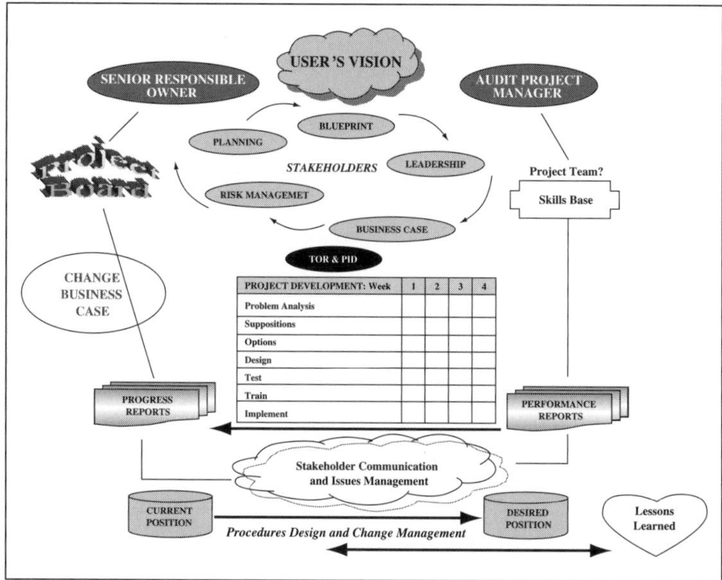

Current versus Desired Position

Our model suggests that there is a clear framework in place to determine how far a business needs to change to move from its current position to a position that reflects the benefits from implementing the project products. This concept needs to be kept in mind because it helps clarify the original vision that created the project in the first place. The desired position should also be communicated to all those affected by the project as a way of promoting good buy-in from all parties. One matter that pops up where audit lead on projects is the ability of the audit staff to document existing systems through years of performing such work for standard audit engagements. This documenting process can be used to record the current system, required arrangements, and the way that necessary movement from one to the other can be progressed.

Procedures Design

One matter that is often missed in poorly managed projects is the need to change, develop, or reinforce standards and procedures in ensuring the changes made by the project are understood and applied. It is always a good idea to set up a small working party to assess whether new procedures need to be written in or old ones amended as part of the project. This not only helps confirm the understanding of the new arrangement but also helps support staff training programs that come about because of the project. Procedure design needs to take on board several important considerations:

- Procedures should reflect the way the organization needs its workforce to perform.
- They should be practical and workable.
- Procedures should be required so that they guard against risks that would materialize in the absence of such procedures. They should be flexible and easy to apply in difficult circumstances.
- They should make sense to everyone who uses them, including the customer.

The auditors need to be careful about drafting detailed procedures as this may affect their ability to audit such arrangements in future and it may be an idea to contract this task out to a dedicated team of nonauditors.

Change Management

Some projects fail because those involved in the work feel that a great idea sells itself and that all sensible changes mean everyone will do their job more efficiently. The reason they fail is because people affected by the project changes do not always act in a way that can be predicted from the outset. This is why it is necessary to develop a change management strategy to consider resistance to change, and the ways in which these problems can be overcome. Often such resistance happens because the operations people do not understand or know about the project aims or because there is a low level of trust amongst managers and workteams, or because there are elements of project products that have not been properly thought through. One way forward is to include operations staff and systems users in the risk workshops to get their input in identifying risks and suitable risk management strategies and controls.

Lessons Learned

All projects should incorporate a "lessons learned" component so that the project manager, and those involved in the work may grow and develop their skills base knowing what went well and what could have been done in a better way. A competent auditor has much to offer an organization and implicit in this competence is the ability to learn to grow with the work that is being performed:

> Internal auditors should apply the care and skill expected of a reasonably prudent and competent internal auditor. Due professional care does not imply infallibility.[6]

Note that a good "lessons learned" policy can enable an organization to move away from a "blame culture" where each project includes someone who can act as the scapegoat when anything goes wrong. In developing lessons learned, the CAE should be wary of the need to report noncompliance with professional standards if this is the case during a consulting project:

> Although the internal audit activity should achieve full compliance with the *Standards* and internal auditors with the *Code of Ethics*, there may be instances in which full compliance is not achieved. When noncompliance impacts the overall scope or operation of the internal audit activity, disclosure should be made to senior management and the board.[7]

There is some crossover between consulting and assurance work and information gleaned from one can be used when performing the other:

> Internal auditors should incorporate knowledge of risks gained from consulting engagements into the process of identifying and evaluating significant risk exposures of the organization.[8]

SUMMARY

Auditors are getting involved in larger projects as their unique skills are being applied to help sort out significant corporate issues. As such, project management becomes an important tool to help direct the auditor's work and one way to realize the benefits from good project management is to go through the following five steps:

Step 1. The CAE should agree on a project management methodology with the audit committee for audit engagements that are significant enough to be deemed projects rather than straightforward audit engagements.

Step 2. The project management approach should incorporate all good principles of planning and running projects, including project boards, SROs, a project manager, and suitable ongoing review mechanisms.

Step 3. Projects should be justified through a formal business case that has clearly stated aims and defined end products that have been developed in consultation with key stakeholders.

Step 4. All projects should incorporate a risk management process, including the identification, and management of risks that impact the project, along with regular reviews, lessons learned, and updates to the project risk register to underpin the successful delivery of project objectives.

Step 5. All projects should specify set tasks in conjunction with a planning schedule that is agreed with the project team and which recognizes the need to make effective change that will need to be carefully reflected in altered procedures and approaches to work.

Note that Appendix A contains a checklist that can be used to assess the overall quality of risk-based audit planning.

NOTES

1. Internal Auditing's Role in Sections 302 and 404 of The U.S. Sarbanes-Oxley Act of 2002, May 26, 2004, IIA.
2. Institute of Internal Auditors, Practice Advisory 2340-1.
3. Institute of Internal Auditors, Glossary of Terms.
4. Moeller, Robert and Witt, Herbert (1999), *Brink's Modern Internal Auditing*, 5th edition, New York: John Wiley & Sons, page 238.
5. Institute of Internal Auditors, Practice Advisory 1000.C1-1.
6. Institute of Internal Auditors, Standard 1220.
7. Institute of Internal Auditors, Standard 1340.
8. Institute of Internal Auditors, Standard 2110.C2.

7

KEEPING THE ACCENT ON RISK

Risk—The possibility of an event occurring that will have an impact on the achievement of objectives. Risk is measured in terms of impact and likelihood.

—IIA Glossary of Terms

INTRODUCTION

We have used the term "risk-based audit planning" throughout this book to highlight the way audits can be aligned to the risk management process that operates within the organization in question. This short chapter seeks to reinforce the focus on risk by developing a suitable model. Risk-based audit planning is about:

- Targeting high-risk areas for audit coverage.
- Promoting a discussion of risk with the management.
- Starting with risk as the first step in the risk-based auditing process.
- Building a role for internal auditing within the ERM framework.
- Developing good knowledge of risk appetite, risk triggers, and the corporate approach to risk management.
- Enabling audit to validate the risk management process that runs across the organization.

One view suggests that there are several different approaches to planning audit work:

Systematic risk scoring. Here, key factors are developed to reflect the audit view of risk and then the entire organization is scored against these factors. The approach is logical and can be consistently applied across the organization. A database of relevant factors can be compiled to represent the risk assessments, which can be weighed and updated as new information comes on line. The drawback is that the approach is old fashioned and suggests that audit's perspective on risk does not coincide with the views of the senior management who assess their risks using a different approach.

Stakeholder assessment. Here, audit's approach to planning involves asking for views from important stakeholders such as the audit-committee members, the senior management, the CEO, and board members, external audit, and others. These views are compiled in a discussion paper that develops high-risk issues of concern to the business and sensitive matters that need to be addressed. This approach can be dynamic and involve a high-level engagement with senior people within the organization in a sensible and flexible manner. The drawback is that auditing can end up being used as a political football and loose much of its objectivity as it is simply told what to look at by a few powerful corporate players.

Risk management based. This approach uses the planning forum to look at the entire risk management process. The risk cycle is assessed and examined in some detail and audit plans simply focus on aspects of this cycle and the way it is being applied within the organization across different business teams and support systems. The auditors look at ways that ERM can be improved and also present formal assurances on aspects that were performing well and those that were not good enough. The focus on ERM as a generic process makes for high-level plans that cut across the day-to-day running of the business and will be appealing to the board as it assumes a strategic approach to the progress made by the organization. The drawback is that the audit work can become superficial as it examines concepts and high-level policy, while missing some of the real problems resulting from significant risks that are already impacting the business.

Corporate risk register. The final approach is based on a mature organization that has developed robust risk profiles and reliable risk registers. Audit simply adopts whatever appears in the corporate register that is used by the board and uses this as the basis for the annual audit plan. In this way, the audit resource sits completely in line with the board priorities and the senior management can buy into the audit process as it coincides with what they have defined as important. As the registers change, the audit plans alter in tandem. The drawback is that audit eventually falls behind schedule and their work is entirely dependent on the extent to which the corporate risk register is able to take on board all relevant issues. It also assumes that management understands soft risks relating to ethics, control frameworks, antifraud measures, security concerns, poor communications, unclear targets, and so on. At the extreme, auditing may be seen as the poodle for the board as it takes whatever appears on the corporate risk register and tries to help sort out resulting problems.

RISK FOCUS MODEL: PHASE ONE

Our first model looks at a framework for developing a focus on risk in Figure 7.1.

Figure 7.1 Risk Focus Model: Phase One

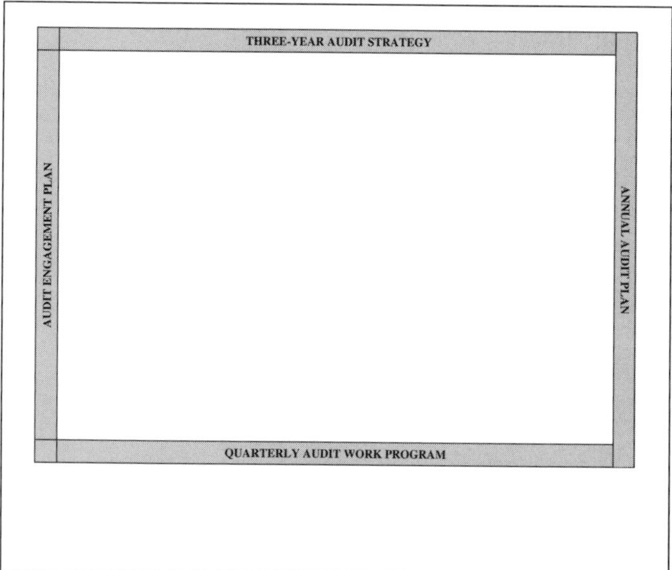

Each aspect of the model is described in the following paragraphs.

Three-Year Strategy

Each audit team needs to think about a long-term audit strategy that reaches out into the future, based on the premise: What do we need to do to ensure that our organization becomes a world-class leader in ERM?

COSO ERM argues for a powerful role for both external and internal audit:

> Internal and external auditors and advisors regularly provide recommendations to strengthen enterprise risk management. Auditors may focus considerable attention on key risks and related responses and design of control activities.[1]

CASE STUDY

Using the Risk Cycle

A private sector audit section developed their three-year audit strategy based on the following principles:

Risk identification. This was part of the preplanning process that involved assessing how risk was being identified by the key business units.

Risk assessment. The main audit-planning stage considered the way risks were being assessed in terms of prioritization to identify high-risk areas.

Risk mitigation. The actual auditing process considered the detailed way that risk mitigation, in the form of good controls, was being applied.

Risk management implementation. Here, the audit reports addressed the extent to which risk management was being applied across the enterprise.

The above stages were built into the three-year strategy:

Year one—mainly looked at the way risk was being identified and assessed across all business units.

Year two—considered the state of controls in response to risk assessment and whether these controls could be relied on to promote the achievement of business objectives.

Year three—audit would be at the stage where they could give firm assurances on the overall state of ERM in the organization.

Risk can be built into the three-year audit plan by ensuring that:

- The auditor assesses where the organization stands in terms of development of an effective ERM process.
- Targets are set for moving forward into a more progressive ERM.
- Audit fits into the way ERM is developing in line with the set targets.
- The three-year audit strategy moves from a consulting base toward a more assurance-based work format as the organization becomes more adept in managing risk.
- The above is reported back to the audit committee in the annual audit report.

Annual Audit Plan

The next side of the model places a clear role for the annual audit plan that will address the audit task over the next twelve months. Risk should be firmly based within the planning framework and therefore lead the audit resource into the heart of the corporate agenda.

> The CAE should develop a proposed audit plan normally for the coming year that ensures sufficient evidence will be obtained to evaluate the effectiveness of the risk management and control processes. The plan should call for audit engagements or other procedures to gather relevant information about all major operating units and business functions. It should include a review of the major risk management processes operating across the organization and a selection of the key risks identified from those processes. The audit plan should also give special consideration to those operations most affected by recent or expected changes. Those changes in circumstances may result from marketplace or investment conditions, acquisitions and divestitures, or restructures and new ventures. The proposed plan should be flexible so that adjustments may be made during the year as a result of changes in management strategies, external conditions, major risk areas, or revised expectations about achieving the organization's objectives.[2]

CASE STUDY

IT Risks

An IT service company's audit team developed a risk-based format for preparing the annual audit plan, as shown in Figure 7.2.

IT Risks *(continued)*

Figure 7.2 Risk-Based Plan

FACTOR	RATING 1–5	SCORE	RANK	IMPACT ON ANNUAL AUDIT PLAN
1. Nature of data and transactions				
2. Operating environment				
3. Human resource issues				
4. Critical impact assessment				
5. Adequacy of internal controls				
6. Physical logical security				
7. Management oversight				
8. Previous audit coverage				
9. Legal provisions				
10. Complexity of Software				

Risk can be built into the annual audit plan by ensuring that:

- The auditor understands the way the organization applies risk management.
- The audit plans are based at the outset on the above process.
- Targets are set for improving ERM and audit's role is clarified therein.
- As corporate risk changes, the annual audit plan should be updated accordingly.
- Audit issues relating to compliance, security, fraud, and sound controls should become management issues that are reflected in the risk profiles used by the board and senior management.

Quarterly Audit Work Plan

The third corner of the model takes the annual audit plan and breaks it down into four thirteen-week periods, that is, the quarterly audit plans. Risk here can be given greater clarity and it is possible to flex the plan to respond to the latest developments as the organizational context itself responds to both internal and external risks.

> The chief audit executive (CAE) should submit activity reports to senior management and to the board periodically throughout the year. Activity reports should highlight significant engagement observations and recommendations and should inform senior management and the board of any significant deviations from approved engagement work schedules, staffing plans, and financial budgets, and the reasons for them.[3]

Risk can be built into the quarterly audit plan by ensuring that:

- The auditor does not become obsessed with the issues from the annual audit plan as these will be dated.
- The auditor uses the quarterly audit-planning process as the key timeframe for getting to grips with risk in the business as it is short enough to reflect the dynamic nature of new and emerging risks.
- Audits are rescheduled as a result of further discussions with the board, audit committee, and external auditors so that they continue to represent the best use of audit resources.
- The quarterly plan takes into account the risk of assigning the wrong type of auditor to the planned work, by ensuring that staff availability is carefully organized around the planned audits.
- The quarterly plan responds well to changes in the extent to which ERM has been implemented in the organization so as to ensure there is a good balance between consulting and assurance work.

Audit Engagement Plan

The final side of the model takes the action into the actual engagement where operational risk may be acknowledged and addressed.

> The internal auditor should exercise due professional care by considering the:

Extent of work needed to achieve the engagement's objectives.

Relative complexity, materiality, or significance of matters to which assurance procedures are applied.

Adequacy and effectiveness of risk management, control, and governance processes.

Probability of significant errors, irregularities, or noncompliance.

Cost of assurance in relation to potential benefits.[4]

Risk can be built into the audit engagement plan by ensuring that:

- The auditor uses all the available information from the annual audit plan to form an initial view of inherent risk in the area.
- The auditor talks to the manager of the area in question and discusses some of the risks that are emerging and causing concerns, including the risk of failing to take risks.
- The auditor takes into account efforts made by the client to effect risk management within the area in question and assesses the extent to which this assessment can be used to help focus the audit plan.
- The engagement plan is flexible enough to allow the auditor to respond to developments in the area in question as and when they arise during the conduct of the audit.

RISK FOCUS MODEL: PHASE TWO

Our model continues in Figure 7.3.

Each new aspect of the model is described in the following paragraphs.

ERM Wheel

The audit-planning horizons revolve around the centerpiece—that is what we have called the ERM wheel. The idea is to use our primary mission to help develop and improve an ERM system and argue that there are four main components that can be considered to assist this task. The ERM components are:

1. Awareness
2. Standards

Figure 7.3 Risk Focus Model: Phase Two

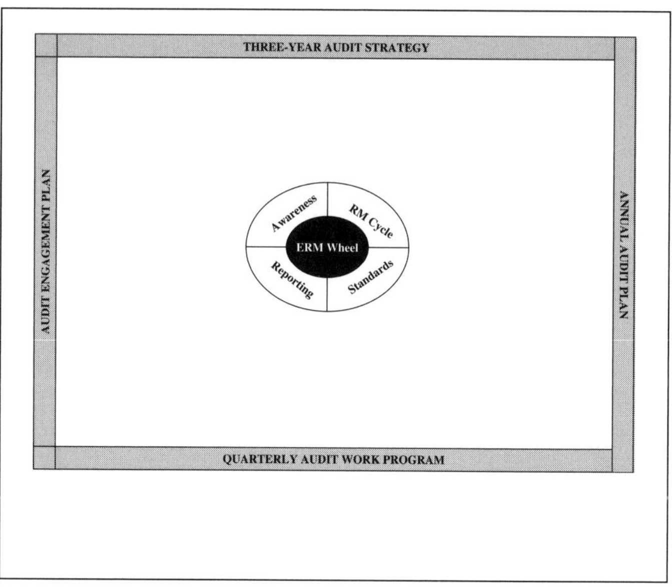

3. RM cycle
4. Reporting

These are each dealt with in separate sections below.

Case Study

Supporting Business Units

In one public-sector body, the auditing team focused their efforts on helping each business unit establish their version of the risk management cycle. Auditors facilitated the process and helped prepare the necessary documentation and templates as well as introduce voting technology, online risk logs and reporting software. The risk cycle was extended to incorporate inputs from internal customers, partners, and regulators and focused on improving the value chain that delivered the defined services.

Risk can be built into the ERM wheel by ensuring that:

- The wheel is promoted by the auditor as an important component of ERM.

- Audit work reviews the extent to which the wheel is in place.
- The auditor provides advice and support on getting the wheel in place whenever audit work is performed.
- The auditor is able to provide assurances on the extent to which a suitable version of the wheel is in place in the organization.

Awareness

The starting place for good ERM is the knowledge and understanding of risk management throughout the workforce. The auditor should develop a template for assessing the extent to which staff in the area under review understand, and are competent to implement the organization's risk management policy and:

- Check the template with the line manager as a fair way of assessing staff awareness of risk management.
- Implement the survey among a sample of the workforce in the area under review.
- Analyze the results and determine whether the position is acceptable or not.
- Use the results to help focus the audit on aspects of the business that can be improved.

Standards

Having achieved a degree of staff competence, the next issue is to set standards and procedures for ensuring that risk is considered in planning, decision making, and designing controls. Many organizations prepare a risk policy and then communicate various approaches such as CSA for getting risk assessment into the business and back-office support services. The auditor should ensure that there is good compliance with the corporate risk management standards in the area under review by:

- Securing a copy of the corporate risk management policy and standards.
- Obtaining any further advice or procedures introduced in the area under review to promote effective risk management.
- Determining whether there is compliance with the above mentioned standards and guidance by reviewing risk management

activity that has been recently carried out, or identifying a lack of such activity.
- Using the results to help focus the audit on aspects of the business that can be improved.

RM Cycle

All organizations will need to establish a version of the risk management cycle to deliver effective ERM and this will vary depending on the way the organization works and its environment and support services. The auditor should assess the extent to which the risk cycle is being operated in the area under review by:

- Checking the way the manager and staff identify risks to the achievement of their set objectives.
- Reviewing the way risks are assessed for impact and likelihood as a way of identifying those that should be prioritized.
- Determining whether the risk management strategy is appropriate in the context of the risks that have been identified as high priority and whether significant risks have been mitigated in such a way as to fit the corporate risk appetite that relates to the area of the business in question.
- Using the results to help focus the audit on aspects of the business that can be improved.

Reporting

The final component of the ERM wheel is the reporting mechanism that is based around outputs from the various risk management activities throughout the business. If this is well developed and sound, then we are on the way to internal control disclosure reporting. The auditor should verify the reliability of reports that derive from the risk management process that is employed in the area under review by:

- Reviewing the database tools in use to determine whether they are appropriate for capturing the data that comes from risk workshops, surveys and management's risk assessments.
- Reviewing the reporting tools in use and whether they represent an appropriate manner for capturing the data that comes from risk workshops, surveys and management's risk assessments.

- Checking the accuracy of risk reports and assessing whether they represent a reliable record of the risk profiles and strategies in the area in question.
- Using the results to help focus the audit on aspects of the business that can be improved.

RISK FOCUS MODEL: PHASE THREE

Our model continues in Figure 7.4.

Each new aspect of the model is described in the following paragraphs.

Awareness

We need to consider the risk management awareness in more detail and look at the subprocesses that form the wider concept.

Competence. There should be set competence for dealing with risk management built into the role for all staff in the organization.

Training. There should be suitable training programs that recognize the need to develop skills and expertise in ERM.

Figure 7.4 Risk Focus Model: Phase Three

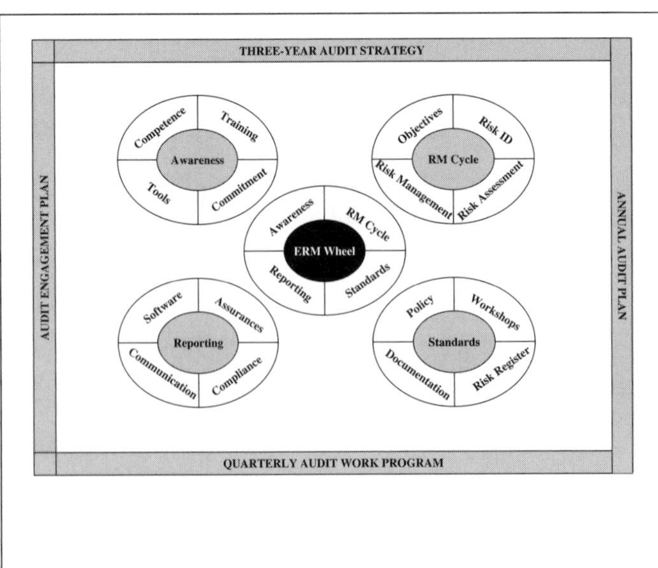

Commitment. Staff should have an honest belief in risk management and believe that this approach can help them perform well and succeed, notwithstanding the risks that may arise now and in the future.

Tools. Staff should have access to suitable tools and techniques such as voting technology, risk registers, and forecasting tools to help them manage risk.

Standards

We need to consider the RM standards in more detail and look at the subprocesses that form the wider concept.

Policy. The organization needs to prepare and publish a set of clear standards covering the way ERM should be developed in all parts of the business.

Workshops. The standards should be used to promote workshops for identifying and assessing risk and working through suitable measures in response to the results.

Risk registers. Each manager should be responsible for preparing an account of the way risk has been addressed in their part of the business.

Tools. Suitable tools and resources should be acquired to support the implementation of the risk policy.

Rather than simply take the risk register and use this for audit plans, some audit teams are developing a set of guiding principles that are applied to the planning process as shown in the next case study:

CASE STUDY

Procedure-Based Planning

A small audit section applied twenty basic criteria, agreed with the audit committee in setting their audit plans:

1. The audit team was there to review the risk management process and provide reports to the board, audit committee, and management.
2. Audit will resource efforts to improve the risk management process through facilitating control self-assessment workshops and activity under its consulting arm.
3. The risk assessment plus consulting work will form the audit plan that is approved by the audit committee.

Procedure-Based Planning *(continued)*

4 Risks are based on the materiality, sensitivity, complexity, and past audit cover for each part of the organization.
5. The audit plans will provide a platform for delivering the audit products and take on board all relevant audit standards.
6. Audit plans will also provide targets that should be achieved to judge the extent to which the audit resource is successful.
7. Audit plans will take on board the results of risk registers, data interrogation exercises, employee survey, the results of the corporate compliance program, and information received from the whistleblowers hotline.
8. Audit will also resource fraud awareness training as part of the audit plan.
9. Hidden risks relating to, say, the reliability of human resource management programs, employees' attitude toward compliance, risks to regulators, legal exposure from poor management decisions, and fears of business managers will be factored into the audit plan even if they do not appear on the corporate risk register.
10. Draft plans will be discussed with the management before they are finalized.
11. The approved audit budget will be based on planning considerations.
12. Audit will investigate irregularity and abuse where these have been identified, including data matching exercises. In terms of fraud-risk management, auditing will ask each unit under review a series of questions to assess awareness levels of the various measures that may be adopted to help guard against fraud.
13. Part of the plan will focus on reviewing internal controls over financial systems, IT systems, compliance programs, and the published disclosures.
14. Audit will consider the way performance is managed in the company and whether the system is reliable and is leading to better business results.
15. All major new developments will include an initial assessment by internal audit to determine whether there are sufficient controls in place to guard against the risk of failure.
16. All planned audits will include a paragraph on the area in question, risk issues, and why the audit is included in the plan.
17. Steps will be taken to move away from a rigid cycle of audit visits.
18. Internal audit will share their information with the external auditors and, where possible, seek to rely on each other's work.
19. The results of audit work will enable audit to formulate a view on the state of governance across the organization.
20. Audit will respond to requests from management for consulting projects or input into ongoing management projects where this would be a good use of audit time and effort.

RM Cycle

We need to consider the RM cycle in more detail and look at the sub-processes that form the wider concept.

Objective setting. Each part of the business with specific objectives should review the way these objectives have been set and whether they reflect the best way to add value to the wider organization.

Risk identification. Each business should have in place a robust process for identifying all risks that could impact on the delivery of the set objectives in a way that might undermine their delivery, or restrict the ability to innovate.

Risk assessment. Each business should have in place a robust process for weighing their risks in a way that provides a reliable method for isolating those that need to be given immediate attention.

Risk management. Each business should have in place a robust process for establishing controls that mitigate unacceptable levels of inherent risk.

Reporting

We need to consider the RM reporting in more detail and look at the sub-processes that form the wider concept.

Software. Reporting software should be in place to support the need to provide certifications on internal controls in conjunction with an assessment of risk to the business.

Assurances. Assurances derived from the reporting system should be sufficiently sound to satisfy the regulators and the board.

Compliance. There should be a compliance system in place to ensure that all reports are derived from careful analysis and based on reliable evidence.

Communications. The ERM reporting process should fit in with the wider communication systems and should not provide information that is inconsistent with those messages that come from other formal and informal sources regarding corporate priorities and what is seen as acceptable behavior.

Audit work will need to be planned to take on board the above mentioned issues and the auditor will need to have a view on whether defined components of ERM are in place or whether they need to be further developed. In this way, risk is retained as a central feature of the audit process as controls are reviewed to ensure that they are sufficient, suitable, and not onerous.

RISK FOCUS MODEL: PHASE FOUR

Our model continues in Figure 7.5.

Each new aspect of the model is described in the following paragraphs.

Facilitation

There are several other items that must be superimposed over our model to give it more form and direction. Facilitation is an important part of audit planning because there is always the potential for audit to revert to a consulting role, where it seeks to help management get to grips with risks to their business.

Figure 7.5 Risk Focus Model: Phase Four

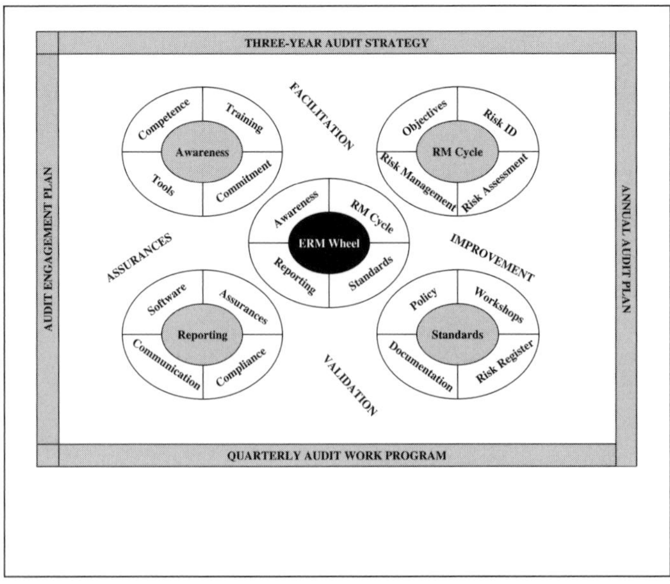

CASE STUDY

CSA and Risk

The annual audit plan of a new audit unit was based on a great deal of CSA facilitation. The auditors offered a wide range of CSA-based services where they would provide risk awareness presentation, workshop support and preparation, and full-blown facilitation for senior management teams. The CSA programs were rolled out across all parts of the organizations, including many overseas operating units.

Improvement

There are several other items that must be superimposed over our model to give it more form and direction. Continuous improvement is important and this requires a clear focus on risk and different types of risk.

CASE STUDY

A Three-Dimensional View

In one audit department, risk-based audit planning used a wide three-dimensional view of risk: that the audit goes well, that controls are working, and that there is good risk management in place. The planning process focuses on these three levels of risk and the plans are aimed at reducing audit risk, detecting control risk, and assessing the adequacy of the management of business risk.

1. **Audit risk.** It is that risk to the audit objectives and professionalism where there is a need to ensure that audit:
   a. *Is professional:* with competent staff who comply with set standards.
   b. *Is delivered*: they are able to meet clients' and stakeholders' expectations.
   c. *Adds value*: with a clear definition of value and measurable inputs and outputs.
   d. *Contributes to assurance framework*: where a defined framework is in place and provides a robust commentary on the status of this framework.

   e. *Achieves enhanced audit reputation*: based on feedback from stakeholders.
   f. *Delivers audit plan*: based on KPIs, completion rates, and good use of audit resources.
2. **Control risk.** Objectives throughout the organization have a reasonable chance of being achieved, where there is a need to ensure:
   a. *Reliable controls*: where error, failure, fraud, and abuse are minimized.
   b. *Enhanced control environment*: against a set benchmark or defined framework.
   c. *Good compliance*: based on user-friendly procedures and well-trained staff.
   d. *Clear and transparent procedures*: that are documented, flexible, understood, and consistently applied.
   e. *Business success*: using suitable measure of value for money and minimal burdensome procedures.
   f. *Solid business reputation*: based on sensible client-friendly controls.
   g. *Unacceptable risk is mitigated*: based on reliable risk management practices.
3. **Business risk.** All parts of the business are able to identify their risks and deal with the fallout, where there is a need to ensure:
   a. *Risk capture*: identify all relevant risks to the business objectives.
   b. *Assessment*: assesses which risks are significant, using CSA or other methods.
   c. *Management of major risks*: by setting acceptable levels of exposure.
   d. *Assurance reports*: based on a quality reporting system.
   e. *Regular review*: to ensure the process is kept relevant.
   f. *Ongoing improvement*: with a strategy in place to maintain good progress.

Validation

There are several other items that must be superimposed over our model to give it more form and direction. The importance of validation is illustrated below:

CASE STUDY

Validating ERM

One audit team developed an audit plan based on validating the ERM process. After having spent two years facilitating risk workshops and driving home the message that people are responsible for their work and employees need to implement as many controls as necessary to ensure they are successful. This strategy having been achieved, the following year the auditors established their validation process. The plans entailed a program of assessing whether each business unit had a professional ERM infrastructure in place, judged against a template that was agreed with the audit committee. Each business unit and operations section was scored from one to ten and given an agreed improvement plan where the score was poor. Consistently bad scores led to an accelerated process that explored the possibility of managerial neglect at the extreme. Meanwhile, high scoring managers were invited to contribute to ERM training programs for new starters and areas where there was more development required.

Assurance

There are several other items that must be superimposed over our model to give it more form and direction. Assurances are provided by the auditors on the reliability of risk management and internal control and much of this can be done through examining the type of assurances that are given by front line management.

CASE STUDY

Assurance Reports

A small, two-person audit team focused on the assurance reports that were presented by line managers to support their disclosures on internal control. The auditors would verify these reports and check their veracity and overall usefulness. Reports that contained Red risks were given more attention and reports that came from high-profile parts of the business were again given a more detailed examination. Parts of the business where there had been changes to staff, reported fraud, low previous audit cover, variances in achieving targets, and known problems were reviewed in some depth, again through the control sign off that the line managers were required to provide.

RISK FOCUS MODEL: FINAL

Our complete model is presented in Figure 7.6.

Each new aspect of the final model is described in the following paragraphs.

Intelligence

We have aligned intelligence with the quarterly planning process because this is a convenient timeframe in which audit plans can be realigned with the realities of changing risk profiles. Good intelligence is about:

- *Audit-committee views.* The concerns of the audit committee will need to be fed into the audit-planning process if the CAE is to have any chance of delivering a successful service.
- *Corporate risk register.* The contents of the corporate risk register and, in particular, emerging risks, should likewise be fed into the audit-planning process. What is important to the organization must surely be of importance to the auditors.

Figure 7.6 The Complete Model

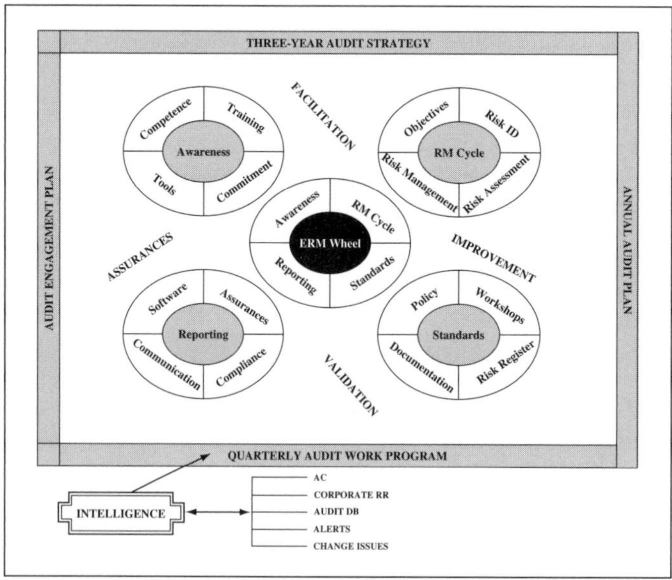

- *Audit alerts.* The CAE will need to keep a close watch on developments in the practice of professional internal auditing to ensure that there are no gaps in the in-house audit strategy.
- *Change issues.* Factors that hit an organization or that lurk in the dark and then hit the business must be watched and plans that fail to recognize this factor will be impoverished.

Intelligence is about resourcing a facility that acts like a satellite. This facility is on guard for anything that cannot be left alone, without damaging the business. Moreover, there is one view that suggests that audit should not need to develop this intelligence, but it is something that all good organizations should have in place to ensure that they keep ahead of threats, and can also take on opportunities. The argument regarding who should set up what information capture system revolves around the definition of respective responsibilities for dealing with risk, which, in turn, relates to what is seen as acceptable and what is seen as not tolerable. Audit can warn about risk but it has no authority to force stringent risk management systems onto management:

> Management is responsible for deciding the appropriate action to be taken in response to reported engagement observations and recommendations. The chief audit executive is responsible for assessing such management action for the timely resolution of the matters reported as engagement observations and recommendations. In deciding the extent of follow-up, internal auditors should consider procedures of a follow-up nature performed by others in the organization.[5]

The auditor has to live with the realities of corporate life but it may help to keep the accent on risk in planning, performing, and reporting all audit work:

CASE STUDY

Risk Factors

Another audit team used an array of factors to assess risk in audit planning, as shown in Figure 7.7.

Most of the values assigned to the risk factors were based on judgment and the scores were the result of discussion and consideration, at times, in a workshop format before each audit unit was given a final score and rating.

Risk Factors *(continued)*

Figure 7.7 Sample Risk Factors

	High/Medium/Low Risk		
	Audit's View	**Management's View**	**Final Score**
Complexity of the system			
State of controls			
Compliance issues			
Specific concerns			
Date last audited			
Impact on business			
Regulatory risk			

SUMMARY

Risk appears throughout the audit-planning process and not just as a one-off consideration during long-term planning. One way to realize the benefits from retaining a focus on risk during audit planning is to go through the following five steps:

Step 1. Risk-based audit planning should retain a focus on risk throughout the planning process and the way that plans are broken down and implemented.

Step 2. Risk-based audit plans should be responsive to the risk management cycle and take on board the extent to which this cycle is in place and able to cope with changing risks to the business.

Step 3. Any planned facilitation of risk management activities should be applied in conjunction with the need to improve ERM and provide a validation on aspects of risk management and internal control that are being relied on by top management as they form their view on the adequacy of internal control.

Step 4. Risk-based audit planning should be based on good intelligence regarding risks facing the organization and changing perspectives of key stakeholders to ensure that audit plans are aligned with corporate priorities.

Step 5. Risk-based audit planning should incorporate attempts to promote the view that risks relate to the way the entire organization operates and are not just related to compliance and regulatory matters.

Note that Appendix A contains a checklist that can be used to assess the overall quality of risk-based audit planning.

NOTES

1. Committee of Sponsoring Organizations, *Enterprise Risk Management*, September 2004, page 77.
2. Institute of Internal Auditors, Practice Advisory 2120.A1-1.
3. Institute of Internal Auditors, Practice Advisory 2060-1.
4. Institute of Internal Auditors, Standard 1220.A1.
5. Institute of Internal Auditors, Practice Advisory 2600-1.

8

A HOLISTIC APPROACH TO RISK-BASED AUDIT PLANNING

> The audit work performed during the year should obtain sufficient information to enable an evaluation of the system of controls and the formulation of an opinion.
>
> —IIA Practice Advisory 2120.A1-1

INTRODUCTION

This final chapter attempts to summarize and draw together all the material we have discussed in the previous chapters. In this way, we can formulate a holistic approach to risk-based audit planning and use this to feed into appendix A where we provide a best practice checklist. It is a good idea to repeat the definition of internal auditing before we draft the first stage of our final model:

> Internal auditing is an independent, objective assurance and consulting activity designed to add value and improve an organization's operations. It helps an organization accomplish its objectives by bringing a systematic, disciplined approach to evaluate and improve the effectiveness of risk management, control, and governance processes.[1]

A risk-based approach to audit planning simply means that the audit resource is focused on those aspects of the business that are key to its success. This is a concept that is aimed at shifting the audit process onto the boardroom's agenda and so allows the auditors to audit new horizons.

HOLISTIC RISK-BASED AUDIT PLANNING MODEL: PHASE ONE

Our first model looks as in Figure 8.1.

Each aspect of the model is described in the following paragraphs.

Corporate Governance Arrangements

The organization's governance arrangement is the high-level arch that sits above the entire organization. All else is derived from world-class governance, which means excellent performance coexists with excellent corporate behavior. The audit role in governance has been described as:

> The internal audit activity should assess and make appropriate recommendations for improving the governance process in its accomplishment of the following objectives:
>
> Promoting appropriate ethics and values within the organization.
>
> Ensuring effective organizational performance management and accountability.

Figure 8.1 Holistic Risk-Based Audit Planning Model: Phase One

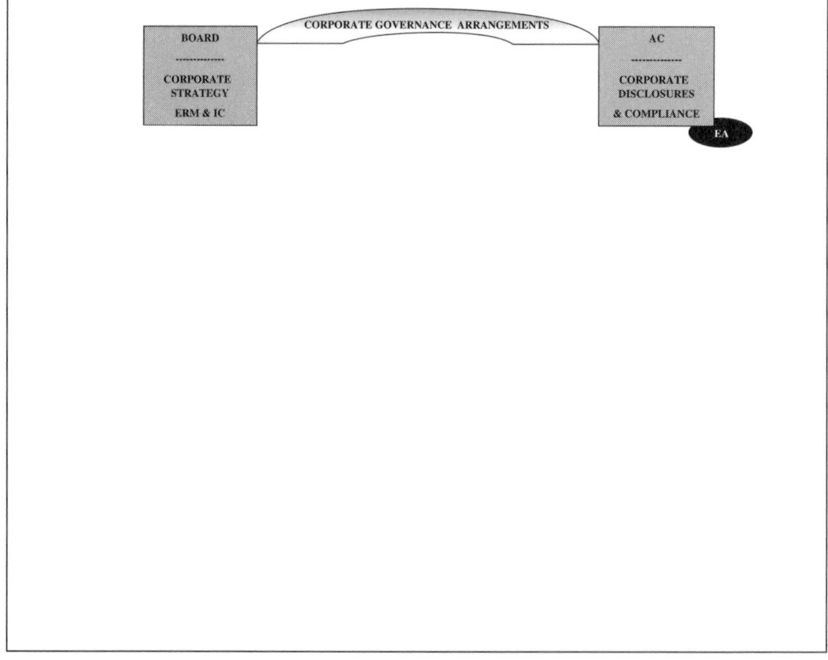

> Effectively communicating risk and control information to appropriate areas of the organization.
> Effectively coordinating the activities of and communicating information among the board, external and internal auditors and management.[2]

The audit planning model should start with these ideals if it is to reach out to the highest levels of performance.

CASE STUDY

Using the Governance Framework

One approach to audit planning used by a small audit team involved using the governance framework as the main driver. The organization in question disclosed their governance arrangements in the annual report and these arrangements were reviewed by the audit team to make sure that they were as reported. The risk profile developed by the audit team became a repository for all risks related to a failure in the governance arrangements and these risks changed as circumstances altered. In this way, the risk registers became a living document for recording risks and decisions made to ensure the organization not only performed well but also behaved in an acceptable manner. The risk registers contained the following information:

- Risk
- Date in register
- Entered by
- Reason
- Source of risk
- Ranking
- Existing controls
- Assessment of reliability of controls
- Responsible person
- Location
- Action plans
- Assurances on controls

Board

The next item to feed into the audit planning process is the expectations and requirements of the board. The board is defined as:

> A board is an organization's governing body, such as a board of directors, supervisory board, head of an agency or legislative body, board of governors or trustees of a nonprofit organization, or any other desig-

nated body of the organization, including the audit committee, to whom the chief audit executive may functionally report.[3]

As is clear from the above, the board is a wide concept that relates to private and public sector organizations. While each board has different responsibilities, they have similar pressures in terms of the need to ensure:

1. They discharge their statutory responsibilities in terms of protecting the welfare of the organization.
2. They discharge their statutory responsibilities in terms of ensuring compliance with relevant laws and regulations.
3. They discharge their responsibility to deliver a set of strategies that promote the achievement of corporate objectives.
4. They discharge their statutory responsibilities to account for the results of the above-mentioned matters through published returns and disclosures.
5. They employ an adequate system of internal controls that guard against the risks of failing in any of the above mentioned matters.

The auditors will need to consider how they impact on items 1–5 above, and how the audit service can be planned to take on board the risks that the board faces in this respect. Moreover, for listed companies, there is a real and present danger for the CEO and PFO in failing to live up to Sarbanes-Oxley's disclosure requirements:

> Section 302 requires management to evaluate and report on the effectiveness of disclosure controls and procedures with respect to the quarterly and annual reports. The principal executive and financial officers must certify that:
>
> - They have reviewed the report, believe that the report does not contain untrue statements or omitted material facts, and the financial statements and other financial information are fairly presented.
> - They (1) are responsible for establishing and maintaining disclosure controls and procedures; (2) have designed such disclosure controls and procedures to ensure that they are aware of material information; (3) have evaluated the effectiveness of the company's disclosure controls and procedures; and (4) have presented in the report their conclusions about the effectiveness of the disclosure controls and procedures.
> - They have disclosed to the auditors and audit committee (1) all significant deficiencies in the design or operation of internal

controls which could adversely affect the issuer's ability to record, process, summarize, and report financial data and have identified for the issuer's auditors any material weaknesses in internal controls; and (2) any fraud, whether or not material, that involves management or other employees who have a significant role in the company's internal controls.

- They have indicated whether there have been significant changes in internal controls over financial reporting or in other factors that could significantly affect internal controls subsequent to the date of their evaluation, including any corrective actions with regard to significant deficiencies and material weaknesses.[4]

Audit plans that do not indicate how the audit process fits into the above agenda may well be relegated to the minor league.

Audit Committee

The audit committee should be firmly linked into the audit planning process. Not only will the committee approve the draft plans, but they will also wish to view the auditors as allies and comrades in the fight against failure, fiasco and fraud, and lawsuits. The audit committee is established by the board to provide advice on many governance issues such as:

- *Corporate disclosures.* The organization needs to establish a system for providing disclosures regarding matters such as internal controls over financial reporting and corporate ethics.
- *Compliance.* The organization also needs to be sure that the system above is fully understood and applied throughout the organization.

Audit planning needs to take on board the needs and expectations of the audit committee members as they strive to achieve the two objectives noted above. IIA guidance provides more details on the three main areas in which the auditor can provide support for the audit committee, that is, financial reporting, corporate governance, and corporate control:

A. *Financial reporting*:

Providing information relevant to the appointment of the independent accountants.

Coordinating audit plans, coverage, and scheduling with the external auditors.

Sharing audit results with the external auditors.

Communicating pertinent observations to the external auditors and audit committee about accounting policies and policy decisions (including accounting decisions for discretionary items and off-balance-sheet transactions), specific components of the financial reporting process, and unusual or complex financial transactions and events (e.g., related-party transactions, mergers and acquisitions, joint ventures, and partnership transactions).

Participating in the financial reports and disclosures review process with the audit committee, external auditors, and senior management; evaluating the quality of the financial reports, including those filed with regulatory agencies.

Assessing the adequacy and effectiveness of the organization's internal controls, specifically the controls over the financial reporting process; this assessment effectiveness should consider the organization's susceptibility to fraud and the effect of programs and controls to mitigate or eliminate those exposures.

Monitoring the management's compliance with the organization's code of conduct and ensuring that ethical policies and other procedures promoting ethical behavior are being followed; an important factor in establishing an effective ethical culture in the organization is when members of senior management set a good example of ethical behavior and provide open and truthful communications to employees, the board, and outside stakeholders.

B. *Corporate governance*:

Reviewing corporate policies relating to compliance with laws and regulations, ethics, conflict of interests, and the timely and thorough investigation of misconduct and fraud allegations.

Reviewing pending litigation or regulatory proceedings that have a bearing on organizational risk and governance.

Providing information on boardroom decision making, employee conflicts of interest, misconduct, fraud, and other outcomes of the organization's ethical procedures and reporting mechanisms.

C. *Corporate control*:

Reviewing the reliability and integrity of the organization's operating and financial information compiled and reported by the organization.

Performing an analysis of the controls for critical accounting policies and comparing them with preferred practices (e.g., transactions in which questions are raised about revenue recognition or off-balance-sheet accounting treatment should be reviewed for compliance with appropriate accounting standards).

Evaluating the reasonableness of estimates and assumptions used in preparing operating and financial reports.

Ensuring that estimates and assumptions included in disclosures or comments are in line with underlying organizational information and practices and with similar items reported by other companies, if appropriate.

Evaluating the process of preparing, reviewing, approving, and posting journal entries.

Evaluating the adequacy of controls in the accounting function.[5]

When formulating audit plans, the CAE needs to think about how the audit team can feed into the above and how the audit committee can get involved in the planning process.

External Audit

The external auditors appear on the planning model because of their relationship with internal audit. It is essential that the internal audit plans fit with the work of the external audit team and that there is no unnecessary duplication:

> Planned audit activities of internal and external auditors should be discussed to assure that audit coverage is coordinated and duplicate efforts are minimized. Sufficient meetings should be scheduled during the audit process to assure coordination of audit work and efficient and timely completion of audit activities, and to determine whether observations and recommendations from work performed to date require that the scope of planned work be adjusted.[6]

The role of external auditing for quoted companies has been codified over the years through Sarbanes-Oxley and the resultant listing rules, to enhance the independence and impact of the audit process. The relationship with internal audit in turn has had to alter as the new provisions have come into play. For external audit the new rules include the following matters:

> Section 404 of Sarbanes-Oxley requires an issuer's external auditors to evaluate management's assessment of internal controls and to issue a report thereon. In addition, Title 2 of Sarbanes-Oxley establishes certain independence requirements for external auditors. Section 201 makes it unlawful for an issuer's external auditor to provide certain types of

nonaudit services to an issuer concurrent with the audit. Section 203 requires the external auditor to rotate every five years the lead audit or coordinating partner and the reviewing partner on the engagement. Section 204 requires the external auditor to report to the audit committee: "(1) all critical accounting policies and practices to be used; (2) all alternative treatments of financial information within generally accepted accounting principles that have been discussed with management officials of the issuer, ramifications of the use of such alternative disclosures and treatments, and the treatment preferred by the registered public accounting firm; and (3) other material written communications between the registered public accounting firm and the management of the issuer, such as any management letter or schedule of unadjusted differences."[7]

HOLISTIC RISK-BASED AUDIT PLANNING MODEL: PHASE TWO

So far our model has provided an outline of the high-level context within which the audit plans are set. We turn now to the work required to get the corporate issues into and inside audit plans in a way that makes good sense. Our model is further enhanced in Figure 8.2 in recognition of this fact.

Figure 8.2 Holistic Risk-Based Audit Planning Model: Phase Two

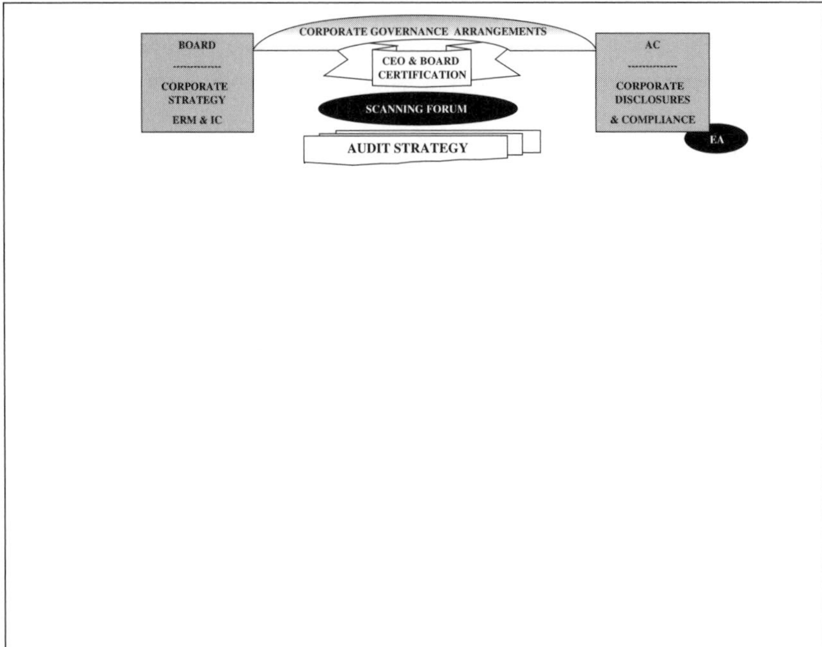

Each new aspect of the model is described in the following paragraphs.

CEO and Board Certification

There is no escaping the fact that all types of boards are now seen as pivotal to good corporate governance. The CEO, as the lead officer, has the onerous task of ensuring that controls make sense and work well, and then communicate this fact to the stakeholders. Most accept that certification is based partly on assessing the type of control environment that is in place across the organization, and this has been defined as:

> The attitude and actions of the board and management regarding the significance of control within the organization. The control environment provides the discipline and structure for the achievement of the primary objectives of the system of internal control. The control environment includes the following elements:
>
> Integrity and ethical values.
>
> Management's philosophy and operating style.
>
> Organizational structure.
>
> Assignment of authority and responsibility.
>
> Human resource policies and practices.
>
> Competence of personnel.[8]

This control certification process is well known, and the auditor cannot really put together an annual audit plan without working out how the audit team will contribute to good controls, either in a consulting or an assuring role:

> Adequate criteria are needed to evaluate controls. Internal auditors should ascertain the extent to which management has established adequate criteria to determine whether objectives and goals have been accomplished. If adequate, internal auditors should use such criteria in their evaluation. If inadequate, internal auditors should work with management to develop appropriate evaluation criteria.[9]

The final point to note is that the CEO's certification should be based on steps to document the system of internal control over financial reporting and then to test these systems to ensure they work properly. The testing process rests with management but the auditor may well be asked to make a contribution and build this work into the audit planning process:

> If management has not documented their control environment and does not have adequate resources needed to do so within the time period required, then internal auditors may be requested to aid management in documenting their internal controls. If the internal auditor is working closely with management in documenting internal controls and slides into more of a decision making role (e.g., implementing internal controls during the documentation process), then objectivity will be impaired. Section 404 rules require management to test the design and operating effectiveness of its internal controls over financial reporting, and reach an opinion as to whether they are effective to support the assertion they are required to provide under the law. Ideally, management should design the test of controls to validate the effectiveness of such controls, and testing should be performed by someone objective or other than the owners or operators. The internal audit activity may aid management in the design or execution of tests for control effectiveness. The degree to which the internal audit activities constitute management's testing of controls should be clearly specified and agreed to by management, internal audit, and the audit committee. In all cases, management should make the final decision on control design, and operating effectiveness, whether and what to remediate, and the sufficiency of information produced from which their assertions are to be made.[10]

Scanning Forum

In the earlier chapters, we suggested that a representative group may be used to assess the different risks that confront the organization and seek to align these risks with the internal audit plans for the coming year. This approach has been used by a few audit departments to develop a multifaceted perspective on risk that takes the concept outside the audit team, but still recognizes the importance of audit independence.

CASE STUDY

Horizon Scanning

A large audit team developed a scanning forum of audit managers, business managers, and other key employees to assess the way a risk profile may be developed for audit planning purposes. The CAE defined:

- The set objectives for the audit service.
- The audit products based on assurance, consulting, and investigatory work.
- How to measure achievements.
- The audit universe.

Horizon Scanning *(continued)*

The scanning forum defined:

- The risk framework applicable to the audit universe.
- How to assign scores.
- The high-risk priorities.
- Those audits that should be short-listed for the audit plan.

Taking this information, the CAE and audit managers would prepare a draft audit plan for the audit committee, and for consultation with the senior management. The audit committee then signs off the annual audit plan. Meanwhile, the scanning forum would continue to re-assess risk factors on a quarterly basis, and is in constant contact with stakeholders to glean information of any concerns it may have.

Audit Strategy

Using the governance context and pressures placed on the board and audit committee as a benchmark, along with a high-level forum for assessing risks to the organization, it is now possible to develop a suitable audit strategy. The adopted strategy will be one that is relevant to the individual audit unit and it is difficult to recommend any one approach. Our model simply suggests that audit strategy takes on board all those elements that are found in the model as it is developed. Strategy should really ensure that audit delivers:

- Assessments of risk management best practices.
- Support and advice on governance, risk, and controls.
- Validation of internal controls disclosure reports issued by management.
- Measures that promote compliance with procedures across the organization.
- Continuous development in the quality of audit work.

CASE STUDY

Dynamic Risk-Based Planning

A CAE ran an audit service that was partly outsourced to a large firm of accountants. In conjunction with advice from the firm, the CAE developed a dynamic risk-based planning model that was fairly interactive. The process entailed:

Dynamic Risk-Based Planning *(continued)*

Developing a corporate risk register.
Conducting workshops with audit and top management based on the organization's overall strategy.
Completing a revised risk register that was then fed into the audit plans.

Meanwhile a three-year audit strategy was adopted as shown in Figure 8.3. The annual audit plan included audits from four main sources:

Formal risk assessments—coded A, B, C, D, E, or F depending on risk scores.
Reviews of all significant financial systems.
Themed audits in line with three-year strategy (controls, risk, fraud, and financial management).
Strategic systems covering compliance, leadership, and human resources.
Fraud risk management consulting reviews.
Previous audit reports and follow-up of outstanding key issues.

Figure 8.3 Sample Three-Year Audit Strategy

YEAR	CONTEXT	AUDIT WORK
ONE	Enhance the control environment	Intelligence gathering on best practice control models
TWO	Focus on risk management and fraud prevention strategies	Facilitation workshops to increase staff awareness
THREE	Enhance financial management and financial controls	Surveys on financial controls efficiency and reviews of weak aspects

For routine audits, the audit universe was risk assessed using data scores, staff surveys, interviews, and intelligence gathering:

Code	Impact	Likelihood	Inclusion in audit plans
A	H	H	all
B	H	M	some
C	M	H	some
D	M	L	minor
E	L	M	minor
F	L	L	none

(Key: H = High; M = Medium; L = Low)

HOLISTIC RISK-BASED AUDIT PLANNING MODEL: PHASE THREE

Our model continues in Figure 8.4.

Each new aspect of the model is described in the following paragraphs.

Risk Management Levels

The overall audit strategy needs to be related to where the organization stands in terms of the development of the ERM. The left-hand pyramid of our model suggests that there are three levels of risk management maturity, and a different audit approach is required depending on the level at which the organization (or parts of the organization) stands. The overriding principle is:

> The scope of internal auditing work encompasses a systematic, disciplined approach to evaluating and improving the adequacy and effectiveness of risk management, control, and governance processes and the quality of performance in carrying out assigned responsibilities. The purposes of evaluating the adequacy of the organization's existing risk management, control, and governance processes is to provide: (1) rea-

Figure 8.4 Holistic Risk-Based Audit Planning Model: Phase Three

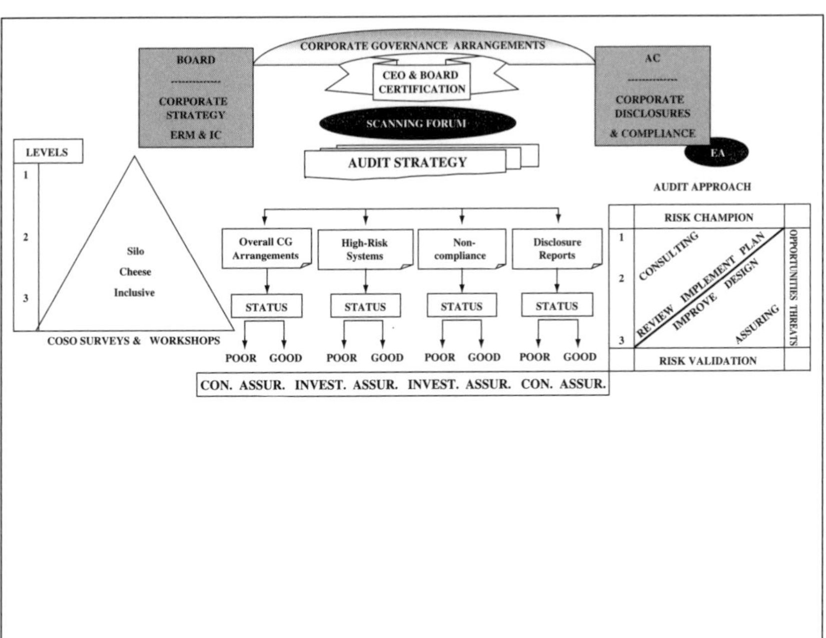

sonable assurance that these processes are functioning as intended and will enable the organization's objectives and goals to be met, and (2) recommendations for improving the organization's operations, in terms of both efficient and effective performance. Senior management and the board might also provide general direction as to the scope of work and the activities to be audited.[11]

1. **Level 1 (Silo).** At this early stage in the development of an ERM process, the various parts of the organization work on their risk assessments in isolated pockets, that is, in silos that have no interaction or linkage with each other. The health and safety staff assess risk; the IT security people likewise carry out risk assessments, as do the insurance teams. But there is no common ground through which these different people assume any degree of consistency in the way they view risk, assess priorities, and seek to manage unacceptable exposures.
2. **Level 2 (Cheese).** This stage is likened to a chunk of Swiss cheese with holes in it. There is a great deal of furious risk-based activity going on in the organization, but again this is not related to an enterprise's wide approach or common standard. There are ad hoc meetings with people who discuss their approach and concerns and there will be a possibility of ongoing dialogue where common problems are debated, if there is time. What is missing is a corporate standard that pulls the disparate efforts together.
3. **Level 3 (Inclusive).** The final stage is what most refer to as ERM, where the entire enterprise is tuned into a common appreciation of risk concepts, recommended methodologies, available tools, and a clear view of risk appetites for all parts of the business.

CASE STUDY

Three-Year Planning

The CAE for the university audit team set up a focus group to consider the way auditing would be applied to the way the ERM process was beginning to emerge in the university. The audit service was set for the next three years as follows:

Year one: Help isolate parts of the university that were engaged in risk assessment activity and work out the aspects of the best practice.

Year two: Develop a center of expertise and spread awareness and training about risk management across all departments in line with a

Three-Year Planning *(continued)*

common understanding of risk and different risk categories relating to strategic, operational, change, regulatory, financial, and compliance risk.

Year three: Help establish the risk policy and facilitate risk workshops and ways of embedding risk into the way work was planned, delivered, and monitored in all parts of the university.

As the university moved from a silo to cheese through to an inclusive risk management approach, auditing resumed its assurance role and stood back from the action as a chief risk officer was eventually appointed.

Five Key Elements of Planning

The next consideration on our model is a set of five elements that the auditor will wish to consider as part of the plans that are developed each year. For each element, the auditor will want to be able to express an opinion on the status of each element—as to whether the arrangements within the organization are poor, good, or a range in between these two ends.

1. **Overall corporate governance arrangements.** Whether there is in place all the necessary components of the governance arrangements that are accepted for the type of organization.
2. **High-risk systems.** Whether there is in place suitable internal controls to guard against high levels of risk that exceed or have the potential to exceed the accepted risk tolerance for the organization in question.
3. **Noncompliance.** Whether there is in place a sound process for ensuring compliance with all relevant rules, systems, and procedures that impact the business of the organization.
4. **Disclosure reports.** Whether there is in place sound arrangements that ensure published disclosure reports meet the needs of all relevant users and fulfill all relevant legal and regulatory obligations.

CASE STUDY

Following Procedures

An audit team used the following procedures to ensure the audit plan made best use of the scarce audit resources:

Following Procedures *(continued)*

The audit committee would sign off the annual audit report, but would listen to requests to make changes in the planned work. Urgent changes were carried out and subsequently reported back to the chair of the audit committee and mentioned at the next meeting.

The plans acknowledged which areas of the organization were not covered and why.

The focus of the plans was on strategic success for the organization in the context of its obligations to all key stakeholders and not just to shareholders and investors.

The audit team prioritized prevention in terms of good controls as the best way to promote success and to proactively anticipate and respond to risk.

Robust control models were developed by the audit team and used to compare and contrast parts of the organization, and each year several aspects of the control model were reviewed against current business practices.

The auditors developed a formal business risk portfolio that was based on the board's own model and this was updated each quarter.

Control awareness training was provided in each quarterly plan based on reaching most parts of the organization over a set time frame.

Management involvement was encouraged in the planning process, and there were quarterly meetings with senior employees to secure views, concerns, and explanation of performance reports that suggested problems or inconsistencies.

The performance appraisal targets for the audit team were based around many elements of the quarterly audit plans.

Succession planning was built into the quarterly plan to ensure that changes in audit staff did not interfere with the CAE's ability to deliver planned work.

Good techniques were applied to audit work, and there was time planned into each quarter to ensure audit staff had access to the right facilities and training where required.

There was a good balance in the type of audit work performed and this depended much on the extent to which management had got to grips with the ERM agenda and were honest in the way they reviewed controls.

The quarterly plan was flexible, and was changed to take on board all new developments arising from new entries in the corporate risk register.

The quarterly plan was aligned with the available audit resources and steps were taken to fill gaps where required.

Following Procedures *(continued)*

Audit staff competence was factored into the quarterly plan to ensure that people were properly developed and were able to deal with the engagements that were assigned to them.

Audit defined a clear role in fraud work, and although not specialists, they were the first point of contact, and would bring in specialist investigators when a fraud broke rather than simply abandoning planned auditors to unplanned fraud work.

The quarterly plan had a clear focus on business success and ways of helping the business to become leaner and meaner.

The CAE had developed an intimate understanding of stakeholders' expectations and spent most of her time out of the office, talking to important people within and outside the organization.

Most of the quarterly plan was based on risk and focused on high-risk aspects of the organization.

Best practice issues were built into the quarterly plan and emerging issues in good risk management were built into the way the organization's ERM process was assessed.

The audit team built value for money into their work, and looked for ways of improving operational efficiency and effectiveness each quarter.

Specialist data interrogations software was used to help identify weak controls and their implications for the ERM process.

Audit engagements and projects were taken from the quarterly audit plans unless they were urgent requests for work that had been agreed with the audit committee.

Objectives for each audit were set and aligned to the business risk assessments that were carried out by the management in the area under review.

Audit Approach Cube

The right-hand side of the model represents a cube with several different factors coming into play to affect the audit approach that is applied in an organization. Each aspect of this cube is described:

- *Levels 1–3.* These are the three levels, silo, cheese, and inclusive that we have already discussed.
- *Risk champion.* At level one (silo), the auditors may well assume the mantle of a risk champion to help set up the concept of ERM within the organization.

- *Risk validation.* At the other extreme, level three (inclusive), the auditors will assume an assuring role where they are able to furnish the board and audit committee with independent opinions on the adequacy of the existing ERM arrangements.
- *Opportunity/threat.* Many organizations start the ERM build by viewing risk as threats to the business that have to be minimized by additional levels of internal control. As ERM maturity develops, there is a much better understanding of risk, and the risk of failing to do more because of excessive internal control is seen as an additional concern. At this level, managers are encouraged to review their controls in a proactive manner and abandon any procedures that are needlessly cumbersome and tie up the business and make it less competitive.
- *Consulting (review/implement/plan).* The consulting role that audit assumes is then related to the position of the organization as defined by the audit approach cube.
- *Assuring (improve design).* Again, the level of assurance will depend on the factors in the cube.

The above analysis enables the CAE to develop an audit strategy that fits in with the way the organization is placed on the ERM maturity process.

CASE STUDY

Emerging Strategies

The CAE for a large private sector company developed a three-tiered audit strategy that emerged over time to reflect the changing role of internal audit. In the past, the auditors used a basic fixed factor risk index to assign audit work as follows:

Complexity of the system
Regulator requirements
Technology and new projects

The audit approach moved over four different levels:

Old style audit using fixed risk assessments to investigate high-risk areas that suggested non-compliance with set standards.

Audit with risk focus on business risk and the corporate risk register to focus on high-risk areas that posed a threat to the organization.

CSA-based audits where audit facilitated improved ERM processes and sought to equip managers with the right tools and approach to tackle their risks.

Emerging Strategies *(continued)*

Handover, where management continued their self-assessment and audit stood back to review their efforts while also concentrating on reviewing controls in high-risk areas.

This changing approach was announced by audit to the organization through various mechanisms:

Presentations

Web site announcements

Brochures

Published audit plan

HOLISTIC RISK-BASED AUDIT PLANNING MODEL: PHASE FOUR

Our model continues in Figure 8.5.

Each new aspect of the model is described in the following paragraphs.

Figure 8.5 Holistic Risk-Based Audit Planning Model: Phase Four

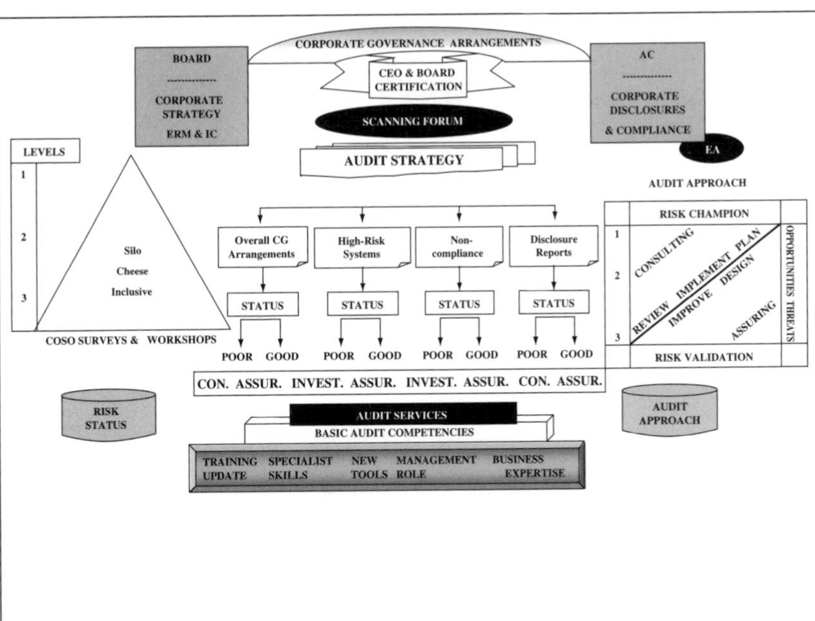

Audit Services

The next part of our model relates to the audit services that should result from the adopted strategy. These are assurance services:

> An objective examination of evidence for the purpose of providing an independent assessment on risk management, control, or governance processes for the organization. Examples may include financial, performance, compliance, system security, and due diligence engagements.[12]
>
> —IIA Glossary of Terms

Consulting services:

> Advisory and related client service activities, the nature, and scope of which are agreed with the client and which are intended to add value and improve an organization's governance, risk management, and control processes without the internal auditor assuming management responsibility. Examples include counsel, advice, facilitation, and training.[13]

And various specialist services, for example:

> Internal auditors should have knowledge of key information technology risks and controls and available technology-based audit techniques to perform their assigned work. However, not all internal auditors are expected to have the expertise of an internal auditor whose primary responsibility is information technology auditing.[14]

These services may include:

- Objective opinions on governance, risk, and controls within an organization.
- Help in developing sound governance, risk, and controls arrangements.
- Training, support, and advice.
- Help on large projects where the type of risks means advice on controls.
- Fraud prevention, detection, and investigation services.
- And a whole range of other related services.

The model suggests that the CAE can only define audit services after having gone through a careful consideration of all the factors that we have so far discussed from our model. Anything less may mean that audit services are poorly conceived, and no amount of planning can overcome this start place.

Basic Audit Competence

Supporting the audit services are competencies that the audit needs to possess to deliver the goods. The IIA's code of ethics makes it clear that internal auditors:

> Shall engage only in those services for which they have the necessary knowledge, skills, and experience.
>
> Shall perform internal auditing services in accordance with the International Standards for the Professional Practice of Internal Auditing.
>
> Shall continually improve their proficiency and the effectiveness and quality of their services.[15]

The auditor also needs to consider:

- *Training update.* Those aspects of audit training that need to be replenished on account of changes that have occurred since the auditor last underwent formal training.
- *Specialist skills.* There are many specialist areas of audit work relating to, say, information technology, procurement, projects, fraud, and operational routines that enrich the audit service.
- *New tools.* Advances in automation mean that new tools are regularly arriving on the shop floor that can help improve the audit process. These tools need to be mastered by good auditors if they are to apply them properly to audit work.
- *Management role.* Audit managers have a special role in the team in that they need to acquire management expertise as well as audit skills.
- *Business expertise.* Big business can be complex and demanding. The auditor needs to keep up to date with operational developments and the type of business environment as a way of maintaining a credible audit role within the organization.

Audit competence covers many areas including:

- Risk management concepts, tools, and standards.
- Audit tools and techniques.
- Common audit methodologies and processes that underpin audit work.
- Championing new corporate initiatives such as fraud awareness, ethics, and ERM related topics.
- And many other aspects of working for large organizations.

A case study illustrates some of these issues:

CASE STUDY

Formal Risk Assessment

A well-developed audit department has for some time been using a formal risk assessment model for planning purposes based on the need to provide assurances on internal control. The planning model assimilated the views of the management as a way of ensuring the plan made sense to the core business lines. The audit committee helped coordinate the plans and asked that the audit cover high-risk areas in their audit work. Some internal audit resources were supplied to assist the external auditors. The risk profile used covered four main categories of risk as shown in Figure 8.6.

Figure 8.6 Sample Risk Profile

High/Medium/Low

A Corporate importance (*)

B Corporate sensitivity (*)

C Inherent risk (**)

D Control risk (***)

(*) risks scored by top management

(**) risks scored by internal audit and business managers

(***) risks scored by internal audit

The formula applied to the risks in Figure 8.6 was:

$$A + B = E \times (C \times D)$$

Plans were used to develop a strategic planning cycle that meant that audit areas were reviewed every year, every two years, every three to five years, or not at all. Meanwhile the annual audit plan was broken down as shown in Figure 8.7.

Risk Status and Audit Approach

The two factors that most affect the audit plans are the risk status and approach that should be applied in response to this status:

1. **Risk status**. The extent to which the organization has been able to implement an efficient and effective ERM process.
2. **Audit approach.** The type of approaches adopted by the CAE to deliver the audit products.

Figure 8.7 Sample Audit Plan

AUDIT DAYS			
Governance disclosures:			
Risk management		x	
Legal compliance		x	
Other Work		x	
Core business reviews		–	x
Business unit A	x		
Business unit B	x		
Business unit C	x		
		–	x
Resources and infrastructure:			
IT audits	x		
Corporate security		x	
		–	x
Regular audit:			
Follow up		x	
Fraud prevention		x	
		–	x
Consulting projects			x
TOTAL AUDIT DAYS			x

The above factors have already been covered in previous chapters. The main point is that the two factors should be interrelated in such a way that the ERM needs of the organization impacts the approach to auditing work. The CAE may use a group approach to help plan the way audit work is directed across the organization.

CASE STUDY

Using a Planning Forum

In a large audit department, the results of formal risk assessments were fed into a planning forum that consisted of the CAE, audit managers, and chair of the audit committee. High scoring systems were identified and special projects of strategic importance were added to the plan if they were deemed important in terms of tackling high-risk aspects of the organization's business development. The output from the audit plan was a level of audit resource required to deliver the defined audits. This was compared with the available audit resource with the following options:

Using a Planning Forum *(continued)*

Plan matches resources. Implement the plan and monitor situation.
Insufficient resources. Buy in more resource and co-source some of the work with external providers using consultants on one-off consulting projects.
Excessive resources. Get rid of contract staff and transfer some audit staff to other parts of the business.

The audit resourcing strategy involved a flexible approach to temporary and short-term contract staff who complement the core audit teams. Meanwhile a three-year strategy was developed that considered factors such as:

- Growth in different types of audit services.
- Refocus on different aspects of consulting and assurance services.
- Transfer of skills to the business in line with the CSA program.
- Development of new audit competencies, as needed, in conjunction with planned changes in audit services, methodologies, and software tools.
- Training and development programs, including qualification-based schemes.
- Future supply of auditors and surveys of satisfaction levels among the audit staff.
- Departure rates and retirement plans of current audit staff.
- Compensation packages and whether they are set to attract the right type of auditor.
- Performance reports and feedback on the quality of auditors in post.

The planning forum considered the above factors and initiated a project to align the three-year staffing strategy with the three-year audit strategy to secure as best a fit as possible between the planned audit coverage and core audit team numbers, experience, and overall competence. The overriding consideration was that the resource profile had to fit the risk-based audit plans and not the other way round. Moreover, auditors who were too far from a good fit with the competence profile generated by the audit strategy were not retained. The audit managers provided a strong sense of continuity and were given a substantial budget for ongoing personal development through training, conferences, and being involved in various national working groups and specialist forums.

HOLISTIC RISK-BASED AUDIT PLANNING MODEL: FINAL

Our complete model is presented in Figure 8.8.

Figure 8.8 The Complete Model

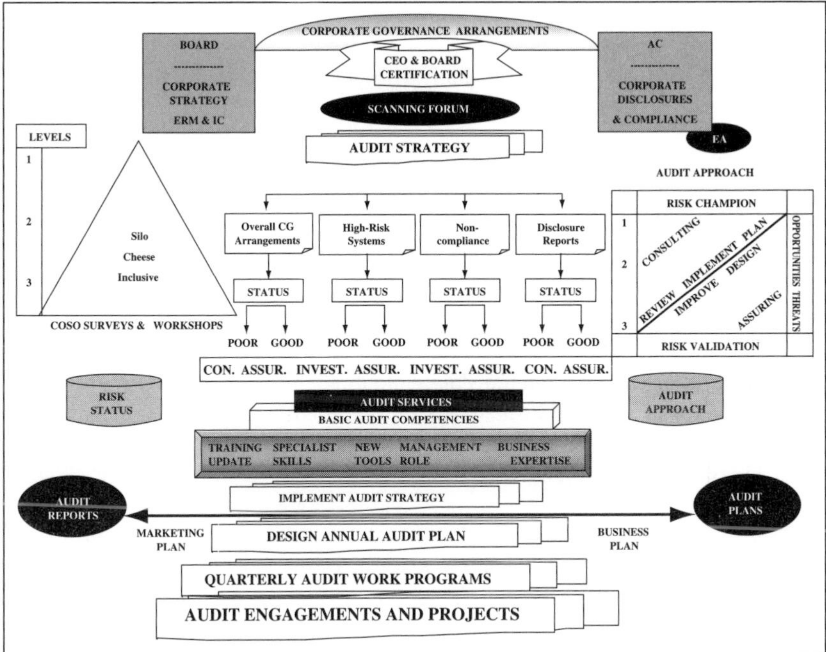

Each new aspect of the final model is described in the following paragraphs.

Implement Audit Strategy

We arrive now at the implementation of strategy. In our model, this has three essential stages.

Design Annual Audit Plan

After having considered all those factors that have so far appeared in the model, the CAE is now in a position to build the annual audit plan. The annual plan has traditionally been seen as the pivotal feature of the audit process since it is this document that may form the basis of an outsourced audit service—that is, what the competition may provide to encourage the audit committee to get rid of the in-house audit team. An example illustrates how one audit team set about the task of developing its annual audit plan:

CASE STUDY

The Risk Index

A team of auditors in an organization with branches scattered throughout the world developed a risk index for audit planning based on:

System changes
Staff changes
Management requests
Potential fraud
Materiality
Last audit
Complexity of the systems

These factors were then translated into three overall elements. The first (A) related to the system and its features, the second (B) related to the controls in terms of their ability to manage risk while the third (C) related to views of stakeholders, shown in Figure 8.9.

Figure 8.9 Sample Risk-Factor Breakdown

A. SYSTEMS	B. CONTROLS	C. INTEREST
Materiality	Date last audited	Requests from management
Complexity	Alleged frauds	External auditing concerns
Recent changes	Complaints	Regulators and media concerns
Importance of system	Known errors	Audit committee concerns
Results:		
High risk	Unreliable	High interest
Medium risk	Neutral	Medium interest
Low risk	Reliable	Low interest

1. Systems risks are taken from the corporate risk register.
2. Control risks indicate where controls may be unreliable or exist to mitigate significant risk.
3. Interests from stakeholders suggest other risks that can be added to the profile and areas where special audit projects can be added to the audit plan.

This risk rating for each of the three factors A, B, and C shown in Figure 8.9 was then applied to each audit unit to arrive at those that will feature in the annual audit plan. See Figure 8.10.

The Risk Index

Figure 8.10 Audit Units and Risk Scores to Feature in Audit Plan

AUDIT UNIT	SCORE: A. SYSTEMS	SCORE: B. CONTROL	SCORE: C. INTEREST	OVERALL SCORE

Quarterly Audit Work Program

We have previously suggested that the quarterly plan may be used to reflect the realities of business life, in that it is a short enough period to incorporate the real life influences on the organization.

CASE STUDY

Quarterly Planning

An innovative audit shop developed a quarter-stop-review approach to audit planning that saw the quarterly planning period as the key to audit's success:

Quarter one: Review aspects of the basic governance framework.
Quarter two: Isolate weaknesses in this framework and review high-risk areas of the organization.
Quarter three: Consider problems arising from weakness in the governance framework.
Quarter four: Investigate these problems and propose improvements to the framework armed with evidence of the implication of weaknesses.

In this way, assurances are given on the governance arrangements, weaknesses therein, whether high-risk parts of the business are well controlled, and how governance is strengthened over the year, particularly bearing in mind audit's evidence of known problems and resulting end recommendations. For example, a review of ethics as an element of governance found gaps in the

Quarterly Planning *(continued)*

workforce's commitment, which resulted in blurred lines regarding overseas contracts. These problems led to potential infringement of anticorruption laws and audit's recommendations were quickly implemented. This approach was also applied each quarter to ERM, financial management, high-level decision making, internal discipline, performance management, compliance oversight, and many other aspects that together go to making a well-run organization, that is, governance issues.

Marketing Plan

Having got a good audit product established through the comprehensive process outlined so far, the results should be marketed. In fact, marketing happens throughout the audit planning process in defining what the stakeholders expect from their auditors and how the proposals are considered and examined before being signed off. The purpose of marketing is to display the product to the clients. For auditing, marketing is about:

- Preparing a good product in terms of defined audit services.
- Making sure the primary stakeholders are happy with these services.
- Complying with auditing professional standards at all times.
- Telling everyone about the services available from the audit team.
- Making clear that consulting services can be requested so long as they fit in with the agreed acceptance criterion.
- Developing a marketing strategy that keep the audit product tight and well received.
- Obtaining feedback from audit client, the board, and the audit committee to ensure the audit's reputation remains second to none.
- Embarking on a formal continual improvement plan to ensure nothing slips out of the constant search for keeping the audit service on top form.
- Making sure plans represent sensible promises that are kept, as far as possible.

Business Plans

We have so far been able to define the audit service and prepare plans to ensure these are delivered to benefit the organization. What is also needed is an additional effort to ensure the underpinning infrastructure is in place to support the planned work. The business plan appears on our model to provide this infrastructure and ensure there is a resource in place that turns promises into action into results. For auditing, business planning is about:

- Considering the outputs that will be delivered as a result of the annual and quarterly audit plans.
- Making sure the resource that is needed to support the delivery of these outputs is also defined.
- Assessing the existing resource for skills, equipment, facilities, location, and budgets that are currently available to the CAE to support audit plans and other drains on audit resources.
- Comparing the existing resource with the required resource and working out whether there needs to be any development or requests for additional funding to meet any predicted shortfalls, or oversupply.
- Documenting the above and discussing the implications with the audit committee to promote decisions required to address any specific concerns therein.

Audit Reports

As we come towards the end of our model, we need to highlight the role of the audit report. Plans should be prepared on the basis of what the reader needs to know, what should be prioritized, what decisions need to be made, and how these decisions should be implemented and monitored. Reports appear in the model because it is the needs of stakeholders that drive the audit service and it is quite possible to work backwards in developing audit plans. Using this approach it is possible to use the following format for developing plans:

- Work out what stakeholders need from their auditors.
- Define the reports that would need to be prepared by the auditors to provide the information required by stakeholders.
- Work backward from the reports required by the audit committee, clients, external auditors, and others to determine what work is required to provide the necessary information.
- The fieldwork will deliver the aims of each audit.
- The audit planning process then swings into action with the compilation of audit strategies, annual plans, quarterly plans, initial surveys, and then the engagement plans for the assurance and consulting work in question.

Using the above steps it may be argued that the results are less about being the final product from the planning process, than about being the reference point from which to develop effective audit plans.

Audit Plans

The final part of the final model captures the essence of the book, which is planning based on an assessment of risk and resulting from a comprehensive set of components that together help ensure a first-class audit service. It is hoped that the plans for a specific audit can be derived from a big-picture thinking where each individual piece of audit work contributes to the growth of good governance, effective risk management, and better internal controls. Notwithstanding the auditor's best efforts to prepare detailed plans for each engagement, there is only so much that auditing processes can achieve:

> The internal auditor should be alert to the significant risks that might affect objectives, operations, or resources. However, assurance procedures alone, even when performed with due professional care, do not guarantee that all significant risks will be identified.[16]

But with good plans, derived from a carefully thought out process that is understood and supported by the audit staff, there is a much better chance that each audit creates the maximum impact on the business in a professional and powerful manner.

SUMMARY

We said in Chapter One that it takes much effort to formulate good risk-based audit plans, and some audit teams are tempted to take short-cuts in getting around planning so that audit staff can spend much more time on actual audit engagements. One way to realize the benefits from a holistic approach to risk-based audit planning is to go through the following five steps:

Step 1. The CAE should adopt a holistic approach to risk-based audit planning that ensures that corporate strategy and disclosure obligations are supported by an effective audit function.

Step 2. An audit strategy should be developed to discharge internal audit's obligation to review and improve the governance, risk management, and internal control arrangements within the organization, taking on board the needs of stakeholders and assurance activities from management and review functions.

Step 3. The risk-based audit planning process should merge the influencing factors of the state of ERM audit services available and the need to apply audit tools in a way that has the most impact on the changing shape of the organization.

Step 4. Risk-based audit planning should be sufficiently robust to enable the CAE to define set competencies and methodologies in response to a defined strategy that is derived from the overall governance arrangements.

Step 5. Risk-based audit planning should be established in such a way that each individual element of audit work has a beneficial impact on the organization and the CAE's obligation to report at the highest level of the organization and position the audit service to maximum effect.

Note that Appendix A contains a checklist that can be used to assess the overall quality of risk-based audit planning.

NOTES

1. Institute of Internal Auditors Professional Practices Framework.
2. Institute of Internal Auditors, Standard 2130.
3. Institute of Internal Auditors, Glossary of Terms.
4. Internal Auditing's Role in Sections 302 and 404 of The U.S. Sarbanes-Oxley Act of 2002, May 26, 2004, IIA.
5. Institute of Internal Auditors, Practice Advisory 2060–2.
6. Institute of Internal Auditors, Practice Advisory 2050–1.
7. Internal Auditing's Role in Sections 302 and 404 of The U.S. Sarbanes-Oxley Act of 2002, May 26, 2004, IIA.
8. Institute of Internal Auditors Glossary of Terms.
9. Institute of Internal Auditors, Standard 2120.A4.
10. Internal Auditing's Role in Sections 302 and 404 of The U.S. Sarbanes-Oxley Act of 2002, May 26, 2004, IIA.
11. Institute of Internal Auditors, Practice Advisory 2100–1.
12. Institute of Internal Auditors, Glossary of Terms.
13. Institute of Internal Auditors, Glossary of Terms.
14. Institute of Internal Auditors, Standard 1210.A3.
15. Institute of Internal Auditors, Code of Ethics.
16. Institute of Internal Auditors, Standard 1220.A3.

APPENDIX A

APPLYING AN RBAP DIAGNOSTIC TOOL

Each chapter of the book has described key aspects of risk-based audit planning and the implications for internal auditing in terms of providing a suitable audit cover. Various models have been developed to help explain some of the issues at hand. Each chapter has been prepared to isolate key issues and describe the way various factors are interrelated to form a picture of the entire audit-planning concept. The final chapter attempted to pull some of the main issues together in a holistic and integrated framework. Appendix A takes on board a great deal of the material from the main chapters and builds a comprehensive checklist that can be used by auditors to assess where they stand in terms of implementing risk-based audit planning. The checklist can be used as a general diagnostic tool, or benchmark, against which to judge the state of risk-based audit planning and decide whether any improvements to the existing arrangement are possible.

We start this appendix by setting out a comprehensive model that can be applied to risk-based audit planning in Figure A.1. Each aspect of this model is addressed by the 100-point checklist that follows the model. Note that each question on the checklist would have to be answered by referring to a further list of more detailed subsidiary questions, which should be prepared by users to suit both the context of the organization and the approach used by the audit department in question. It may also be necessary to develop measures for assessing how the audit team is able to demonstrate that the assigned score is appropriate. Moreover, the checklist has been made fairly general to reflect the fact that the questions are applicable to all types of organizations in the public, private, and not-for-profit sectors.

Figure A.1 Comprehensive RBAP Model

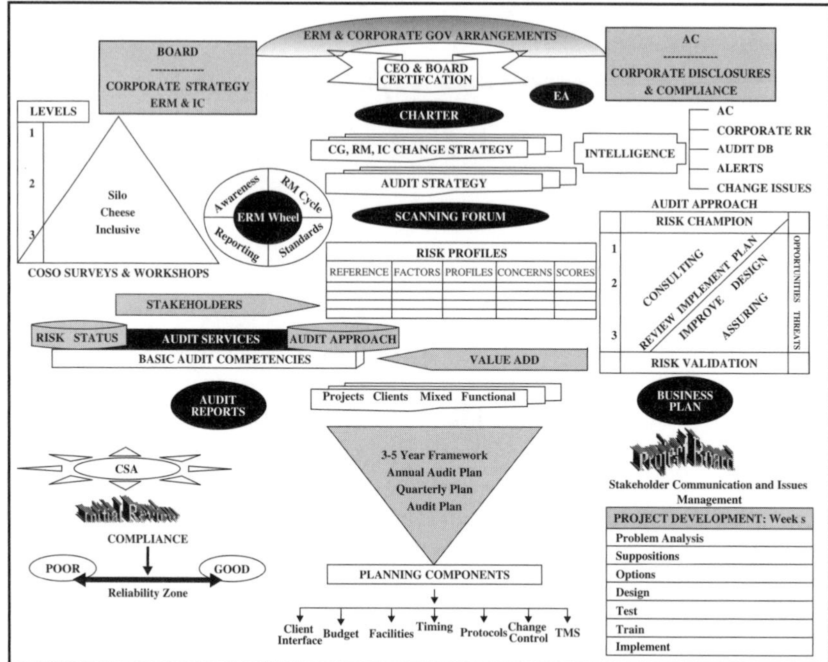

It is possible to assign a score of 1 to 10 for each of the items on the checklist:

1 Does not meet the criteria at all

5 Meets the criteria partially

10 Meets the criteria completely

The scores in between will reflect a best estimate of where the audit department sits in terms of the two extremes (1 and 10).

ASSESSING THE RBAP COMPONENT CHECKLIST

		Score (1–10)	Evidence	Action
A.	**ERM and corporate governance arrangements:** Audit plans should be set within the overall context of the need to ensure there are effective governance arrangements and a robust ERM process established within the organization.			
A.1	Is there a suitable audit strategy on the extent to which internal auditors will champion the use of risk management where the organization or defined parts of the organization are at an early stage in establishing ERM?			
A.2	Is there a suitable audit strategy on facilitating the risk management process where the organization has made some progress in establishing ERM?			
A.3	Is there a suitable audit strategy, including a set criteria for larger audit projects, on the provision of advice and assistance to help senior management develop the establishment and improve governance and ERM within the organization?			
A.4	Is there a suitable audit strategy on the provision of assurance services that is designed to provide a considered view of the effectiveness and efficiency of the governance and ERM processes based on the result of audit work performed over the previous year?			
A.5	Is there a suitable strategy on audit's involvement in governance and disclosures projects that ensures any temporary involvement will not undermine the delivery of a professional and independent audit service based on the result of audit work performed over the previous year?			
Total score:		**Percentage:**		

B.	**Board corporate strategy:** Audit plans should be derived from the overall corporate strategy and they should help move this strategy forward in a dynamic manner.	**Score (1–10)**	**Evidence**	**Action**
B.1	Are the internal audit plans derived from the focus and direction provided by the overall corporate strategy that has been adopted by the organization?			
B.2	Is there a clear and meaningful interface between the aims and objectives of the organization and the aims and objectives of the internal audit department?			
B.3	Is there a good understanding among the audit staff of how audit products add value to the overall drive to implement corporate strategy across the organization?			
B.4	Does the audit mission make clear the need for audit to contribute to the achievement of corporate objectives?			
B.5	Is there a formal process in place that recognizes and takes on board changes to the corporate strategy to ensure that audit plans are fully aligned to current organizational priorities?			
Total score:		**Percentage:**		

C.	**Audit Committee:** The needs and expectations of the audit committee should be duly recognized in the formulation of audit plans.	Score (1–10)	Evidence	Action
C.1	Does the audit committee have a reliable process for assessing the adequacy and effectiveness of internal audit plans?			
C.2	Is an effective procedure in place that ensures the needs and expectations of the audit committee are incorporated into the way auditing plans its work for the ensuing year?			
C.3	Do audit plans take on board and respond to the need to assist the audit committee in meetings its set obligations and responsibilities including the need to provide an oversight of the governance arrangements, corporate controls, financial reporting, and the risk management process?			
C.4	Is an effective mechanism in place for ensuring that changes to the audit plans are duly notified to the audit committee and, if significant, formally submitted to the audit committee for consideration and approval?			
C.5	Is there an effective dialogue established between the auditor and the chair of the audit committee concerning the way audit plans are prepared, and whether there are any problems or issues that arise from the audit planning process, particularly regarding the recognition of competing priorities?			
Total score:		**Percentage:**		

D. **CEO and board certification:** Audit plans should reflect the organization's obligation to formulate disclosures on its systems of internal control and provide a source of reliable assurance on this matter.	**Score (1–10)**	**Evidence**	**Action**
D.1 Does the board have a good understanding of the value that can be derived from objective assurances from the auditors regarding the state of the organization's systems of internal control?			
D.2 Is there a reliable process in place that ensures audit plans make a valuable contribution to the assurance framework used by the CEO and the board in furnishing a formal certificate on internal control?			
D.3 Is a clear methodology in use that ensures all disclosure requirements that are the responsibility of the CEO and PFO are duly considered and evaluated in the formulation of audit plans and setting of key priorities?			
D.4 Does the planned coverage of audit work for the ensuing year ensure that there is a reasonable opportunity to uncover significant weaknesses in internal controls that may be reported to the board and help inform the board's understanding of the overall state of internal controls on a quarterly basis?			
D.5 Do internal audit plans respond properly to significant changes in internal controls over financial reporting to support audit reports to the board on whether such changes have an impact on the reliability of internal controls?			
Total score:	**Points:**	**Percentage:**	

E.	**External audit:** Internal audit plans should be established in such a way as to promote a good working relationship with external audit and ensure that both types of audit services are delivered with maximum impact.	**Score (1–10)**	**Evidence**	**Action**
E.1	Does the CAE have a good working relationship with the Reporting External Audit Partner based around the need to ensure both sets of plans are coordinated in a way that ensures the most effective use of all audit resources?			
E.2	Is there a sound process in place that ensures presentations made to the audit committee from both external and internal audit staff present a consistent message on matters that fall within the remit of the audit committee's responsibilities?			
E.3	Do the internal auditors make a valuable contribution to the external auditor's Section 404 requirement to evaluate management's assessment of internal controls?			
E.4	Is there an effective process in place that can be used by the internal auditors to report any concerns they might have with the professionalism and independence of the external audit process?			
E.5	Does the audit committee have sufficient knowledge of the different aims and objectives of external and internal auditors to be able to appreciate the way each team makes a different, but nonetheless, valuable contribution to corporate governance and management accountability and control within the organization?			
Total score:		**Percentage:**		

F.	**Audit charter:** The audit charter should document the role of audit and drive the focus, direction, and scope of audit plans.	**Score (1–10)**	**Evidence**	**Action**
F.1	Does the audit charter make a good job of establishing the internal audit activity's position within the organization: authorizing access to records, personnel, and physical properties and defining the scope of audit's work?			
F.2	Does the audit charter make it clear that there is a suitable process for ensuring that risk is properly considered when determining which aspects of the organization will be covered in the annual audit plan?			
F.3	Are audit plans sufficiently resourced to ensure the aims and aspirations of the audit charter are achieved now and in the future?			
F.4	Does the audit charter spell out the roles, responsibilities, and accountabilities of the chief audit executive and does it make clear the need to deliver a professional and independent audit service?			
F.5	Does the audit charter make clear the way the audit plans are approved by the audit committee and provide a facility to seek reapproval in the event of any changes that impact the current published plans?			
Total score:		**Percentage:**		

G. **Corporate governance, risk management, and internal control change strategy:** Audit plans should take on board the extent to which the organization has been able to implement better governance, ERM, and internal controls and maximize the impact of the audit function in promoting the necessary degree of change in this respect.	**Score (1–10)**	**Evidence**	**Action**
G.1 Do audit plans incorporate suitable measures of the extent to which the planned audit work will help the organization develop better arrangements to promote good governance in line with accepted best practice?			
G.2 Do audit plans incorporate suitable measures of the extent to which the planned audit work will help the organization design and implement an effective ERM process in line with accepted best practice?			
G.3 Do audit plans incorporate suitable measures of the extent to which the planned audit work will help the organization ensure internal controls are sound and observed across the organization in line with an ongoing assessment of risks to the achievement of business objectives?			
G.4 Do audit plans enable the CAE to provide a perspective on the extent to which change programs incorporate good governance and an assessment of risks and controls that help ensure the programs have a reasonable chance of success?			
G.5 Are audit plans responsive to the corporate risk register and information that comes to light concerning the adequacy and effectiveness of governance, risk management, and the overall control environment?			
Total score:	**Percentage:**		

H.	Intelligence: The audit team should establish a mechanism to ensure that audit plans incorporate, in the audit risk scoring process, new and emerging factors and information that impacts corporate and local risk assessments.	Score (1–10)	Evidence	Action
H.1	Is there an effective mechanism that ensures new and emerging risks that impact the current audit plans are captured and used to update the audit universe and resulting plans to ensure that audit work is vibrant and meaningful?			
H.2	Is there an effective and ongoing dialogue between the CAE and chair of the audit committee that enables any concerns that impact the remit of the audit committee to be considered in terms of any possible revision to the current audit plans?			
H.3	Is there an effective and ongoing dialogue between the CAE and CEO (and board) that enables any concerns that impact the remit of the senior management to be considered in terms of any possible revision to the current audit plans?			
H.4	Has the CAE established a mechanism for ensuring that alerts, new projects, and changes to the corporate risk register are incorporated into the audit risk database and in turn translated into new or revised audit plans with relevant themes that are agreed to by the audit committee?			
H.5	Do members of the audit shop have a clear idea of areas that they should keep under continual review and feed into the audit-planning process in a way that makes the best possible use of the available expertise of the audit staff?			
Total score:		**Percentage:**		

I.	**Risk management maturity:** The type of audit services provided to the organization should reflect the degree to which ERM has been designed, implemented, and improved.	**Score (1–10)**	**Evidence**	**Action**
I.1	For organizations that can be described as having a "Silo" approach to ERM, does the audit plan contain a realistic attempt to move ERM to a more advanced "Cheese" approach?			
I.2	For organizations that can be described as having a "Cheese" approach to ERM, does the audit plan contain a realistic attempt to move ERM to a more advanced "Inclusive" approach?			
I.3	For organizations that can be described as having an "Inclusive" approach to ERM, does the audit plan contain a realistic attempt to assess whether this more advanced approach, based on a strong control environment, can be made even more effective?			
I.4	Do audit staff have a good understanding of the need to provide different types of audit services depending on the extent to which the organization has designed, implemented, and improved the ERM process?			
I.5	Is there an adequate degree of audit independence in place that ensures that consulting work does not impair the ability of the CAE to perform sufficient audit work to enable independent assurances on the state of ERM within the organization?			
Total score:		**Percentage:**		

J.	**Audit strategy:** The auditor should establish a strategy based around all suitable planning techniques that seeks to evolve the audit service over several years.	Score (1–10)	Evidence	Action
J.1	Is the CAE in a position to apply all well-known planning tools to ensure that audit plans are based on the professional application of planning techniques that mean audit plans provide a meaningful and motivating process for applying audit resources to the audit universe?			
J.2	Does the audit team spend sufficient time developing a clear vision of where it needs to be in set future periods, which may last up to several years, and does the audit-planning process ensure that this vision has a good chance of being achieved?			
J.3	Does the audit strategy incorporate clear decisions on whether the audit resource needs to be grown, stabilized, or reduced in line with the need to add value to the organization and avoid waste of resources, or an insufficient level of audit coverage?			
J.4	Has the CAE developed a clear strategy for marketing the audit service that acknowledges the needs and expectations of key stakeholders, the changing nature of internal auditing, and the requirement to observe professional auditing standards?			
J.5	Does the CAE have a formal strategy for meeting the real or potential threat from external providers of internal audit services that has been developed with a careful consideration of how such threats may be countered now and in the future?			
Total score:		**Percentage:**		

K. **ERM wheel and risk profiles:** The auditor should ensure that audit plans incorporate an assessment of ERM through a consideration of factors that have a fundamental bearing on the quality of risk management within the organization.	**Score (1–10)**	**Evidence**	**Action**
K.1 When developing audit plans, is there a reliable process that ensures that the extent to which management is aware of the concept and theory of ERM is incorporated in the need to ensure that the risk wheel is being developed and established within the organization?			
K.2 When developing audit plans, is there a reliable process that ensures that the extent to which management is able to identify, assess, and manage their risks is incorporated in the need to ensure that the risk wheel is being developed and established within the organization?			
K.3 When developing audit plans, is there a reliable process that ensures that the extent to which management has established standards and guidelines on the use of ERM is incorporated in the need to ensure that the risk wheel is being developed and established within the organization?			
K.4 When developing audit plans, is there a reliable process that ensures that the extent to which management is able to report the results of ERM is incorporated in the need to ensure that the risk wheel is being developed and established within the organization?			
K.5 Does the audit-planning process incorporate the results of risk profiles developed by the auditor in the form of a formal database that captures all relevant information to allow a risk-assessed perspective of the organization?			
Total score:	**Percentage:**		

L.	**Scanning forum and stakeholders:** The auditor should consider the use of key personnel and concerns of stakeholders to assist in the task of reviewing the factors that impact the risk profile of the organization and therefore have a bearing on the audit plans.	**Score (1–10)**	**Evidence**	**Action**
L.1	Has the CAE identified select personnel to provide a formal input into the audit-planning process by spending sufficient time meeting with and talking to these stakeholders on an ongoing basis to ensure that audit is able to respond to all relevant issues that sit within the remit of the audit role?			
L.2	Do the select personnel have a good understanding of ERM and the role of internal audit that enables them to provide a valuable input to the audit-planning process in that the CAE has made available sufficient information to these stakeholders concerning the role, responsibilities, approach, and planning process that is used by the audit department to ensure it makes a valuable contribution to the organization?			
L.3	Have the select personnel formed themselves into a forum that meets on a regular basis to engage in a robust deliberation of issues that may have an impact on the audit plans that are being formulated or revised, and do they have a good appreciation of the fact that any specific concerns need to meet the criteria set by the audit-planning standards before these concerns can feature in published audit plans?			
L.4	Has the audit team undertaken an in-depth workshop to arrive at a clear appreciation of the key stakeholders for the audit service and considered individual stakeholder's needs, expectations, and concerns along with concerns of groups outside the organization that depend on the products and services provided by the organization?			

(*continues*)

(Continued)

	Score (1–10)	Evidence	Action
L.5 Does the CAE have a mechanism in place that enables the audit department to ensure the input from any scanning forum does not provide a significant impairment to the auditor's independence?			
Total score:	**Percentage:**		

M. **Audit approach, risk status, and audit services:** The approach adopted by the auditors and resultant services that are provided by the audit team should be consistent with the degree to which risk has been embedded into the organization's processes, products, and people.	**Score (1–10)**	**Evidence**	**Action**
M.1 Does the audit department make a clear analysis of the balance between assurance and consulting work on at least an annual basis in the context of the type of approach that best suits the organization?			
M.2 Does the audit department make a clear analysis of the specific types of audit services that it provides on at least an annual basis in the context of the type of approach that best suits the organization?			
M.3 Has the CAE developed a clear position on issues relating to fraud, compliance, information systems, and value for money in terms of the way audit services incorporate these aspects within the scope of audit work?			
M.4 Has the audit department developed a formal approach for reviewing the ERM framework either in its entirety or in terms of aspects that can be tackled individually over the coming years as the framework is developed and further refined by senior management?			
M.5 Are regular and sufficiently robust meetings held within the audit team to discuss the best approach to audit work and progress that is being made to implement ERM within all parts of the organization?			
Total score:	**Percentage:**		

N.	**Basic audit competence and value add:** The audit team should possess the values, expertise, competence, and tools to deliver the audit plan in a way that maximizes value to the organization.	**Score (1–10)**	**Evidence**	**Action**
N.1	Does the audit department have a formal human resource management strategy that enables it to ensure the challenges implied in the agreed audit plans can be achieved through the use of well-trained and properly focused audit staff now and in the future?			
N.2	Does the CAE have access to a source of specialist skills and expertise in the event that this is required to support the current audit staff in meeting their obligations under the current audit plans for the next few years?			
N.3	Does the CAE bring to bear all relevant and up-to-date tools, techniques, resources, software, and aids that will help equip and motivate the audit staff to deliver carefully developed targets arising from agreed audit plans?			
N.4	Do the audit staff have a sufficiently grounded knowledge of the business and environment within which the organization operates to ensure that audit work recognizes the reality of business pressures and influences that affect operational staff, board members, and senior management?			
N.5	Are the auditors sufficiently well versed in governance, risk management, and internal control to be able to form a source of expertise on these matters and provide an independent perspective on whether these matters are being adequately addressed across the organization?			
Total score:		**Percentage:**		

O.	**Business plans, audit reports, and planning framework:** Professional and valuable audit reports should result from well-formulated business plans and a carefully structured audit-planning framework.	**Score (1–10)**	**Evidence**	**Action**
O.1	Has the CAE compiled a comprehensive list of outputs from the audit service and how these might be measured to provide meaningful targets that act as a roadmap for moving the audit shop from where it currently stands to where it needs to be to excel and be considered world class?			
O.2	Is the audit-planning process properly derived from the audit reporting process, which in turn aims to meet the needs of stakeholders who depend on a professional audit service to help them meet their obligations for ensuring the organization is successful and compliant and that reported results are trustworthy?			
O.3	Has the CAE delivered to the audit committee an acceptable, risk-assessed long-term audit plan that covers up to three years and that demonstrates growth in the audit shop to world-class standards in a way that fits with the context of developments that impact the organization?			
O.4	Has the CAE delivered to the audit committee an acceptable, risk-assessed audit plan that covers the ensuing year and incorporates all relevant sources of risk for the organization and information concerning risk such as the business risk registers and concerns from persons who are in a position to appreciate issues of strategic importance to the organization?			
O.5	Has the CAE delivered to the audit committee a risk-assessed quarterly audit plan that takes on board all significant recent developments and seeks to reconcile the available staff for the period in question with the level of audit coverage needed to deliver a reliable audit opinion on internal control and assist the organization in embedding ERM within the business?			
Total score:		**Percentage:**		

P.	**Audit structure:** The structure of the audit shop should be set having regard to the results of the audit-planning process and the need to focus audit resources in the best possible way.	**Score (1–10)**	**Evidence**	**Action**
P.1	Has the audit department made a careful consideration of the use of project teams within the audit service to help deliver the requirements of the agreed annual audit plan?			
P.2	Has the audit department made a careful consideration of the use of audit teams aligned to specific audit clients within the audit service to help deliver the requirements of the agreed annual audit plan?			
P.3	Has the audit department made a careful consideration of the use of audit teams grouped because of their specials skills and expertise within the audit service to help deliver the requirements of the agreed annual audit plan?			
P.4	Has the audit department made a careful consideration of the strategy of rotating auditors between audit teams to ensure they acquire a variety of expertise over the years as part of their personal development and as a way of promoting the best use of staff to help deliver the requirements of the agreed annual audit plan?			
P.5	Has the CAE developed a strategy, in conjunction with the Human Resource Officer, that means auditors can be temporarily transferred out of the audit team and other staff can be temporarily assigned to the audit team depending on the quarterly work plan to help deliver the requirements of the agreed annual audit plan?			
Total score:		**Percentage:**		

Q.	**CSA, initial review, and reliability:** All audit assurance engagements should start with an initial review of the reliability of the risk management process set out in a formal preliminary survey report, so as to determine the best way to employ audit resources to the engagement in hand.	**Score (1–10)**	**Evidence**	**Action**
Q.1	Does the assigned auditor have a clear procedure for isolating the extent to which risk management has been developed and embedded in the area under review before formulating a terms of reference for the planned audit assurance engagement?			
Q.2	Does the assigned auditor have a clear procedure for isolating the main risks to the achievement of objectives for the area under review before deciding which aspects have to be focused on in the planned audit assurance engagement?			
Q.3	Does the assigned auditor encourage management for the area under review to engage in sufficient dialogue to ensure that any concerns and special factors that they may have related to the way risk in being managed are considered when setting the terms of reference for the planned audit assurance engagement?			
Q.4	Does the assigned auditor consider the use of a facilitated workshop (or staff surveys) with key members of the area under review to help determine any high levels of risk that can be built into the terms of reference for the planned audit assurance engagement in the area under review?			
Q.5	Does the assigned auditor have a clear process for determining any significant risks in the successful completion of the audit and the way these risks may be mitigated through a carefully formulated engagement plan and robust quality assurance process?			
Total score:		**Percentage:**		

R.	**CSA, initial review, and reliability:** All audit- consulting engagements should start with an initial review of the areas of interest and consider the consequences of the reliability of the risk management process before setting out, in a formal preliminary survey report, the best way to employ audit resources to the engagement in hand.	**Score (1–10)**	**Evidence**	**Action**
R.1	Does the assigned auditor have a clear procedure for isolating the extent to which weaknesses in the risk management process have an impact on the issues that are being considered in the planned audit-consulting engagement?			
R.2	Does the assigned auditor have a clear procedure for isolating the main risks that may impact on the terms of reference for the planned audit-consulting engagement?			
R.3	Does the assigned auditor encourage management for the area under review to engage in sufficient dialogue to ensure that any concerns and special factors that they may have are considered when setting the terms of reference for the planned audit-consulting engagement?			
R.4	Does the assigned auditor consider the use of a facilitated workshop (or staff surveys) with key members of the area under review to help determine the issues that should be built into the terms of reference for the planned audit-consulting engagement?			
R.5	Does the assigned auditor have a clear process for determining any significant risks in the successful completion of the consulting audit and the way these risks may be mitigated through a carefully formulated engagement plan and robust quality assurance process?			
Total score:		**Percentage:**		

S.	**Project board:** All longer audit engagements should be treated as projects and therefore incorporate a form of project management to ensure the audit resource is applied in the best possible manner.	**Score (1–10)**	**Evidence**	**Action**
S.1	Has the CAE developed a clear policy for managing longer audits, including a project development plan (incorporating elements from Figure A.1) that takes on board aspects of good project management to ensure that these more substantial engagements can be properly planned and controlled?			
S.2	Has the CAE established a suitable project management methodology that can be applied to larger audits and involves stakeholder analysis, project boards, and a stage reporting arrangement that promotes the most efficient use of audit resources in pursuance of the agreed audit objective?			
S.3	Do all larger audits incorporate the concept of an approved business case that has to be defined and approved before audit resources are committed to the project or when substantial changes are proposed to the ongoing project?			
S.4	Has the CAE approved an effective procedure for ensuring that change management issues are duly recognized and addressed if larger audit engagements have the potential to result in major changes to procedures, working practices, business processes, and team structures?			
S.5	Does the CAE have in place a formal lessons-learned protocol where larger audits can be assessed in terms of identifying areas that can be improved in future audits that are sufficiently similar to warrant such considerations?			
Total score:		**Percentage:**		

T.	**Planning components:** Audit engagement plans should incorporate several basic planning components as a way of managing the risk of poor performance or inappropriate use of audit resources.	**Score (1–10)**	**Evidence**	**Action**
T.1	Is the audit engagement planning process sufficiently robust to allow each planned audit to acknowledge the risk of poor working relationships between auditors and their clients and ensure that this risk is properly addressed through adequate training, professionalism, and the use of suitable tools within the audit department?			
T.2	Has the CAE encouraged a formal process for establishing realistic time and expenses budgets for each audit so that time charged to engagements and other work may be properly accounted for in a timely manner and carefully managed to ensure an efficient and effective audit service?			
T.3	Has the CAE developed suitable protocols that inform the client about audit processes and practices that are made clear at the planning stage and that work to ensure the audit can be completed in a positive and timely manner?			
T.4	Does the audit team have sufficient facilities, including adequate travel, hotel, and expenses budgets to ensure that all audits that have been planned and approved by the audit committee can be carried out in a professional manner?			
T.5	Does the audit-planning process contain sufficient flexibility to ensure that the timing of audits constitute best value bearing in mind the pressures on management and the changing profiles of risk that runs across all parts of the organization?			
Total score:		**Percentage:**		

RBAP Process Scores				
Item	**Title**	**Points**	**%**	**Action Plan Reference**
A				
B				
C				
D				
E				
F				
G				
H				
I				
J				
K				
L				
M				
N				
O				
P				
Q				
R				
S				
T				
RBAP Process Overall Score:				

INDEX